The Disenfranchisement of Ex-Felons

The Disenfranchisement of Ex-Felons

Elizabeth A. Hull

FOREWORD BY
Representative John Conyers, Jr.

Temple University Press
PHILADELPHIA

Elizabeth A. Hull is Professor of Political Science at Rutgers University, Newark. She has written numerous articles on the constitutional rights of women, minorities, and non-citizens, and two books: *Without Justice for All: The Constitutional Rights of Aliens* and *Taking Liberties: National Barriers to the Free Flow of Ideas.*

Temple University Press
1601 North Broad Street
Philadelphia PA 19122
www.temple.edu/tempress

∞ The paper used in this publication meets the requirements of the American National Standard for Information Sciences—Permanence of Paper for Printed Library Materials, ANSI Z39.48-1992

Library of Congress Cataloging-in-Publication Data

Hull, Elizabeth.
   The disenfranchisement of ex-felons / Elizabeth A. Hull.
      p.   cm.
   Foreword by John Conyers, Jr.
   Includes bibliographical references and index.
   ISBN 1-59213-184-0 (cloth : alk. paper)—ISBN 1-59213-185-9
(pbk. : alk. paper)
   1. Political rights, Loss of—United States—States.   2. Ex-convicts–
Suffrage–United States.   I. Title.
   KF9747.Z95H84 2006
   324.6'2'086927–dc22

                                             2005048585

2   4   6   8   9   7   5   3

For Loretta

Contents

Foreword

The United States continues to stand alone among the major industrialized nations in permitting an entire category of citizens–former felons–to be cut off from the democratic process. The practice of many states denying voting rights to ex-felons represents a vestige from a time when suffrage was denied to whole classes of our population based on race, gender, religion, national origin, and property. Over the past two centuries, however, these restrictions, along with post-Civil War exclusions such as the poll tax and literacy requirements, have been eliminated to conform with our basic American notion of equality. I believe that the time has also come to eliminate this class voting restriction and to join the community of nations in this regard.

Almost every state prohibits inmates from voting while incarcerated for a felony offense. Voting rights are not, however, restored with any uniformity upon release from prison, with 36 states prohibiting ex-felons from voting while they are on parole and 31 of these states excluding felony probationers as well. Three states completely deny the vote to ex-offenders. Another 10 states disenfranchise certain categories of ex-offenders and permit application for restoration of rights for specified offenses only after a waiting period through cumbersome administrative proceedings.

The denial of suffrage to these individuals is no small matter and should be the focus of academic scrutiny. A recent study by the Sentencing Project reveals that some 4.7 million Americans, or one in 43 adults have currently or permanently lost their voting rights as a result of a felony conviction. This includes an estimated 1.4 million African American men, or 13 percent of the total population of black adult men, a rate seven times the national average. Hispanic citizens are also disproportionately disenfranchised. These numbers not only illustrate the magnitude of the injustice, they also show the impact of excluding this group from the electoral process. In the state of Florida alone, an estimated 600,000 ex-felons were unable to vote in the 2000 presidential election. Denying their voice may have literally changed the history of this nation.

In addition to diminishing the legitimacy of our democratic process, denying voting rights to ex-offenders is inconsistent with the goal of rehabilitation. Instead of reintegrating such individuals into society, felony voting restrictions only serve to reaffirm their feelings of alienation and isolation. As the National Advisory Commission on Criminal Justice Standards and Goals has concluded, "if correction is to reintegrate an offender into free society, the offender must retain all attributes of citizenship." The purpose of correctional facilities throughout our history has been to make an offender fit to re-enter society. We should honor the principle that once a felon has served his time, he is ready to be a functioning member of society. Voting must then be allowed, as the most basic constitutive act of citizenship.

A growing number of commentators, most recently former Secretary of the Department of Housing and Urban Development Jack Kemp, have taken the position that, as a matter of law, the federal government should act to restore the fundamental right to vote for ex-offenders. Since 1999, I have introduced legislation to assist ex-felons in regaining their voting rights. The legislation would apply only to persons who have been released from prison, and it would apply only to federal elections. As such, my bill is fully consistent with constitutional requirements protecting state prerogatives to establish general voting qualifications. The legislation has been supported by a broad coalition of groups interested in voting and civil rights, including the NAACP, ACLU, National Council of Churches, National Urban League, Human Rights Watch, and Lawyers Committee for Civil Rights.

Many states are also beginning to take the lead on this issue. Alabama, Iowa, Maryland, Connecticut, Delaware, and New Mexico have all scaled back voting bans on ex-felons who have paid the price for their crimes and now want to participate in the democratic process as citizens. The growing roster of states that allow ex-felons to vote is encouraging, but is not a substitute for a uniform federal voting requirement. A person's basic constitutional rights simply should not vary due to geography or their ability to traverse complex administrative proceedings.

Our nation has seen the slow enfranchisement of all of its citizens. Though it has been a painful process, we have always moved forward, giving more and more citizens the right to vote. Still, Elizabeth Hull, in the book you hold in your hands, argues compellingly that the battle for civil rights will not be won until ex-felons are afforded the same voting rights enjoyed by all Americans.

The war on drugs and the explosion of the prison population has created a sense of urgency around this issue because ex-felon disenfranchisement touches an ever-expanding number of families. Along with the razor-thin margins of the past election cycles, these circumstances may finally create sufficient momentum for this issue to receive a fair hearing at the federal level.

Representative John Conyers, Jr.
Member of Congress, Michigan 14th District
Ranking Member, House Committee on the Judiciary

Acknowledgments

I have not looked forward to writing my "acknowledgments." Where can I begin? How can I ever end? What words can I summon to do justice to the many people who have helped me write this book? But here goes!

Thanks to Mary Segers, my dear friend and the chair of my department at Rutgers University in Newark, who lightened teaching loads, somehow managed to squeeze research money out of a tight budget, and helped and encouraged me in every way she could.

Thanks, as well, to Loretta Hardy, the Wonder Woman to whom this book is dedicated. Loretta is theoretically our department's administrative assistant, but in reality she is also its hands, its feet, its heart and its brains. What would we do without her?

I am very grateful to Marc Mauer, who heads the Sentencing Project, a remarkable Washington, D.C.–based research and advocacy group on behalf of prisoners' rights. Under Marc's adroit and indefatigable leadership, the Sentencing Project has already, in its young life, spearheaded many important reforms and put "felon disenfranchisement" on the political agenda. My appreciation extends, as well, to Alec Ewald, a brilliant young scholar whose research on felon disenfranchisement has been a source of inspiration and instruction; to the wise and patient Peter Wissoker, my original editor at Temple University Press; and to Dong-Young Rhee, my research assistant at Rutgers, who in his phenomenally competent and gracious way mined data, reconfigured tables, and transformed an otherwise solitary undertaking into an enjoyably collegial one.

Where would I be without either my son, Hal, or my husband, Jeff Ambers? Hal made me laugh and kept me honest. A twenty-year-old does wonders for anyone who tends to take herself too seriously ("If you start in again about those prisoners, Mom, I'm leaving the table ..."). As for Jeff, no amount of praise suffices. He's been reassuring, funny, and forbearing lo these many months, when my share of domestic chores never got done, and my share of the conversation focused almost exclusively on the plight of parolees.

I've ordered roses and champagne for two people I have never met. The first is my editor, Suzanne Wolk—although calling her an "editor" scarcely captures her many roles. She is indeed a wordsmith, and a sleuth extraordinaire who can spot even the most cleverly hidden error or inconsistency. She also became my confederate, doing everything in her power to make my book as good as it might be. She is a gifted and magnanimous human being who even from a distance has become a treasured friend.

The identity of the second person, the "outside reviewer" whom Temple University Press contracted to read and critique my manuscript, is unknown to me, but, whoever you are, thank you! You obviously spent an enormous amount of time, first reading and re-reading my work, and then finding just what was needed to strengthen my arguments, tighten my prose, tone down my rhetoric, and fill in my gaps. Whoever you are, I marvel not only at your wisdom and tact, but also at your professional duty in undertaking such a time-consuming and tedious chore. You are an estimable person, and I hope I can eventually repay your efforts in a more personal way.

1 Introduction

In the 2000 presidential election, 4,686,539 Americans—more than 2 percent of the voting-age population—were barred from the polls.[1] In a country that has extended the suffrage to virtually every other class of citizens, this group alone was deemed unworthy of exercising what the Supreme Court has called "the right preservative of all other rights," the franchise.[2] We are talking about former convicts, men and women who have completed not only their sentences but often their paroles and the terms of their probation as well, yet in many states are still prohibited from casting a ballot.

Until the 2000 election, disenfranchisement was a "non-issue," something about which even well-educated individuals were largely unaware. The excruciatingly close 2000 presidential election changed that. In what seems record time, the issue ballooned into a "phenomenon," generating editorials, television specials, academic conferences, advocacy groups, proposals for legislative reform, and much public soul-searching, as thoughtful Americans began weighing the human and institutional costs of marginalizing millions of their fellow citizens.

To grasp how many "fellow citizens" are unable to vote because of a felony conviction, imagine this: If all of them congregated in a single geographical area, it would become the nation's second-largest city, right behind New York. It would be larger than Los Angeles or Chicago. If those deprived of their suffrage lived in a single state, it would be the country's twenty-sixth-most populous—right after Kentucky, right before South Carolina.[3] (See disenfranchisement numbers in Table 1.)

Ex-felons pay taxes, go to work, raise their children, and are generally indistinguishable from their fellow citizens in all but one respect: They have no say in the way their communities are governed. Unlike voters, they can't stop the deterioration of their neighborhood schools or prevent yet another waste incinerator from

1

Table 1. Disenfranchisement Rates in the United States (January 1, 2004)

State	Felon Prisoners	Probation	Parolees	Total Ineligible Felons	Voting-Age Population	Disfranchised Rate (%)
Alabama	28,440	39,652	6,950	55,216	3,425,842	1.61
Alaska	4,431	5,406	927	8,061	470,024	1.72
Arizona	30,741	65,805	5,367	69,011	4,194,395	1.65
Arkansas	12,378	28,126	13,694	40,135	2,069,578	1.94
California	163,361	0	110,338	273,699	26,647,974	1.03
Colorado	19,085	0	6,559	25,644	3,456,281	0.74
Connecticut	20,525	0	2,599	23,124	2,684,496	0.86
Delaware	6,879	18,921	529	16,869	629,012	2.68
D.C.	0	0	0	0	448,818	0.00
Florida	80,352	287,641	4,952	229,125	13,441,589	1.70
Georgia	47,004	424,385	22,135	281,332	6,534,901	4.31
Hawaii	5,635	0	0	5,635	980,145	0.57
Idaho	5,825	32,220	2,329	24,264	1,025,470	2.37
Illinois	43,186	0	0	43,186	9,518,511	0.45
Indiana	22,576	0	0	22,576	4,635,693	0.49
Iowa	8,395	20,885	3,099	21,937	2,274,202	0.96
Kansas	9,009	14,551	4,145	20,430	2,049,542	1.00
Kentucky	16,377	28,696	7,572	38,297	3,157,230	1.21
Louisiana	36,091	36,677	25,065	79,495	3,358,475	2.37
Maine	0	0	0	0	1,038,834	0.00

State	Felon Prisoners	Probation	Parolees	Total Ineligible Felons	Voting-Age Population	Disfranchised Rate (%)
Maryland	24,186	77,875	13,742	76,866	4,200,864	1.83
Massachusetts	10,511	0	0	10,511	4,956,251	0.21
Michigan	49,524	0	0	49,524	7,616,370	0.65
Minnesota	7,612	110,725	3,596	66,571	3,872,377	1.72
Mississippi	20,542	19,116	1,816	31,916	2,139,838	1.49
Missouri	30,649	55,610	15,220	73,674	4,344,701	1.70
Montana	3,440	0	0	3,440	715,516	0.48
Nebraska	4,103	18,412	650	13,959	1,316,507	1.06
Nevada	10,527	12,159	4,126	20,733	1,737,785	1.19
New Hampshire	2,483	0	0	2,483	1,000,677	0.25
New Jersey	28,213	124,281	13,248	103,602	6,573,016	1.58
New Mexico	6,173	16,136	2,407	16,648	1,403,012	1.19
New York	65,914	0	55,853	121,767	14,790,563	0.82
North Carolina	33,334	113,161	2,677	92,592	6,414,826	1.44
North Dakota	1,168	0	0	1,168	490,193	0.24
Ohio	45,831	0	0	45,831	8,680,824	0.53
Oklahoma	23,004	28,326	4,047	41,214	2,664,546	1.55
Oregon	12,422	0	0	12,422	2,766,949	0.45
Pennsylvania	40,545	0	0	40,545	9,615,192	0.42
Rhode Island	3,569	25,929	392	16,926	842,974	2.01
South Carolina	24,247	40,047	3,210	47,481	3,174,275	1.50
South Dakota	3,059	0	0	3,059	576,223	0.53
Tennessee	25,409	42,836	7,967	54,794	4,516,712	1.21
Texas	164,222	431,989	102,271	482,488	16,263,943	2.97

(continued)

Table 1. *Continued*

State	Felon Prisoners	Probation	Parolees	Total Ineligible Felons	Voting-Age Population	Disfranchised Rate (%)
Utah	5,594	0	0	5,594	1,645,373	0.34
Vermont	0	0	0	0	488,177	0.00
Virginia	34,733	41,663	4,834	60,399	5,695,264	1.06
Washington	16,284	172,814	105	102,796	4,732,168	2.17
West Virginia	4,703	1,143	6,864	12,139	1,430,277	0.85
Wisconsin	22,366	55,336	11,966	62,000	4,192,517	1.48
Wyoming	1,809	4,662	578	4,718	386,177	1.22
Federal prisons	170,461	86,459	30,599	244,281	N.A.	N.A.
U.S. Total	1,456,927	2,481,644	502,428	3,200,177	221,285,099	1.45

Source: The United States Elections Project, http://elections.gmu.edu/Turnout%20Tables.xls, accessed June 22, 2005.

Note: States vary considerably in their disenfranchisement laws, particularly in regard to parolees and probationers. This table calculates the number of ineligible, disenfranchised felons (column 5) to include all felon prisoners and parolees (columns 2 and 4), as well as half of probationers (column 3), an estimate drawn from Department of Justice reports. In blank cells, persons in the category are not specifically subject to disenfranchisement. Fourteen states have discretionary forms of post-correctional voting restriction; for these states, the total of the disenfranchised is minimally estimated as the number of felon prisoners, since statistics on recidivism, deaths, and migration of felons are largely nonexistent. In Maine and Vermont, where they are allowed to vote, no prisoners are listed. The United States totals include persons in the federal corrections system.

moving in nearby. In a 1951 federal case, Judge Henry Wingate observed that disenfranchisement was "the harshest civil sanction imposed by civil society. When brought beneath the axe, the disenfranchised is severed from the body politic and condemned to the lowest form of citizenship, where voiceless at the ballot box ... the disinherited must sit idly by while others elect his civil leaders and ... choose the fiscal and governmental policies which govern him and his family."[4]

As striking as the sheer number of citizens barred from the polls is the arbitrary and even capricious way they forfeit their fundamental civic right. As the Department of Justice itself has concluded, disenfranchisement laws "governing the same rights and privileges vary widely from state to state, making something of a crazy-quilt of disqualifications and restoration procedures."[5]

A particular act may or may not trigger disenfranchisement, depending upon whether it's classified as a felony or a misdemeanor. Although felonies, in theory, are usually crimes serious enough to warrant at least a one-year prison sentence,[6] in reality it is often anybody's guess why a particular act is classified as such. Moreover, since an act may be considered a felony, misdemeanor, or even permissible conduct, depending upon the state, two people might engage in the same behavior, but only one might lose his right to vote. In Florida someone convicted of "public indecency" might be disenfranchised for life, whereas in New York State such an exhibitionist would receive at most a slap on the wrist.[7]

States also categorize as felonies activities that in many other countries would not rise to "misdemeanor" status—prompting Human Rights Watch to conclude that "the extent of disenfranchisement is even more disturbing given that the right to vote can be lost for relatively minor offenses such as shoplifting."[8] In Maryland, for instance, roughly five hundred offenses are considered felonies, or what the state calls "infamous crimes." They include, in addition to such serious acts as assault and murder, relatively innocuous ones such as passing bad checks, using fake IDs, and possessing fireworks without a license.[9] Alabama denies voting rights to anyone convicted of vagrancy;[10] North Dakota imposes the same fate on those who break a water pipe, and Texas includes scoundrels who steal "any wool, mohair or edible meat."[11]

What are legislators to do if ballots are cast by too many "undesirables"—classes of voters, say, whom they presume would support the "wrong" sort of candidate? They can attach a "felony" label to activity associated with these troublemakers and thereby expunge at least some of their names from the voting rosters. Florida state senator Daryl Jones observed, in one illustrative case, that in 2000 the Republican legislature proposed a bill that would have increased from 365 to 366 days the jail sentence for anyone who cashes two welfare checks after gaining employment. What's the purpose of adding one more day? The offense then becomes a felony, and "you take one more person off the voter rolls ... it's been going on in Tallahassee for years."[12]

Whether or not lawbreakers lose their franchise depends not only on how their misdeeds are classified but on where they are committed (see Table 2). Anyone lucky enough to live, or commit their crime, in Maine or Vermont can vote even while they are behind bars. In the other forty-eight states, however, they lose their ballot while they are incarcerated; when, how, and even whether they can reclaim it once they are released depends upon the vagaries of each state's law. In some places ex-convicts' rights are restored once they complete probation and parole, in others, after they complete the terms of their sentence and then wait a prescribed period of time. A few jurisdictions seldom if ever restore voting rights to applicants who have committed one of several specified offenses,[13] or are recidivists, or fail to complete a cumbersome and often expensive clemency procedure.[14] (See categories of felons disenfranchised under state law, Table 2.)

In Louisiana only ex-felons convicted prior to the adoption of the 1974 state constitution can vote upon their release,[15] whereas in Washington only those convicted after the state enacted statutory changes in 1984 enjoy this privilege.[16] Sixteen other states are particularly unaccommodating to anyone who has broken federal law; they won't re-enfranchise these wrongdoers unless they secure a pardon from the president of the United States.[17]

Among the fifteen states and the District of Columbia that restore voting rights to individuals as soon as they are released from prison, many are relatively liberal—Ohio, Massachusetts, Hawaii, Oregon, Michigan, and Pennsylvania—but some have more conservative political cultures, such as Idaho, Utah, Montana, and

Table 2. Categories of Felons Disenfranchised under State Law
(January 1, 2004)

State	Prison	Probation	Parole	Ex-felons
Alabama	Y	Y	Y	By pardon (prior to 2003: permanent disfranchisement)
Alaska	Y	Y	Y	
Arizona	Y	Y	Y	2d felony
Arkansas	Y	Y		
California	Y		Y	
Colorado	Y		Y	
Connecticut	Y	Prior to 2002	Y	
Delaware	Y	Y	Y	Five-year waiting period (prior to June 2000: permanent disfranchisement)
D.C.	Y			
Florida	Y	Y	Y	Y
Georgia	Y	Y	Y	
Hawaii	Y			
Idaho	Y			
Illinois	Y			
Indiana	Y			
Iowa	Y	Y	Y	Y
Kansas	Y	Y (adopted in 2002)	Y (adopted in 2002)	
Kentucky	Y	Y	Y	Y
Louisiana	Y			
Maine				
Maryland	Y	Y	Y	Three-year waiting period (prior to 2002: three-year waiting period and permanent disfranchisement after 2d violent felony)
Massachusetts	Post-2000			
Michigan	Y			
Minnesota	Y	Y	Y	
Mississippi	Y	Y	Y	Y
Missouri	Y	Y	Y	

(continued)

Table 2. *Continued*

State	Prison	Probation	Parole	Ex-felons
Montana	Y			
Nebraska	Y	Y	Y	
Nevada	Y	Y	Y	All except first-time nonviolent offenders (prior to 2003: All)
New Hampshire	Y			
New Jersey	Y	Y	Y	
New Mexico	Y	Y	Y	Prior to 2002
New York	Y		Y	
North Carolina	Y	Y	Y	
North Dakota	Y			
Ohio	Y			
Oklahoma	Y	Y	Y	
Oregon	Y			
Pennsylvania	Y			
Rhode Island	Y	Y	Y	
South Carolina	Y	Y	Y	
South Dakota	Y			
Tennessee	Y	Y	Y	Prior to 1986
Texas	Y	Y	Y	For two years
Utah	Y			
Vermont				
Virginia	Y	Y	Y	Five-year waiting period for some ex-felons; seven years for drug offenders
Washington	Y	Y	Y	Prior to 1984
West Virginia	Y	Y	Y	
Wisconsin	Y	Y	Y	
Wyoming	Y	Y	Y	All except first-time nonviolent offenders, five-year wait (prior to March 2003: All)
U.S. Total	49	29	32	14

Source: The United States Elections Project, http://elections.gmu.edu/ Turnout%20Tables.xls, accessed June 22, 2005.

Note: Y = Yes

Louisiana. Even so, the general political climate of a particular state is no guarantee that a person will be able to regain the franchise upon release from prison. Ex-felons have a particularly hard time retrieving their vote in historically progressive Washington State.[18]

States that impose restrictions disenfranchise, on average, 1.2 percent of their voting-age citizens.[19] The actual numbers vary greatly, however: In 2000 Florida alone stripped the vote from 827,207 former prisoners—more than 7 percent of its voting-age population. Texas denied suffrage to some 525,967 people—3.54 percent of its electorate; together these two states prohibited some 1,353,174 people from voting—almost 29 percent of the citizens nationwide who were unable to participate in the 2000 presidential election. The top five disenfranchisers—Florida, Texas, Virginia, California, and Alabama—account for more than half this total.[20] (See Table 3 for disenfranchisement rates as a percentage of the voting-age population as of January 1, 1999.)

Still more striking is the racial impact (Table 4). More than 1.8 million of those barred from the polls are African Americans,[21] prompting the U.S. Civil Rights Commission to conclude that the disenfranchisement of ex-convicts is "the biggest hindrance to black voting since the poll tax."[22]

In the 2000 presidential election 7.48 percent of black men were disenfranchised—a rate seven times the national average (Table 4). In southern and border states, collectively, the rate was 25 percent, and in Florida an astonishing 16.02 percent of black men could not cast a ballot.[23] Racial disparities exist in virtually every state that penalizes ex-felons.[24] One out of every four persons who have lost their right to vote in Iowa, Washington, and Wyoming is black or Hispanic, and in New Mexico, according to a Santa Fe newspaper, as many as 45 percent of the state's black males have been barred from the polls—"the highest ratio in the country" (Table 4).[25]

Hispanics lag behind blacks, but they're catching up; as I note in Chapter 3, they now constitute more than 10 percent of the disenfranchised population. They are now more likely than African Americans to have lost their vote in seven states, and they fare particularly badly in three—California, Florida, and Texas (which in 2000 disenfranchised 104,597, 107,194, and 156,564 Hispanics, respectively).[26]

These statistics are worrisome. Democracy is dealt a blow whenever citizens are prohibited from voting, but the blow is even more damaging when a disproportionate number of these citizens are racial or ethnic minorities. Even at full voting strength they have difficulty safeguarding their interests through the political process, and when hundreds of thousands of their members are stripped of the franchise, these difficulties are vastly compounded.

Table 3. Disenfranchised Population as a Percentage of Voting-Age Population (January 1, 1999)

State	Disenfranchisement rate (%)	State	Disenfranchisement rate (%)
Alabama	6.21	Montana	0.44
Alaska	1.70	Nebraska	0.56
Arizona	3.58	Nevada	4.56
Arkansas	2.61	New Hampshire	0.26
California	1.18	New Jersey	2.40
Colorado	0.69	New Mexico	5.52
Connecticut	1.85	New York	1.00
Delaware	5.63	North Carolina	1.31
D.C.	2.44	North Dakota	0.20
Florida	6.24	Ohio	0.60
Georgia	2.80	Oklahoma	1.93
Hawaii	0.42	Oregon	0.38
Idaho	1.40	Pennsylvania	0.40
Illinois	0.51	Rhode Island	2.09
Indiana	0.46	South Carolina	1.72
Iowa	4.14	South Dakota	0.47
Kansas	0.76	Tennessee**	2.03
Kentucky	4.24	Texas	3.64
Louisiana	1.10	Utah	0.57
Maine	0.00	Vermont	0.00
Maryland	3.20	Virginia	5.33
Massachusetts*	0.00	Washington**	3.33
Michigan	0.65	West Virginia	0.60
Minnesota	1.07	Wisconsin	1.32
Mississippi	5.28	Wyoming	4.55
Missouri	1.84	National Total	2.09

Source: John Mark Hansen, "Disenfranchisement of Felons," in "To Assure Pride and Confidence in the Electoral Process" (August 2001), report of the Task Force on the Federal Election System, Task Force Reports to Accompany the National Commission on Federal Election Reform (Ford/Carter Commission), part 8, 4–5. http://millercenter.virginia.edu/programs/natl_commissions/commission_final_report/task_force_report/complete.pdf, accessed June 15, 2005.

*In November 2000, Massachusetts voters passed an initiative to disenfranchise convicted felons during the period of their incarceration.

**Tennessee and Washington State deny the franchise to felons convicted before these states eased their laws in the 1980s.

Table 4. Disenfranchisement Population as a Percentage of Voting-Age Population, Categorized By Race (January 1, 1999)

State	All (%)	Black (%)	White, Latino, and other non–African American (%)
Alabama	6.21	12.41	4.26
Alaska	1.70	5.65	1.55
Arizona	3.58	11.75	3.29
Arkansas	2.61	7.60	1.78
California	1.18	4.84	0.87
Colorado	0.69	4.07	0.55
Connecticut	1.85	6.42	1.73
Delaware	5.63	15.60	3.45
D.C.	2.44	4.18	0.58
Florida	6.24	13.77	5.07
Georgia	2.80	6.08	1.62
Hawaii	0.42	0.26	0.42
Idaho	1.40	4.05	0.47
Illinois	0.51	2.39	0.21
Indiana	0.46	5.24	0.07
Iowa	4.14	22.52	3.81
Kansas	0.76	5.22	0.50
Kentucky	4.24	14.96	3.46
Louisiana	1.10	2.87	0.36
Maine	0.00	0.00	0.00
Maryland	3.20	7.57	1.62
Massachusetts	0.00	0.00	0.00
Michigan	0.65	2.72	0.34
Minnesota	1.07	7.54	0.91
Mississippi	5.28	9.71	3.06
Missouri	1.84	6.56	1.31
Montana	0.44	3.33	0.43
Nebraska	0.56	3.83	0.42
Nevada	4.56	16.53	3.66
New Hampshire	0.26	1.91	0.25
New Jersey	2.40	9.73	1.25
New Mexico	5.52	24.78	5.00
New York	1.00	3.11	0.57
North Carolina	1.31	3.72	0.68
North Dakota	0.20	1.04	0.20
Ohio	0.60	3.10	0.30
Oklahoma	1.93	8.00	1.47
Oregon	0.38	2.74	0.32
Pennsylvania	0.40	2.56	0.19

(continued)

Table 4. *Continued*

State	Disenfranchisement rate		
	All (%)	Black (%)	White, Latino, and other non–African American (%)
Rhode Island	2.09	11.68	1.65
South Carolina	1.72	3.90	0.88
South Dakota	0.47	2.64	0.46
Tennessee	2.03	5.86	1.36
Texas	3.64	8.77	2.95
Utah	0.57	5.01	0.53
Vermont	0.00	0.00	0.00
Virginia	5.33	13.82	3.35
Washington	3.33	12.32	3.01
West Virginia	0.60	2.70	0.54
Wisconsin	1.32	10.61	0.86
Wyoming	4.55	14.94	4.46
Total U.S.	2.09	6.57	1.49

Source: John Mark Hansen, "Disenfranchisement of Felons," in "To Assure Pride and Confidence in the Electoral Process" (August 2001), report of the Task Force on the Federal Election System, Task Force Reports to Accompany the National Commission on Federal Election Reform (Ford/Carter Commission), part 8, 4–5. http://millercenter.virginia.edu/programs/natl_commissions/commission_final_report/task_force_report/complete.pdf, accessed June 15, 2005.

U.S. Disenfranchisement Policy in Comparative Perspective

Virtually every other democratic nation in the world considers America's disenfranchisement laws unjust and punitive. By virtue of these laws, ironically, the modern world's first democracy now lags behind the same countries it once inspired—most of which have severely limited or abolished altogether restrictions on ex-felon suffrage. The trend among them, in fact, is to extend voting rights to individuals who are still behind bars—as South Africa, Canada, Israel, Japan, Kenya, Peru, Zimbabwe, Puerto Rico, and eighteen European countries now do.[27] In a recent Israeli election, an imprisoned felon even led the Shas Party in its successful campaign to win seats in the Knesset.[28]

Even among the few developed countries that continue to impose some voting restrictions, the United States is exceptional. In

Finland and New Zealand ex-felons are barred from the polls for a few years following their discharge from prison—but only if they have been convicted of electoral fraud.[29] In Australia and New Zealand, Austria, Belgium, Italy, and Norway, released prisoners forfeit their voting rights only for major crimes. In this country, as noted above, the commission of even minor offenses, or offenses bearing no relationship to the electoral process, can result in long-term or even lifetime disenfranchisement.[30]

Judges in France, Germany, and Greece can order the suspension of voting rights as an additional punishment for serious crimes—but, notably, the suspension is temporary and it is imposed only in a deliberate and calibrated manner. In many American states, conversely, convictions automatically trigger disenfranchisement. Often, neither judges nor defendants even realize that the vote, the constituent act of citizenship, is forfeited when a guilty verdict is announced.[31]

With respect to its disenfranchisement policies, the United States not only parts company with most other democracies but aligns itself with many of the world's most authoritarian regimes. Among the first actions Chilean dictator Augusto Pinochet took upon seizing power in 1973, for example, was to push through a constitutional amendment prohibiting ex-prisoners from voting for the rest of their lives.[32] In contrast to authoritarian regimes, the bulk of which silence former prisoners, many countries that have thrown off totalitarian rule—such as Armenia, Bulgaria, the Czech Republic, Estonia, Hungary, Romania, and Russia—have restored ex-convicts' right to vote.[33] In this one respect the United States has more in common with Chile under Pinochet than with the newly liberated polities of eastern Europe.

Unlike the Chilean policy, however, which is fairly recent, many U.S. disenfranchisement provisions have been in force since the country's founding; indeed, they are apparently sanctioned by the Constitution itself. They have historically been justified on theoretical and practical grounds—that individuals who flout the social contract forfeit their right to participate in communal decision making, for instance, or that convicted felons might imperil the general welfare by supporting disreputable candidates or anti-social policies. (A more recent justification, discussed at some length in Chapter 5, is seldom stated out loud: In the absence of disenfranchisement laws, ex-felons might swell the ranks of the Democratic Party.)

The Prospects for Reform

Members of this country's large and growing reform movement are mapping their strategy with care. They know that Americans have little sympathy for convicted felons in the abstract, but they take heart from two recent studies showing that such is the public's commitment to democratic principles that it supports—"by overwhelming majorities"—the restoration of voting rights to individuals who have completed their sentences and the terms of their parole.[34]

Public support doesn't necessarily translate into public policy, of course. Whether a given state will in fact restore voting rights depends upon its particular history and political culture: Has it practiced wide-scale disenfranchisement in the past? Does its electorate favor policies that are relatively lenient or "tough on crime"? The party affiliation of a state's governing powers also influences its response: Would enfranchising former prisoners endanger incumbents or otherwise challenge the status quo? Would it antagonize key constituents?

The prospects for reform also depend on a host of other unpredictable and idiosyncratic factors, among which are the outcome of legal challenges mounted by public interest law groups and the presence of well-mobilized and savvy political action coalitions. International condemnation could also be a factor, accelerating reform the same way it did in the 1950s, when it targeted institutional racial segregation in the United States.

In this book I discuss the arguments for and against disenfranchisement policies and examine these policies from historical, political, penological, and philosophical perspectives. I also examine reform efforts undertaken by Congress and individual states, particularly those initiated after the 2000 presidential election.

In the final third of the book I examine the extent to which felon disenfranchisement is consistent with statutory, constitutional, and international law, and in the penultimate chapter I crawl out on a limb and suggest that conferring voting rights even on citizens still behind bars might not be altogether outlandish.

While I would like to see ex-felons regain the vote, I respect those who support disenfranchisement on thoughtful and public-spirited (as opposed to merely reflexive or punitive) grounds, and I make a good-faith effort to accord their points of view due consideration.

2 The History of Disenfranchisement Laws

Early History

Former Supreme Court Justice Felix Frankfurter once observed that people have a tendency to confuse the familiar with the necessary.[1] His observation explains why many laws—those delineating gender roles, say, or prohibiting miscegenation—were so widely assumed to reflect necessities that for centuries they went almost unchallenged. So it is with laws that disenfranchise ex-felons: They, too, have deep roots, and until recently few questioned whether they were indeed necessary—let alone just.

At least as far back as ancient Greece and Rome, polities engaged in *infamia* ("ignominy" or "disgrace"), subjecting members who committed "infamous" crimes to "civil death."[2] These malefactors were denied the perquisites of citizenship, such as the right to vote, participate in court proceedings, or defend the homeland.

After the fall of the Roman Empire, the practice spread throughout Europe, manifesting itself in the German practice of "outlawry" (under which an outlaw was a "bando" or wolf, for if he did not flee to another country he was forced to dwell in the forest like a wild beast) and in the English common-law tradition known as "attainder."[3] Once convicted of a heinous crime, an English citizen was pronounced "attainted" and was subject to three penalties: forfeiture, so-called "corruption of the blood" (which prohibited the guilty party from retaining, inheriting, or passing an estate to his heirs), and loss of civil rights. An attainted individual's marriage was dissolved and he was forbidden to bring suit or enter into contracts. Like his counterparts on the continent, he experienced "civil death."

The possibility of civil death was intended to discourage illegal and immoral behavior. While continental Europe, England, and even colonial America punished miscreants by hanging, burning at the stake, branding, and pillorying, disenfranchisement provided a different kind of deterrent. As Nora Demleitner has observed, "the stigma of the loss of civil rights in the small community of those times increased the humiliation and isolation suffered by the offender and his family and served as a warning to the rest of the community, all of whom probably knew the offender."[4]

In the course of settling North America, the English colonists transplanted much of their common-law heritage, including the imposition of civil disabilities and forfeiture of property that resulted from attainder. Indeed, Alec Ewald points out that early Plymouth would not admit as a freeman "any opposer of the good and wholesome laws of the colonie," and seventeenth-century Massachusetts judges could at their discretion disenfranchise anyone guilty of fornication or any "shamefull and vitious crime."[5]

Following the American Revolution, the newly independent states continued to subject miscreants to civil death, although they rejected England's severe common-law strictures. The framers of the Constitution, for example, specifically prohibited forfeiture and corruption of blood except for those convicted of treason. In the second half of the twentieth century, states also abolished many of the remaining consequences of civil death, such as prohibitions against entering into contracts or inheriting property.[6]

The states, however, retained one remnant of civil death: disenfranchisement. As early as 1776 Virginia passed a law prohibiting ex-felons from voting. Before the Civil War, nineteen of the thirty-four states in the Union had adopted similar legislation, and by 1869 twenty-nine had done so. The trajectory has continued upward; by 2004, forty-eight states imposed some limits on the voting rights of ex-felons.[7]

Disenfranchisement was not widely practiced during the early days of the American Republic, since at that time only white men of property were entitled to vote. When a member of this privileged group *was* singled out for civil death, however, his offenses were presumably considered particularly deleterious to the commonwealth, and his banishment was intended as much to deter others from engaging in similar behavior as to stigmatize him.

Disenfranchisement after the Civil War

John J. Miller noted in a recent *National Review* article that "[b]ans on [ex-felon voting] are as old as the Constitution. Unlike a literacy test in 1965 Mississippi, this form of discrimination doesn't grow out of malign intentions."[8] Roger Clegg, general counsel for the Center for Equal Opportunity, agrees, arguing that the fact that all but two states have disenfranchisement laws "indicates that something other than racial discrimination was the motive."[9]

Miller and Clegg are partially right: Most of the disenfranchisement laws enacted before 1865 were not racist in intent. They're wrong, however, in claiming that the statutes enacted in the decades following the Civil War were similarly innocent. As investigative reporter Nicholas Thompson has observed, many of these measures remain "anachronistic remnants of the hideous post–Civil War Reconstruction period."[10] Indeed, between 1890 and 1910 many states adopted new laws or reconfigured preexisting laws to handicap newly enfranchised black citizens whose rights had been expanded by both the Fourteenth and Fifteenth Amendments. In fact, after performing a statistical analysis of the circumstances surrounding the adoption of disenfranchisement laws in the United States, three sociologists concluded that most of these laws resulted from a backlash against the Fifteenth Amendment, which was ratified in 1870 and extended the suffrage to black males.[11]

Southern states held constitutional conventions, particularly in the years between 1890 and 1910, at which they adopted provisions that both reflected and reinforced the backlash—literacy tests, grandfather and "understanding" clauses, property qualifications, and poll taxes. The purpose of these various measures, as the president of Alabama's all-white 1901 convention explained, was "within the limits imposed by the Federal Constitution to establish white supremacy."[12]

The conventions also adopted disenfranchisement provisions—which, in an ironic twist of history, were encouraged by the adoption, in 1868, of the Fourteenth Amendment, which guarantees "all persons," including newly freed blacks, the "equal protection of the laws." Section 2 of the amendment, however, permits states to withdraw suffrage rights from anyone engaged in "rebellion or other crimes"—language that enabled the former slave states to subvert the amendment's very purpose. They did so, first, by criminalizing a host of activities that blacks were supposedly more likely than whites to commit, and then by permanently stripping the franchise from every person convicted of any of these wide-ranging offenses.[13] As Missouri senator Charles D. Drake observed in 1868, "it is a very easy thing in a State to make one set of laws applicable to white men, and another set of laws applicable to colored men."[14]

Mississippi led the way. At its 1890 constitutional convention it replaced an 1869 provision disenfranchising citizens convicted of "any crime" with a narrower one barring only those found guilty of certain petty offenses for which blacks had an apparent proclivity. The move was enthusiastically endorsed by the state's supreme court:

> The Convention swept the circle of expedients to obstruct the exercise of the franchise by the Negro race. By reason of its previous condition of servitude and dependence, this race had acquired or accentuated certain particularities of habit, of temperament and of character, which clearly distinguished it, as a race, from that of the whites—a patient, docile people, but careless, landless, and migratory within narrow limits, without forethought, and its criminal members given rather to furtive offenses than to the robust crimes of the white. Restrained by the federal Constitution from discriminating against the Negro race, the convention discriminated against its characteristics and the offenses to which its weaker members were prone .... Burglary, theft, arson, and obtaining money under false pretenses were declared to be disqualifiers, while robbery and murder, and other crimes in which violence was the principal ingredient, were not.[15]

Until 1968 Mississippi allowed convicted rapists to retain their franchise—rape being considered, along with murder, among those "robust" crimes to which whites were susceptible. Anyone found guilty of the kind of "furtive offenses" to which blacks were reputedly inclined, however—such as bribery, perjury, bigamy, or miscegenation—forfeited their voting privileges into perpetuity.[16] As Nicholas Thompson points out, "for almost a century, then, you wouldn't lose your right to vote in Mississippi if you committed murder or rape, but you would if you married someone of another race."[17]

When Alabama revised its constitution in 1901 it included "wife-beating" among the offenses triggering disenfranchisement, because, as one drafter explained, that crime alone "would disqualify sixty percent of the Negroes."[18] Another provision of the Alabama constitution, section 182, denied voting rights to anyone convicted of a crime involving "moral turpitude." The U.S. Supreme Court invalidated this section in 1985, noting that among the Alabamans who participated in this convention the "zeal for white supremacy [had run] rampant."[19]

South Carolina, similarly, stripped the suffrage from anyone convicted of crimes "to which [the Negro] was especially prone: thievery, adultery, arson, wife-beating, housebreaking, and attempted rape." Significantly, such crimes as murder and fighting, to which the white man was as disposed as the Negro, were omitted from the list.[20]

Some southern states disempowered anyone judged to be a landless laborer, a vagrant, or a farmer who allowed his animals to graze on common lands; historian Eric Foner notes that blacks could also be denied access to the polls if they were jobless, "vagrant," if they used "insulting gestures or language," or "preach[ed] the Gospel without a license."[21] In Mississippi black workers who quit their jobs before their contract expired could be arrested by any Caucasian. In Florida, as John Vile points out, it was a felony to report falsely a bomb threat but only a misdemeanor to issue a false fire alarm. It was felonious for unmarried persons to cohabit "lewdly and lasciviously" but a misdemeanor to commit adultery, a felony to kill another person's animal but a misdemeanor to deprive a child "of necessary food, clothing, or shelter."[22]

Disenfranchisement clauses were intended to provide states with "insurance if courts struck down more blatantly unconstitutional clauses."[23] They have worked precisely as intended. While the poll tax has been eliminated by the Twenty-Fourth Amendment, and while such devices as literacy tests and grandfather clauses have been struck down by the courts or outlawed by the Voting Rights Act of 1965, disenfranchisement provisions have held their ground.

They have also been remarkably effective, contributing—along with poll taxes, literacy tests, and outright intimidation—to the rapid decline of black voting: In Louisiana, after the Civil War, blacks made up 44 percent of the electorate; by 1920, they constituted less than 1 percent. Almost 70 percent of eligible blacks were registered to vote in Mississippi in 1867; two years after the state ratified its new criminal code, in 1890, fewer than 6 percent were registered. The effect was equally stark among black elected officials: In the eleven former confederate states, 324 blacks sat in the state legislature and the U.S. Congress in 1872; eighteen years later, after the bulk of disenfranchisement statutes had been adopted, only five black officeholders remained.[24]

Northern States

Racist laws were not exclusive to the South. When New York adopted its first constitution in 1777, it extended the vote only to free men and property holders. In 1821, after a few black men managed to acquire property, the state duly amended the document to impose stiffer requirements solely on people of African ancestry. New York also denied voting privileges to anyone found guilty of "an infamous crime," and as spokespeople for one organization pointed out, the "infamous crime" disqualification was periodically renewed by legislators well aware that blacks were thirteen times more likely than whites to be convicted of offenses under this rubric.[25] (The "infamous crime" disqualifier has never been repealed.)

After the ratification of the Fifteenth Amendment, New York and other states adopted policies such as poll taxes, literacy tests, and all-white primaries that were less transparently discriminatory than the ones they replaced. Many of these laws remained in force until passage of the Voting Rights Act. (When the Voting Rights Act was enacted in 1965 the Department of Justice concluded that Hispanic citizens in three New York City counties were so disadvantaged under prevailing electoral procedures that they qualified for federal protection under this act.)[26]

Most states in regions outside the South enacted disenfranchisement laws, however, less to disqualify blacks than to prevent those who lacked moral integrity from contaminating the electoral process. In 1899, for instance, New Jersey denied voting rights to anyone convicted of "blasphemy, treason, murder, piracy, arson, rape, sodomy, or any infamous crime against nature, bigamy, robbery, conspiracy, forgery or larceny." The state supreme court found no fault with this all-embracing statute, concluding in 1948 that "its intent was to maintain the purity of our elections by excluding those would be voters whose status was deemed to be inimical thereto."[27]

By 1850, apparently as a consequence of this "purification" movement, roughly one-third of the states subjected ex-felons to lifetime voting bans; by 1920 more than 75 percent did.[28]

Liberalization Movement

Before the remaining states could respond in kind, however, reigning penal theories were temporarily deposed. By the early 1950s criminal justice scholars and practitioners, seeking ways to discourage recidivism, began to emphasize the importance of rehabilitating offenders and reintegrating them into the community. They consequently regarded disenfranchisement provisions as counterproductive.[29]

Yet even with exhortations from prominent public interest groups and support from influential lawmakers, Congress failed to enact legislation re-enfranchising federal offenders upon the completion of their sentences. Several states, however—in what may be a harbinger of current trends—eliminated some mandatory sentences, adopted alternatives to incarceration in a few circumstances, and otherwise liberalized their laws.[30]

This era of relative liberality was short-lived, however—overtaken in the 1970s by a "get-tough-on-crime" movement that replaced rehabilitative measures with policies emphasizing deterrence, retribution, and collateral penalties such as disenfranchisement. In response to this conservative resurgence, state and federal lawmakers determined that the use or sale of even relatively small amounts of illegal drugs would hereafter be considered a felony rather than a misdemeanor. Since felony convictions trigger disenfranchisement, the result has been a continuously expanding cohort of individuals—particularly young men of color—who are denied access to the polls.

Yet, in penalizing drug use, lawmakers were responding the same way legislators in the past have done—that is, by criminalizing activity that influential members of society, at any particular time, consider alarming. As the Supreme Court noted in *Otsuka v. Hite*

(1966), what constitutes a "felony at common law" is usually determined by "historical contingency."[31]

In the congressional debates preceding the ratification of the Fourteenth Amendment, for instance, Nora Demleitner points out that lawmakers stressed the importance of prohibiting pirates from exercising the franchise since they threatened the states' maritime commerce.[32] By the end of the nineteenth century, Americans looked upon Mormonism as a fount of immorality, and as a consequence both Congress and several state legislatures disenfranchised convicted polygamists.[33]

In the coming decades a range of new activities, inspired by technological innovations, will acquire the "felony" imprimatur—the way the deliberate creation of computer viruses already has. But when young technocrats leave prison and attempt to vote, they may benefit from a phenomenon unavailable to the ex-felons who preceded them, the vast majority of whom lacked their social and economic advantages—a public no longer willing to tolerate disenfranchisement laws any more than poll taxes or all-white primaries.

That day has not yet come, however, and in the meantime disenfranchisement laws, for a variety of reasons examined in the next chapter, are again debilitating minority communities as relentlessly as they did at the height of Reconstruction.

3 The Toll on Minority Communities

Even if policies that deny ex-felons the vote are eventually abandoned, their legacy will endure for decades to come—particularly in minority communities. Over the past thirty years these communities have been particularly hard hit by disenfranchisement laws because of two unfortunate and concurrent trends. First, as a by-product of the country's "war on crime," the number of people saddled with felony convictions has mushroomed. Second, this war has been waged disproportionately against racial minorities. The combined effect has been a lamentable decline in the voting strength of America's least privileged citizens.

For roughly fifty years, from the 1920s to the early 1970s, incarceration rates in the United States remained more or less constant at roughly 110 prisoners for every 100,000 people.[1] During this half century, as noted above, rehabilitation was the primary goal of the criminal justice system, and as a result, probation, parole, and indefinite sentencing were emphasized as appropriate tools to reform lawbreakers and reintegrate them into their communities.[2]

Then came the late sixties, with their antiwar and civil rights protests. Richard Nixon, who won the presidency in 1968, exploited the predictable public backlash that followed by taking a severe stand on law and order. Ronald Reagan and George H. W. Bush accelerated the conservative momentum, and from 1980 until 1992 the country experienced the largest increase to date in its prison population.[3]

Still, this increase paled beside the one that took place during the two-term presidency of Bill Clinton. Clinton, a so-called "New Democrat," realized that by encouraging severe crime-control measures he could expunge the long-held public perception that his party was "soft on crime," and at the same time curry favor with a presumptively ever-more-conservative electorate.[4]

By the time Clinton left office, according to Department of Justice statistics, the number of state and federal prisoners had climbed more than 60 percent.[5] It continues upward: At the close of 2003 there were roughly 6.9 million people under the control of the American criminal justice system, or roughly 3.2 percent of this country's adult population. The same year there were 691,301 people in local and county jails and 1,387,269 in state and federal prisons, representing a 3.9 percent rise in the jail, and a 2.3 percent rise in the prison, population. By the end of 2004, moreover, there were 4,073,987 Americans on probation, a 1.2 percent increase from the end of 2002, and 774,588 on parole, a 3.1 percent increase.[6] This massive increase since 1973 prompted one authority to observe that such a rise is unprecedented among democracies, certainly in so short a time.[7]

The War on Drugs

There is one overarching reason why prison populations are bulging—the "war on drugs." In 1980 one out of fifteen people in jails and prisons was incarcerated for a drug offense; by 2002 the number was one out of four, a twelve-fold increase.[8] This war, moreover, has focused on racial minorities, which explains in large part why so many people of color have ended up not only as convicted felons but stripped of their right to vote as well.

Although white and minority youths sell and use drugs at about the same rate, black youths are twenty-five times more likely to end up behind bars for drug-related crimes.[9] In at least fifteen states, remarkably, black males in general were imprisoned on drug charges at rates anywhere from twenty to fifty-seven times those of white men, thereby making up, nationwide, fully 74 percent of those incarcerated for drug offenses.[10] The author of an article in *The Economist* maintains that, given these disparities, the "war on drugs" could more accurately be called a "war on minorities,"[11] and in August 2001 more than a hundred politicians, celebrities, and religious leaders wrote a letter to UN Secretary General Kofi Annan urging acknowledgment of the drug war as a "de facto form of racism."[12]

Racist Law Enforcement

Whether or not the drug war deliberately targets people of color, through virtually every step of the criminal justice process they are treated more severely than whites. Police target low-income, street-level drug offenders, who are predominantly black or Hispanic, rather than white suburbanites.[13] Prosecutors use their ample discretion to thwart plea bargaining that might allow minorities to be charged with a misdemeanor rather than a felony, or to be sentenced to community service or drug counseling in lieu of time behind bars.[14]

This disparate treatment has been abundantly documented. The Justice Policy Institute found, for instance, that in the Los Angeles area, white youth, from arrest to sentencing, were treated more leniently than nonwhites.[15] Both a Human Rights Watch study[16] and a 1995 report by New York's Division of Criminal Justice Services similarly concluded that in the country at large Caucasian youth received preferential treatment.[17]

Other factors also contribute to the racial disparity: Both the public at large and criminal justice officials tend to regard as suspect any activity primarily associated with urban minorities. Marijuana possession was stiffly penalized during the first half of the twentieth century, when blacks were its major users; only when white middle-class college students started smoking the substance in the late sixties were these penalties softened.[18] Today, similarly, crack-cocaine use, for which urban blacks are disproportionately convicted, tends to result in felony convictions and the resulting disenfranchisement far more often than does the use of powder cocaine, the drug of choice among suburban whites.[19]

Significantly more whites than blacks can afford to hire a capable attorney, a fact that also contributes to the racial disparity.[20] A competent attorney, if nothing else, can usually get a felony charge reduced to a misdemeanor. Most African Americans charged with drug-related offenses, however, must rely on overworked public defenders.[21]

Jim Crow Redux?

Not all disenfranchisement laws are intentionally racist, as I noted earlier, but they have nevertheless succeeded in banning blacks from the polls at rates last seen during the heyday of the Jim Crow era. According to the Leadership Conference on Civil Rights, in fact, the rate of black disenfranchisement "threaten[s] to negate fifty years of hard-fought civil rights progress."[22]

Forty-eight of the fifty states prohibit felons from voting while they are in prison, and many extend the prohibition indefinitely upon their release (see Table 4 in Chapter 1). Not surprisingly, given their conviction rates, more than 1.8 million of the disenfranchised are African American men—13 percent of their population in the United States.[23] By comparison, 7 percent of Hispanic males and 5.9 percent of white males have lost their vote.[24] African American women are also dramatically overrepresented: In 2004 they had the dubious distinction of being disenfranchised at four times the rate of other females.[25]

Bad as this is, it will get worse: The Bureau of Justice Statistics predict, based on current rates of incarceration, that an estimated 32 percent of black males will enter prison during their lifetime, and among them nearly three in ten will temporarily or permanently lose their vote.[26] Yet even this estimate is probably low. Tens of thousands of felons are sentenced to parole or probation rather than incarceration, and many among them are also stripped of their voting rights. According to predictions made by the Bureau of Justice, if they are included, then fully 29 percent of the upcoming generation of black men are likely to lose their vote for at least some period of their lives.[27]

This adds insult to injury. Blacks, the victims of egregiously discriminatory criminal justice policies, are incarcerated at staggering rates. Upon their release they discover that it's harder than ever for someone saddled with a prison record to find a job.[28] They return to communities, moreover, that are themselves caught in a vicious cycle: Their electoral representation declines as their disenfranchised population swells, rendering them increasingly incapable of treating the social pathologies that breed crime in the first place.[29]

Dissenting Voices

Not everyone agrees that disenfranchisement policies necessarily harm the black community. According to Todd Gaziano, director of legal studies at the Heritage Foundation, banning convicted felons from the polls actually benefits law-abiding residents of high-crime neighborhoods, where a high percentage of racial minorities often live, by preventing malefactors from diluting their vote.[30] Roger Clegg, general counsel for the Center for Equal Opportunity, agrees: Erstwhile felons, if allowed to cast ballots, would put minority neighborhoods in "real danger" by voting as a bloc for "anti-law-enforcement" policies and candidates. Clegg charges, moreover, that re-enfranchisement would allow the "race card" to trump the claims of "individual responsibility." Just because racial minorities are overrepresented among those denied voting privileges does not mean that the laws themselves need changing, he argues. Rather, "if there is a large number of young black males engaged in antisocial behavior, the answer is to change the behavior, not the laws."[31]

Massachusetts state representative Francis L. Marini does Clegg and Gaziano one better. He was the primary legislative sponsor of an ultimately successful 2000 bid to strip voting rights from Massachusetts prisoners, and he thinks opposition to disenfranchisement can itself be discriminatory. In response to the charge that prohibiting inmates from voting would inordinately penalize nonwhite voters, he retorted that "[t]he idea that average minorities share a community of interests with incarcerated felons who may have the same skin color is insulting, at best. At worst, it is racist."[32]

Some blacks, as well, resent the suggestion that disenfranchisement laws are implicitly racist. Noting that African Americans are disproportionately the victims of crime, they have little sympathy for its perpetrators, whatever their color. Others, while not necessarily opposing restoration drives, consider other issues more pressing: "If I had to weigh what to put my energies into, it would be in increased opportunities [for former prisoners] in affordable housing, treatment and job training," says James Kelly, president of the Urban League of Metropolitan Seattle.[33]

Roger Clegg, Todd Gaziano, and Francis Marini may be right that disenfranchisement laws do not deliberately target blacks and

Hispanics. But they and like-minded commentators can scarcely deny the toll these laws exact on minority communities. Perhaps they would argue that they're worth it anyway. In the next chapter I will attempt to determine whether disenfranchisement provisions are indeed "worth it anyway"—that is, whether their benefit to society at large is sufficient to offset the damage they do to particular individuals and neighborhoods.

4 Collateral Damages and Clemency

Disenfranchisement laws wreak particular havoc on minority communities, but they encumber everyone with a felony record, whatever their color—so much so, in fact, that two-thirds of the men and women released from prison end up behind bars again within three years.[1] These laws foster recidivism by sapping the political power of former prisoners, as a class, making them easy targets for politicians who can restrict their access to jobs and social service benefits whenever they must cut the budget or brandish their "get tough" credentials. Of course, these restrictions, some of which are discussed below, make it all the more difficult for ex-felons to gain a foothold in law-abiding society.

Public Service

The thought of convicted felons determining the fate of their fellow citizens is unnerving to many public officials. As one after another has said, in so many words: "Do you want a serial killer, or a sex fiend, sitting in judgment of you?" In many states, accordingly, ex-prisoners forfeit not only their franchise but also the right to serve on a jury unless they are granted administrative or judicial dispensation. In Florida, given its reluctance to issue pardons, the vast majority of convicted felons remain ineligible for life; in New York they remain similarly disqualified unless and until the state awards them a certificate of relief from disabilities.[2]

Whether offenders can hold public office depends upon both state and constitutional law, as illustrated by the plight of former congressman James Traficante Jr. When this Ohio Democrat was convicted in April 2002 of several federal offenses, he refused to relinquish his House seat and vowed to run for re-election as an independent.[3] As it turned out, however, he couldn't run, since he would be serving his sentence in a Pennsylvania rather than an Ohio prison, and the Constitution requires that House members reside in the district they serve.[4] But what if he *had* been imprisoned in an Ohio facility, and the people of his district, well aware of his criminal history, reelected him anyway?

The Constitution does not prohibit either convicts or parolees from serving in the U.S. Congress or even as president of the United States as long as they are otherwise qualified. As Bill Kimberling, a Federal Election Commission director, explains, "The founding fathers thought about that but didn't include it in the Constitution because they were afraid a sitting president could have all the members of his opposition arrested. They could be convicted felons and then nobody could run against him."[5]

The House of Representatives' code of official conduct stipulates that members found guilty of crimes carrying prison terms of two or more years *should* "refrain from voting" and "refrain from taking part in the business of all committees of which they are members." The rules don't bar convicted lawmakers from attending or addressing legislative sessions, however, or from running for re-election. The House Ethics Committee can also impose punishments—ranging anywhere from light fines to expulsion. Yet in the entire history of the House of Representatives, only four members have actually been expelled (three of them for conduct traitorous to the Union in the Civil War era).[6] Perhaps this is because members, serving in what they consider "the people's chamber," are reluctant to defy the will of the voters by ejecting their freely chosen delegate.

Upon his release from prison, Traficante could run for state—as distinct from federal—office, provided that he chose the right jurisdiction. He should avoid Pennsylvania, since according to its constitution "no person hereafter convicted of embezzlement of public moneys, bribery, perjury or other infamous crime, shall be eligible to the General Assembly, or capable of holding any office of trust or profit in this Commonwealth."[7] He might consider campaigning in New York, however, where the right to hold office is automatically restored as soon as prisoners complete their sentences and parole.[8]

Whether to run for office is not a consideration for most of the 630,000 state and federal inmates who were discharged into their various communities in 2002.[9] They tend, rather, to be preoccupied with matters of basic survival.

Most offenders enter prison with little in their favor. They are apt to be black or Hispanic and more than likely poorly educated. (According to a recent survey, more than 50 percent of California inmates were functionally illiterate.)[10] They are probably ill equipped for any decent-paying job, and chances are they suffer from drug addiction, alcoholism, or mental illness.[11] Still, they have not yet reached bottom—that comes when they get out.

Upon release, these former inmates experience what criminologists call "invisible punishments," that is, the punitive and often counterproductive barriers that restrict their rights and opportunities no less than steel bars once restricted their movement.[12] They discover that as ex-convicts they are no longer entitled to their pensions, disability, or Veterans Administration benefits.[13] They find it difficult to secure affordable housing, food, health care, educational loans, a gun permit, or employment. The American Bar Association, acknowledging the devastation imposed by these "invisible sentences," has adopted guidelines calling for states to disclose post-release penalties at any plea-bargain or sentencing hearing.[14]

These consequences are "invisible" because most defendants, lawyers, and even sentencing judges—let alone the public at large—are unaware that they exist. Like disenfranchisement sanctions, they are imposed administratively rather than by the sentencing court, and as a result their wisdom is rarely debated or their impact weighed. They are slipped into congressional bills at the last moment, often as riders or amendments, and they typically mandate that jurisdictions failing to impose the prescribed penalty forfeit federal money.[15] When Congress passed the Welfare Reform Act, for instance, one of its caveats prevented anyone with a drug conviction from receiving its benefits. This consequential provision was introduced and approved in just two minutes.[16]

Employment

The dearth of decent-paying jobs available to ex-convicts is the major cause of recidivism. Even the few inmates who emerge from prison trained as computer programmers, teachers, or barbers soon discover that the handful of positions open to them are low-paying dead ends. However well they perform on job interviews, moreover, ex-felons are rarely called back once employers check their records (which, by virtue of digital technology, can be easily accessed through credit reporting agencies or other investigative services).[17]

Many employers consider background checks indispensable, particularly in the aftermath of the September 11 terrorist attacks, and worry that without such checks they themselves could incur liability by hiring an ex-convict who then committed a new crime. (They needn't worry unduly: Employers are usually insulated from culpability as long as they could not have foreseen the crime.)[18]

A survey of employers in five large cities found that 65 percent would not knowingly hire anyone with a prison record. Many couldn't even if they wanted to, since as part of the latest "get-tough-on-crime" movement states themselves now prohibit ex-convicts from working in scores of professions. Illinois, for instance, bars them from fifty-seven different positions, and as a result they are no longer allowed to cut hair or polish nails.[19]

Although no federal law explicitly forbids employers to blackball anyone with an arrest or conviction record, the Equal Employment Opportunity Commission has ruled that many across-the-board bans violate the Civil Rights Act of 1964 because of their disparate impact on minority applicants.[20] This act is so laden with exceptions, however, and the relief it provides so hard to come by, that disappointed job seekers would be better advised to seek redress under state law.

Not that most state law is much better, although many jurisdictions forbid employers to discriminate against job applicants solely because of their arrest or conviction records (unless the position requires bonding). Employers *are* allowed to disregard anyone whose offenses are directly relevant to the job for which they are applying, however (Chase Manhattan needn't hire convicted embezzlers), or whose backgrounds render them an unacceptable risk for vulnerable populations (public schools needn't hire pedophiles), or that are otherwise particularly susceptible to abuse.[21] In a 1960 case, for instance, the Supreme Court upheld a statute forbidding ex-convicts to receive longshoremen's licenses because, it said, the restriction was "a reasonable means for achieving a legitimate state aim, namely, eliminating corruption on the waterfront."[22] Other tribunals have also permitted states to deny licenses to ex-felons seeking to work as plumbers, palm readers, or food caterers, where the link to corruption seems less tenable.[23]

Education

In order to make college affordable, the Higher Education Act (HEA) was passed in 1965 to provide poor students with federal loans, grants, and work-study programs. In 1998, however, Congress attached an amendment to the HEA denying federal aid to anyone with a drug conviction. The period of ineligibility is one year for a first conviction and two years for a second; third-time "users" forfeit educational benefits for life.[24] Under federal law, moreover, no one found guilty of drug possession can ever qualify for a "Hope Credit," which ordinarily allows $1,500 in tax deductions.[25]

Since 2000 almost 88,000 students have been denied access to financial aid because of the HEA amendment.[26] (The John W. Perry Fund awards financial assistance to needy students who lose federal aid under this policy, as do some colleges and universities, such as Hampshire, Swarthmore, and Yale.)[27]

Social Welfare

Ex-felons are denied many other government benefits as well. Under Section 115 of the 1996 Personal Responsibility and Work Opportunity Reconciliation Act, as noted above, individuals convicted of a drug-related offense that occurred after August 22, 1996, are prohibited from receiving, for at least five years, Temporary Assistance for Needy Families (TANF), Social Security, Medicare, food stamps, or any other federal health benefit.[28] States are free to modify these prohibitions, but as of March 2002 almost half were enforcing total bans.[29]

Public Housing

Individuals with felony convictions are also out of luck if they need affordable lodging. They are often ineligible for federal housing subsidies, including Section 8 assistance, which provides vouchers to low-income, elderly, and disabled people so that they can afford private rentals. Worse, former offenders frequently lack the money to put down a security deposit, or even the ability to provide the credit references that the owners of many rental units require.[30]

Partly as a result, ex-felons are well represented among the homeless population. At any given time, according to one study, men and women under parole supervision constitute between 30 and 50 percent of the homeless in Los Angeles and San Francisco. At least 11 percent of the inmates released from state prisons who settled in New York City between 1995 and 1998 similarly ended up living in homeless shelters within two years of their release.[31]

Foster Care

Felon disabilities extend even to the intimacies of family life. According to the Sentencing Project, two-thirds of women in prison have children under the age of eighteen, and many among them are also single parents.[32] Once they are released, they often have trouble maintaining parental rights or reuniting with their children, who might have been placed with relatives or foster parents during their absence. They may also have difficulty caring for other people's children, since the federal Adoption and Safe Families Act of 1997 prohibits individuals with drug and certain other convictions from becoming foster or adoptive parents.[33] By 1999 every state had passed legislation either as tough as or tougher than its federal counterpart.[34]

Clemency

Without the franchise, then, ex-felons can't protect themselves or their families, get a leg up, *matter*—witness the plight of southern blacks before passage of the Voting Rights Act in 1965. Until then, literacy tests, grandfather clauses, and poll taxes decimated their voting power, and as a consequence their needs went virtually unaddressed. Once the Voting Rights Act assured African Americans relatively unimpeded access to the polls, however, few officeholders could any longer ignore their interests without jeopardizing their own political futures.[35] So it is with ex-felons. They will continue to be denied decent housing, tuition vouchers, professional licenses, secured loans, and even some parental privileges until they are able to protect themselves through the electoral process.

Reclaiming their voting rights is therefore crucial, and in states where these rights are not automatically reinstated, former inmates can usually retrieve them by receiving either clemency or, on rare occasions, a gubernatorial or presidential pardon. Securing such privileges, however, is usually a formidable undertaking. For instance, according to a headline in the *New Times*, a Florida newspaper, "The Process for Restoring the Civil Rights of Felons in Florida Works Perfectly—If *Not* Restoring Their Rights Is the Goal."[36]

A congressional "finding" concludes that the situation nation-wide is not much better than it is in Florida: "In those States that disenfranchise ex-offenders who have fully served their sentences, the right to vote can be regained in theory, but in practice this possibility is often illusory."[37] Indeed, for many ex-felons the attempt to redeem the franchise is a burdensome, tortuous, often demeaning, and usually futile undertaking—requiring unusual stamina, perseverance, political savvy, and financial resources.

Individual states determine whether, and how, voting rights can be restored. South Dakota, Ohio, and thirty-five other states automatically reinstate these rights when convicts have completed the terms of their sentences and any requisite probation or parole.[38] The remaining thirteen states, however, have adopted wildly variant re-enfranchisement procedures. Eight require a pardon from the governor;[39] Mississippi requires many pardon seekers to win support from two-thirds of the legislature.[40] Some deny clemency to everyone who has not undergone some sort of judicial or administrative procedure at which they have exhibited remorse or demonstrated adequate rehabilitation.[41]

Several states deny absolution to individuals convicted of specified offenses, most commonly murder, arson, child molestation, treason, or election chicanery.[42] Some withhold re-enfranchisement from anyone who has not paid a hefty application fee—sometimes as much as $1,000. Washington State won't process anyone who still owes court costs or restitution fees; at the close of 2001, as a consequence, approximately 46,500 Washingtonians who had completed their sentences were still not eligible even to apply for the reinstatement of their voting rights.[43] Alabamans must not only pay their outstanding debts but must also finance the costly DNA test required of every clemency seeker. (This requirement is difficult to satisfy, in addition to being expensive, since in 2000 only four of the state's sixty-seven counties had equipment capable of processing DNA samples.)[44]

In some jurisdictions claimants must wait a certain number of years following their discharge before they can even apply for the restoration of their voting rights. In a move hailed as a "reform," Wyoming, which until recently disqualified ex-felons for life, now allows those convicted of nonviolent offenses to apply for re-enfranchisement five years after completing their prison sentence or probation.[45]

In Arizona probationers can seek re-enfranchisement through either administrative or judicial procedures; the former requires no waiting period, the latter, a full two years.[46] Residents of Washington State convicted after June 30, 1984, are automatically re-enfranchised, but whether a person who committed his or her crime before that date can ever vote again depends upon an array of variables.[47]

Individuals attempting to regain their suffrage in Alabama, Arizona, Florida, Kentucky, and Tennessee must first notify prosecuting authorities, law enforcement officials, or victims—and sometimes all three. Aspirants in Mississippi must publish—for thirty days—their petitions for pardon in a newspaper of record, and in Virginia they must produce three letters of reference from "reputable" people in the community and "demonstrate" civic responsibility. Pardon seekers in Iowa must receive a favorable evaluation from their prison wardens, and ex-convicts in Maryland must convince clemency boards that there is nothing untoward in their marital histories, religious observances, or leisure activities.[48]

Ex-convicts in Mississippi must either secure an executive order from the governor or persuade a state legislator to introduce a bill on their behalf and then convince two-thirds of the members of both houses to support it, and then receive the governor's signature.[49] Would-be voters in Tennessee have it even worse: Because successive amendments to the criminal statutes were not made retroactive, they must now follow one of five different procedures, depending upon the crime itself and the date of conviction.[50]

Pity anyone convicted of a federal crime who lives in New Jersey, Hawaii, California, or any of thirteen other states that have interpreted the Constitution's supremacy clause to mean that only the president of the United States, exercising his pardoning powers, can grant them absolution. (Most of these states, as a consequence, have no procedure for re-enfranchising residents convicted of a federal offense, although some, like Florida, permit their governor to restore rights granted under state law.)[51]

Using his statutory power, Florida governor Jeb Bush restored the privileges of state citizenship to Charles Colson—the man who encouraged the Nixon administration to firebomb the Bookings Institute and who later served time in prison for his role in the Watergate scandal.[52] Bush is one of eight chiefs of state who must grant a formal pardon before ex-felons within their jurisdictions can retrieve the franchise, and by bestowing this privilege on Colson he illustrated their common tendency to favor individuals who are politically well connected.

Under state law, Jeb Bush, like many of his counterparts, has "unfettered discretion to deny clemency at any time and for any reason."[53] Even where administrative bodies decide who deserves a pardon, however, the process is conducted behind closed doors, in the absence of any standards, accountability, or transparency. Under such circumstances there is nothing to restrain decision makers from considering an applicant's race, religion, or political affiliation. At the very least, such veiled procedures create the appearance of impropriety. For instance, while Governor Bush and his Republican allies on Florida's Board of Clemency may be scrupulously fair-minded in their deliberations, by operating in private and answering to no one they inevitably arouse suspicion that their decisions are influenced by partisan calculations.

Given the hoops through which clemency seekers must jump, the wonder is not that so few succeed but that any do at all! The success rate is generally dismal, however: Seven months after Alabama liberalized its law, only eight hundred applicants—a fraction of its disenfranchised population—recaptured their suffrage;[54] among their counterparts in Tennessee, only one-half of 1 percent regained the vote. A full year after Nevada eased its restrictions, only four petitions had been granted.[55]

In Nevada, Maryland, and presumably in other states as well, the high failure rate is a direct result of procedures that one researcher described as "not only tedious, but extremely complex, incorporating a level of sophistication daunting for the literate and illiterate alike." Not surprisingly, more than half the people who request an application never submit it.[56] Even the intrepid souls who persevere discover that one technical misstep on their part can nullify the whole procedure, forcing them to start all over again.

There is another major reason why so few succeed: Officials seldom tell offenders, upon their release, how to go about regaining their franchise—which, as Elizabeth Simson observes, should be regarded as "[their] bare minimum responsibility in creating civic-minded citizens of ex-felons."[57] According to two recent studies, one by the Brennan Center for Justice at New York University Law School and the other by the NAACP, election authorities are themselves often ignorant of the law and, as a result, sometimes provide erroneous information or require felons to produce documentation that is either unnecessary or nonexistent.[58] The principal investigators of a third study, this a nationwide one conducted by the Prison Reform Advocacy Center and Human Rights Watch, reached the same conclusion, and noted that ignorance of the law was not confined to the election boards, parole officers, or social service agencies: "We even found a breakdown in communication coming from the pulpit of prison ministries."[59] In Ohio, therefore, as in several other states, the likelihood of regaining the vote sometimes depends on something as arbitrary as the competence of local officials. Applicants seeking assistance in Cleveland or Cuyahoga County are fortunate because authorities there, reportedly, dispense accurate information. They are less fortunate if they solicit help in certain other regions, including Cincinnati, because there they will be told that their franchise is irretrievable. According to Davis Singleton, executive director of an Ohio-based prison-reform organization, "This is absolutely unacceptable, that people who are supposed to know the law ... are giving misleading, inconsistent and flat-out wrong information to ex-offenders."[60]

California is no better, according to the director of a prisoner-assistance agency there. "Who gets to vote," he said, "it's the best kept secret in town." California law provides that voting rights are automatically restored once prisoners complete their sentences, parole, or probation, and although correction officials are legally mandated to note this in a prisoner's discharge papers, they frequently neglect to do so. As one ex-felon mused, "isn't it ironic—voting is the fabric of our democracy—yet the one restored right listed on my discharge papers is 'you have the right to own a firearm.' "[61]

Reforms

Although clemency seekers still face daunting odds, their circumstances have improved marginally in some states by virtue of modest reforms recently enacted. Texas and Nevada have reduced the time that one-time offenders must wait, upon completion of their sentences, probation, or parole, before becoming eligible to apply for the restoration of their franchise,[62] and Texas, Kentucky, Missouri, Nebraska, Delaware, Arkansas, and Florida now require corrections officials to provide convicted felons, on a timely basis, with application forms and instructions for reactivating their voting rights.[63] While some of these changes were instituted with little prodding, in Florida they came about only in response to a court order.

Florida: A Case Study

Ex-felons in the Sunshine State forfeit their franchise for life unless they are granted clemency, an unlikely outcome because, as Randall Berg, executive director of the Florida Justice Institute, points out, "The Rules of Executive Clemency established by the Governor ... assure that very few ex-offenders, acting on their own, will be successful."[64]

Until 2002 most former inmates were unaware that a restoration procedure even existed, let alone of how to comply with it. Although the Department of Corrections (DOC) was legally mandated to provide assistance to all inmates approaching the end of their prison terms, during the course of a lawsuit brought by the ACLU it conceded that it had in fact failed to help any of the 124,769 offenders who were released between 1992 and 2001. The ACLU won its suit in August 2002, and a federal court commanded prison officials to fulfill their statutory obligation.[65]

Florida accordingly agreed to create and publicize a new website and toll-free number for anyone needing assistance. In April 2002, the DOC also simplified the application form pardon seekers must complete—this is the good news. The bad news is that DOC employees process these forms in slow motion. Moreover, in 2003 the DOC added another eight crimes to the more than two hundred that already trigger disenfranchisement, thereby ensuring that each year an additional two thousand people or so will be added to the backlog. At the same time, inexplicably, the Florida Board of Clemency refused to hire new staff.[66]

The Board of Clemency itself, which meets only four times annually, considers at most two hundred applications a year. The *Miami Herald* reports, moreover, that since Jeb Bush became governor it has rejected 85 percent of them. As a consequence, the paper said, nearly forty thousand people—80 percent of the fifty thousand felons released from custody between 2001 and 2003—were still unable to vote in the November elections. Most of these clemency seekers, what's more, are nonviolent offenders who served little if any time in prison—the very people board members themselves say should quickly regain their franchise. Jeffrey Jansen, who retired in 2003 after more than twenty-five years with the Florida Parole Commission, which administers the clemency process, concluded that "[t]he whole system is in chaos." "They're making rules that are stopping almost everybody from voting."[67]

The District Court of Appeals for the First District of Florida agreed. In August 2004, responding to another lawsuit brought by public interest groups, it unanimously ruled that Florida was still derelict and it ordered the DOC to implement substantive changes. According to Judge Peter D. Webster, the restoration process then in operation "sounds to me like [one] … intended to continue to disenfranchise a number of these felons."[68]

Shortly after this ruling Governor Bush and the Clemency Board agreed to allow ex-felons who remain crime-free for five years, or whose offenses were relatively minor, to regain their voting rights on an expedited basis.[69] These reforms could indeed be the "substantive" ones the district court ordered—although Randy Berg of the Florida Justice Institute has called them "a complete joke."[70] Why such ingratitude? Because, as Howard Simon, executive director of the ACLU in Florida said, "[t]hose who have successfully completed their sentence, including any probation and parole, should have their full civil rights restored automatically."[71] "If the overall goal is to bring people back as a productive citizen, any waiting period at all is inconsistent with that." Besides, the vast majority of former prisoners will still have to wait years for their hearings, and even then there is no assurance they will regain their rights. Meanwhile, says Berg, Florida still has more ex-prisoners unable to vote than some states have voters.[72]

Regaining the Franchise: A Rite of Passage

Since most ex-felons encounter only misinformation and resistance in their quest for re-enfranchisement, it seems almost hypocritical to suggest honoring the few who succeed. Still, given the centrality of the franchise in a democratic polity, it should be a notable occasion when Charles Colson or anybody else regains his or her voting rights. What Kai Erikson observed in the 1960s, however, is still the case in 2005: One is "ushered into the deviant position by a decisive and often dramatic ceremony, yet is retired from it with hardly a word of public notice. And as a result, the deviant often returns home with no proper license to resume a normal life in the community."[73] Harrison Trice and Paul Roman, among other penologists, accordingly recommend that an offender's readmission to the political community be formally commemorated in what they call a "delabeling," or a "deviant decertification" rite.[74]

Such a rite, however, seems almost fanciful, given that it celebrates an attainment that is beyond the reach of so many ex-felons. At the least, the clemency process should first be purged of its numerous gratuitous and onerous hurdles, and pardon seekers should be provided with considerably more assistance than they are receiving even in the states that recently modified their procedures. Only then will regaining the franchise represent a civic milestone and not the fruit of a decathlon.

5 Justifications for Disenfranchisement, Pragmatic, Principled, and Philosophical

There must be solid reasons to support disenfranchisement laws, considering that at one time 75 percent of the states enforced them, and that even now fully 64 percent continue to do so. Certainly in the South, during the Reconstruction era, these laws served a baldly racist purpose. As we saw in Chapter 3, however, their present-day proponents insist that they now promote a variety of nondiscriminatory and salutary objectives, from deterring crime to rewarding good citizenship to strengthening the social fabric. Are they right? Does stripping ex-convicts of their voting rights indeed further any or all of these goals?

The Pragmatic

According to some criminologists, the prospect of losing one's vote serves as a deterrent, discouraging malefactors from engaging in further crime once they are released from prison and prompting would-be offenders to "think twice" before breaking the law.[1] There is not a shred of evidence to support this claim, however, in part because most criminals don't even know that by robbing a store, say, or selling drugs on the street corner, they might imperil their voting rights; disenfranchisement is consequently a "low-visibility" sanction. Indeed, disenfranchisement is rarely even mentioned in a state's criminal code; it is cited only in those sections of its constitution or sentencing statutes that concern voter qualifications.[2]

Even if aspiring lawbreakers *did* realize that criminal behavior might cost them their vote, they would scarcely be fazed. The vast majority of offenders are well under age thirty, and every study of voting behavior concludes that young people don't value the franchise nearly as much as their elders do.[3] Ironically, then, in being deprived of their ballots, they are losing something they will miss only later in life.

To be sure, it is always difficult to gauge the extent to which a given penalty serves as a deterrent. Yet criminologists know that the likelihood of a long prison sentence, or even the death penalty, does not appreciably discourage crime. It thus seems reasonable to assume that the prospect of losing one's vote won't, either. Certainly states that disenfranchise ex-felons experience no less crime or recidivism than states that do not.[4]

Among its advocates, a few even claim that disenfranchisement encourages rehabilitation, presumably by motivating ex-felons to adopt so responsible a lifestyle that even the least charitable clemency board will see fit to reinstate their voting privileges.[5] Yet even criminologists who agree on virtually nothing else agree that depriving erstwhile convicts of the ballot in no way encourages them to embrace community norms. As Justice William Brennan explained in a 1958 Supreme Court case, referring to the revocation of citizenship but using logic equally applicable to disenfranchisement, the practice "constitutes the very antithesis of rehabilitation." "Instead of guiding the offender back into the useful paths of society," Brennan wrote, "it excommunicates him and makes him, literally, an outcast. I can think of no more certain way in which to make a man in whom, perhaps, rests the seeds of serious antisocial behavior more likely to pursue further a career of unlawful activity than to place on him the stigma of the derelict, uncertain of many of his basic rights."[6]

Re-enfranchisement, conversely, might actually *encourage* rehabilitation. After reviewing research on factors that counter recidivism, criminologists Jeremy Travis and Christy Visher suggest a plausible connection between voting rights and successful reintegration.[7] The National Advisory Commission on Criminal Justice Standards and Goals similarly found that the ex-offender's "respect for law and the legal system may well depend, in some measure, on his ability to participate in that system." Moreover, the commission concluded, "[l]oss of citizenship rights [including] the right to vote … inhibits reformative efforts. If corrections is to reintegrate an offender into free society, the offender must retain all attributes of citizenship."[8]

It seems counterintuitive that merely possessing the franchise would have so regenerative an effect on former prisoners, especially considering how few of them actually show up at the polls. According to several studies, however, including the one conducted by the National Advisory Commission cited above, regaining the vote has enormous symbolic importance because it signifies that one is again entitled to the same rights and privileges that any other member of the community enjoys. Don't most people, moreover, attempt to prove themselves worthy of the privileges society has bestowed upon them?

Abrogating someone's voting privileges is perverse as well as counterproductive. After all, who suffers? Not the unrepentant ex-con who wouldn't waste his time on such a chump ritual, but only those who have reformed, who are now law-abiding citizens eager to exercise their civic responsibilities.

Retribution

Perhaps disenfranchisement constitutes a valid form of "retribution" against those who have unlawfully harmed individuals or the larger community. Among the pragmatic justifications for disenfranchisement, this is the most persuasive. Certainly retribution itself is an age-old practice. As far back as 1750 b.c. Hammurabi instructed his subjects to retaliate against wrongdoers in essentially the same way the Old Testament God commanded his people to respond—i.e., by exacting "an eye for an eye and a tooth for a tooth."[9]

Given its ancient roots and near universality, some criminologists speculate that the need for retribution may be both an inborn human trait and a necessary component of communal society. Supreme Court Justice Potter Stewart suggested as much when he wrote in a 1972 concurring opinion that "the instinct for retribution is part of the nature of man, and channeling that instinct in the administration of criminal justice serves an important purpose in promoting the stability of a society governed by law. When people begin to believe that organized society is unwilling or unable to impose upon criminal offenders the punishment they 'deserve,' then there are sown the seeds of anarchy—of self-help, vigilante justice, and lynch law."[10]

Virtually no decent society, however, condones blind vengeance or retaliation far in excess of the instigating offense. Even the "eye for an eye" reference in Exodus, understood in context, calls for a just—which is to say a "proportional"—response.[11] But that's the rub: Disenfranchisement is rarely "applied judiciously."[12] There is no sliding scale: People who write bad checks forfeit their political rights as readily as someone who slays a bank teller.

Retribution, properly understood, seeks punishment that fits the crime. Exiling former prisoners to the margins of society long after they have completed their sentences is so excessive as to constitute not retribution but unreasonable cruelty. Senator Harry Reid, a former prosecuting attorney, implicitly made this point when he urged his colleagues to support a bill restoring voting rights to ex-felons in federal elections: "We have a saying in this country: If you do the crime, you have to do the time. I agree with that. But if you do the time, and do it completely, why should you have to do more time?"[13]

Perhaps long-term disenfranchisement, scraped of its varnish, is really intended "not for preventive purposes but solely to exclude an offender from society," as law professor Nora Demleitner suggests, or, alternately, simply to stigmatize.[14] Indeed, the sanction was originally instituted in seventeenth-century America to shame and ostracize members of the governing elite who had violated the community's moral or legal code in a particularly objectionable way.[15] Yet what may have been an effective sanction in a small New England village where everyone knew one another becomes merely punishment for its own sake in today's mass society.

The Principled

Although disenfranchisement does not further the traditional ends of criminal justice, perhaps the practice serves other important values. So argued Judge Charles Doherty Gonthier in an eloquent dissenting opinion written in response to a ruling by the Supreme Court of Canada in 2000 invalidating a parliamentary act that suspended the voting rights of certain prisoners.[16] The act had applied exclusively to offenders convicted of serious crimes, and even then only during the period in which they were actually incarcerated.[17] Given its limited application, Judge Gonthier defended the act, and his reasons for doing so merit examination because they are considerably more thoughtful and nuanced than the ones commonly invoked in support of disenfranchisement.

In an effort to define its identity, virtually every country in the world limits the franchise in some way, Gonthier said, and he quoted the renowned American legal scholar Laurence Tribe:

> Although free and open participation in the electoral process lies at the core of democratic institutions, the need to confer the franchise on all who aspire to it is tempered by the recognition that completely unlimited voting could subvert the ideal of popular rule which democracy so ardently embraces. *Moreover, in deciding who may and who may not vote in its elections, a community takes a crucial step in defining its identity. If nothing else, even though anyone in the world might have some interest in any given election's outcome, a community should be empowered to exclude from its elections persons with no real nexus to the community as such.* (Emphasis added.)[18]

Tribe's analysis explains why every country considers citizenship and/or residency a reasonable minimum requirement for voting, Gonthier pointed out, since these attributes frequently signify familiarity with and attachment to a particular commonwealth.

Whereas Canada's charter guarantees fundamental freedoms, legal and equal rights to "everyone," it confers the right to vote only upon "citizens." According to Judge Gonthier, this limitation "reflects the special relationship, characterized by entitlements and responsibilities, between citizens and their community." It is this special relationship that serious criminals have betrayed.

Chief Justice Beverley McLachlin, who spoke for the majority, asserted that disenfranchisement necessarily undermines a prisoner's inherent "worth" and "dignity." Gonthier scoffed at this premise. On the contrary, he said, the very notion of punishment is based on criminals' dignity because it acknowledges them as "rational, autonomous individuals who have made choices." When their choice is to abuse their freedom, the community imposes a correlative penalty. Moreover, is it possible to "punish" serious criminals without undermining their "worth"? If not, why would the Canadian charter condemn only punishment that is "cruel and unusual?"[19] Temporarily withdrawing voting privileges from serious offenders not only "reiterates society's commitment to the basic moral values which underpin the *Criminal Code*, but also respects the inherent value of fellow-citizens who have been or may become victims of crime."[20]

The chief justice further asserted that denying prisoners their voting rights constitutes "an additional and gratuitous punishment that serves only to assuage those not behind bars by further stigmatizing prisoners as disconnected social outcasts."[21] Again Gonthier disagreed. In his view, temporary disenfranchisement deters anyone contemplating crime, encourages ex-felons to forswear further illegal activity, and alerts both the public at large and prospective malefactors that serious breaches of the law will not be tolerated. "When society rejects serious crime it draws a 'moral line' that safeguards the social contract and enhances the relationship between individuals and their community."[22]

Ultimately, Gonthier concluded, both those who support and those who oppose disenfranchisement have "accept[ed] logically prior political or social philosophies about the nature and content of the right to vote."[23] Yet both parties seek the same objective—i.e., to underscore the fundamental importance of the franchise; and in seeking support for their convictions both can point to the practices of the various Canadian provinces, the policies pursued by other liberal democracies, and the theoretical ruminations of scholars. There is accordingly a range of acceptable practices that decent people can support. This being the case, a court called upon to choose among competing social and political theories should define the parameters within which the acceptable reconciliation lies, but then defer to Parliament as long as its choice is an acceptable one "amongst those permitted under the Charter."[24]

John Silber, the former chancellor of Boston University, expressed sentiments similar to Judge Gonthier's when, in October 2000, he urged his fellow citizens to repeal a law then on the books in Massachusetts that permitted felons to vote during the period of their incarceration. "Fundamentally," Silber wrote,

> we imprison them for having broken the social contract that binds
> citizens together. All citizens have an implied obligation to obey the

law with regard to others along with an implied right to expect that others will obey the law with regard to them. In most of the country, the exercise of the vote is understood not merely as conferring the right to govern oneself, but a right to share in the governing of others. When felons demand the right to vote, they demand the right to govern others while rejecting the right of others to govern them. In this they exhibit patent hypocrisy.[25]

Silber, again like Judge Gonthier, emphasized the importance of re-enfranchising prisoners as soon as they had completed their sentences. A failure to do so, he said, would "deny the possibility of redemption and rehabilitation." All sentences, apart from those committing someone to life in prison without parole, are based on the expectation that at some future time the offender will return to the community. "Permanent disenfranchisement," therefore, "makes a mockery of the notion that the term has been served." "Without the vote, they return to society still prisoners to a degree." Society, moreover, is strengthened when former prisoners honor the social contract by respecting the rights of other people. They are less likely to show such respect if they are deprived of their own "correlative rights."[26]

Not all thoughtful people agree with Gonthier and Silber's contention that citizens who have "paid their debt" should regain the franchise. Spokesmen for the Heritage Foundation and the Center for Equal Opportunity maintain, for instance, that simply serving a prescribed term does not necessarily render ex-felons trustworthy or qualified to vote on issues affecting the common good.[27] This is why federal law prohibits erstwhile convicts from possessing firearms, and why most public schools refuse to employ convicted pedophiles. Indeed, as Roger Clegg points out, the Justice Department's Office of the Pardon Attorney publishes a 144-page binder (plus two appendices) enumerating the civil disabilities that the states and federal government impose on ex-felons.[28] "Society is not required, and should not be required, to ignore someone's criminal record once he gets out of prison."[29]

Surely there's a middle ground, however, between ignoring someone's criminal record and using this record as a pretext for denying fundamental rights unrelated to a person's offense. It doesn't follow that just because pedophiles forfeit their right to teach in public schools, or ex-prisoners their right to own handguns, they should also forfeit their right to vote. The one is reasonable, the other, simply punitive.

The Philosophical

Civic Republicanism

Disenfranchisement is also justified by two broad political theories. One, often referred to as "civic republicanism," posits that society's physical and moral health depends upon the virtue of its citizens. A judge articulated this line of reasoning when he explained that ex-felons are prohibited from exercising the franchise because they "lack the character on which the survival of the community depends."[30]

In this country civic republicanism dates back at least to the seventeenth century, when, as Alec Ewald pointed out, the governing fathers in Plymouth, Massachusetts, would not admit as freemen "any opposer of the good and wholesome laws of the colonies." Neither would judges in New England grant voting privileges to anyone convicted of fornication or any "shamefull and vitious crime." Nearly four hundred years later, "celebration of civic virtue and vigilance against corruption are [still] among republicanism's central elements."[31]

Voting, then, becomes a privilege rightfully available only to those who have shown themselves worthy. As a district court judge declared in 1844, "One rendered infamous by conviction of felony, or other base offense indicative of great moral turpitude, ... is unfit to exercise the privilege of suffrage, or to hold office, upon terms of equality, with freemen who are clothed by the State with the toga of political citizenship"[32] (or, as some wags paraphrased it, "you've been bad and no longer deserve a spot on the team").[33]

The noted historian Gordon Wood has observed that underlying the concept of "civic republicanism" is the premise that the American Republic is extremely "delicate," demanding "an extraordinary moral character" in the people. "Whereas no regime could survive unless its members possessed at least a modicum of virtue," he wrote, "a republic which rested solely on the people absolutely required it."[34]

Not only are ex-felons themselves impure, according to this way of thinking, but in the absence of firm boundaries their impurity might infect others. Judges have equated former criminals with contagions, suggesting that by casting ballots they could contaminate the electoral process in the same way a carcinogen could sully a cranberry crop. As one state court reasoned, the "manifest purpose" of denying suffrage to ex-felons "is to preserve the purity of the ballot box, which is the only sure foundation of republican liberty, and which needs protection against the invasion of corruption, just as much as against that of ignorance, incapacity, or tyranny. The evil infection of the one is not more fatal than that of the other."[35] More recently, Texas state representative Harold Dutton sounded a variation on this theme when he warned that "40,000 ex-felons with registration cards is more of a threat than 40,000 ex-felons with guns."[36]

Some courts have carried this reasoning to extremes, portraying convicts as lacking rational capacities as well as moral virtue. In one illustrative case, a judge averred that the suffrage should be denied ex-felons no less than "idiots, insane persons, and minors," who similarly "lack the requisite judgment and discretion which fit them for the exercise."[37]

The Social Contract

A second theory is based on the political constructs of Thomas Hobbes, Jean-Jacques Rousseau, and, in particular, John Locke. They not only provided democratic government with theoretical legitimacy by basing it on an imagined "social contract" but also supplied disenfranchisement policies with an intellectual burnish by suggesting that anyone who violates the contract be sanctioned.[38]

Contract theories posit that autonomous individuals, living freely but precariously in a state of nature, agree to relinquish some of their liberty in exchange for a government that will protect their lives and property. As Locke said, by agreeing to the covenant, every man "authorizes the society, or ... the legislature thereof, to make laws for him as the public good of the society shall require, to the execution whereof his own assistance ... is due."[39]

Covenanters who violate these rules—who "break the terms of the contract"—forfeit their right to participate in communal decision making. Hobbes asserted that a "banished man is a lawful enemy of the commonwealth that banished him";[40] and Locke that a "man who breaks the laws he has authorized his agent to make for his own governance could fairly have been thought to have abandoned the right to participate in further administering the compact."[41]

Courts often use contractarian language to justify disenfranchisement. In one notable 1968 ruling, for instance, circuit court judge Henry Friendly justified the practice by quoting liberally from Locke's second treatise.[42] A Maryland lawmaker similarly paraphrased the philosopher, albeit with considerable license, when he recently argued against liberalizing his state's disenfranchisement laws on the ground that "people convicted of some heinous crime" have "broken their contract with society, and ... even if God forgave them, they shouldn't regain certain societal rights."[43]

The social-contract theory, however—certainly as Locke and Hobbes conceived it—honors the principle of proportionality. As noted above, most disenfranchising states honor this principle only in the breach. Locke made clear in his writings that the power to strip someone of his political rights extends only "so far as calm reason and conscience dictate what is proportionate to [the] transgression, which is so much as may serve for reparation and restraint." Elsewhere he asserted that the damages or punishment individuals suffer "will be proportionate to the breach."[44] In *Leviathan* Thomas Hobbes similarly emphasized the importance of commensurability: "[R]evenge without respect to the example and profit to come is a triumph, or glorying, in hurt of another, tending to no end (for the end is always somewhat to come); and glorying to no end is vainglory, and contrary to reason."[45]

Under the social contract's own terms, individuals relinquish power to the state under the assumption that their transgressions will be punished rationally and equitably. As a district court noted in 1965, "it is hardly likely that free and informed individuals would enter into a contract in which a single failure to execute payment by one party would constitute a forfeiture of all goods previously obtained under the contract."[46]

How many citizens would in fact sign a contract knowing that a single transgression could deny them any future say in their own governance? Yet in many states that is precisely what happens. Even individuals who commit relatively minor offenses can be disenfranchised indefinitely, or sometimes for life.

The Problems

Most of the arguments invoked in support of disenfranchisement are baseless. The notion that denying ex-felons the vote constitutes a deterrent, for instance, is trumped only by the claim that purging them from the voting rosters serves a rehabilitative function. The suggestion that ex-felons lack the moral virtue requisite for civic participation is similarly objectionable: It is antidemocratic, and it presupposes that mere mortals are capable of distinguishing the "meritorious" from the "nonmeritorious." Even the proposition that disenfranchisement reinforces the social contract is bogus, certainly in those states where offenders remain disempowered long after they have completed their sentences, since any contract imposing baldly incommensurate penalties is unjust and maybe even unenforceable.

No less an authority than James Q. Wilson, a conservative who is among the country's foremost criminologists, concedes that "a perpetual loss of the right to vote serves no practical or philosophic purpose."[47] In 1972 an appellate tribunal similarly concluded that "courts have been hard pressed to define the state interest served by laws disenfranchising persons convicted of crimes. The temptation to identify the interest as state concern for additional punishment has been resisted because the characterization creates its own constitutional difficulties. Search for modern reasons to sustain the old governmental disenfranchisement prerogative has usually ended with a general pronouncement that a state has an interest in preventing persons who have been convicted of crimes from participating in the electoral process."[48]

Neither courts nor philosophers nor criminologists nor politicians, then, have been able to provide a convincing rationale for disenfranchisement. Yet that is not to say no such rationale exists. Members of a polity often share deeply felt values, and as long as these values are not invidiously discriminatory they are entitled to respect. Citizens can surely conclude—without being either irrational or unjust—that there is a valuable relationship between exercising the franchise and the obligations of citizenship, or that individuals who break the law, or who engage in harmful or even heinous behavior, should forfeit the right to engage in communal decision making.

Of course there is no way to prove that allowing lawbreakers to vote demeans the franchise, just as there is no way to prove that prohibiting them from doing so accomplishes the opposite. But according to Judge Gonthier, whose defense of disenfranchisement was discussed above, the "rightness" or "wrongness" of many cherished values is incapable of "scientific proof."[49]

Nor do these values necessarily lack legitimacy because they conflict with others that are more rationally defensible. Again, to quote Judge Gonthier: "There is a flaw in an analysis which suggests that because one social or political philosophy can be justified, it necessarily means that another social or political philosophy is not justified: in other words, where two social or political philosophies exist, it is not by approving one that you disprove the other."[50]

Just as the most persuasive argument in favor of disenfranchisement is, at bottom, subjective, so too a major reason for opposing the practice springs less from empirical data than from a gut sense that the practice is unfair.

As we shall see in the following three chapters, the move to re-enfranchise former prisoners is being pushed ahead and pulled backward by many diverse groups that dutifully cite statistics and refer to academic studies. Then, when all is said and done, they ultimately rely on appeals to the public's unquantifiable, inchoate, yet strongly held values.

6 Reform: Interest Groups and Strategies

Although miscreants have been ostracized from the political community in the United States ever since the Pilgrims first landed at Plymouth Rock, only in the last few years have reformers attempted in any sustained way to challenge this practice.

When a handful of scholars first began to research the extent and impact of felon disenfranchisement, they were embarking on a somewhat quixotic mission, because at the time the voting rights of ex-prisoners commanded virtually no public interest.[1] There was some professional debate, but it was limited: Decades earlier the American Bar Association and the American Law Institute had announced their opposition to voting restrictions,[2] and in 1998 the Sentencing Project and Human Rights Watch reported that nearly 13 percent of all African American men in the United States were barred from the political process because of felony convictions.[3] The disclosure prompted a murmur but certainly no outburst.

In the past five years, however, a "non-issue" has been transformed into a *cause célèbre*—one heralded by some public interest groups as *the* "major civil rights struggle" of the new millennium.[4] The precipitating cause was the presidential election of 2000. George Bush apparently won the popular vote in Florida by 537 ballots, enabling him to capture all of the state's electoral votes and therewith the presidency of the United States. The day after the election, Human Rights Watch reported that 31 percent of African Americans in Florida had been prohibited from voting, because they were either in prison or among the more than 400,000 ex-prisoners who had been stripped of the franchise.[5] Since they would have "overwhelmingly" voted Democratic, their exclusion "decisively" changed the outcome of the election.[6]

Soon people who had never heard of "disenfranchisement" not only learned what the term meant but came to understand that it had profound implications for the black community, the political balance of power, even the well-being of democracy itself. Government authorities accordingly sprang into action (albeit reluctantly in some cases), impaneling one prestigious body after another to figure out what had gone wrong and recommend changes.

In June 2001 the U.S. Commission on Civil Rights released a report entitled "Voting Irregularities in Florida during the 2000 Presidential Election." It concluded that the proceedings in the Sunshine State were "marred by voter disenfranchisement," and among its suggestions was one to abolish state policies stripping ex-felons of their suffrage.[7]

A month later the Commission on Federal Election Reform, chaired by former presidents Jimmy Carter and Gerald Ford and composed of establishment titans from both the Republican and Democratic Parties, also released a report, similarly recommending that states restore the franchise to felons once they had fully completed their sentences.[8] As Carter testified during the hearing: "I think we have been far too casual in disenfranchising people due to past felony convictions—not only creating inequalities, but influencing future lack of participation by children of those disenfranchised."[9]

In light of the 2000 presidential election, the recommendations of high-level commissions, the clamor from public interest groups, pundits, and even aroused citizens, the timing seemed ideal for major electoral reform. After all, in campaigns for social justice, as in so much else, timing is everything, something Jimmy Carter stressed at the beginning of his tenure on the Election Reform Commission: "I think if you would have brought up this same kind of discussion four years ago, there would have been very little interest. I think now is the time when there might be enough focus to actually do something. I would guess that four or eight years in the future, that opportunity might have dissipated again."[10]

Yet here it is, more than four years later, another presidential election has come and gone, and Congress has done virtually nothing to ease the plight of ex-felons.[11] As for the states, the NAACP concluded in a 2002 report that most of them had made little substantive headway in reforming their election systems.[12] Although this claim is overstated, since the apparent trend among states is to ease the restoration process (as I discuss in the next chapter), most of their recent reforms have indeed been modest, and at any rate the momentum for change has slowed. What happened?

September 11th happened. Before sluggish or reluctant lawmakers could be prodded or shamed into action, the World Trade Center and a wing of the Pentagon were destroyed by suicide bombers, and the nation has been preoccupied ever since with its "war on terror." Restoring voting rights to erstwhile prisoners no longer seems so pressing.

Still, there are several reasons to believe that the re-enfranchisement movement may yet revive. For one thing, influential newspapers throughout the country continue to support the political empowerment of ex-felons. The *New York Times*, to cite one prominent example, has written several editorials inveighing against disenfranchisement, which it describes as "an archaic practice, at odds with basic American values about both punishment and democracy."[13] The *Washington Post*, the *Christian Science Monitor*, the *Chicago Sun-Times*, the *St. Petersburg Times*, the *Minneapolis Star Tribune*, and *USA Today* have similarly castigated the practice.[14]

Another reason is that "reform" has public opinion on its side. After the 2000 election, many figures in politics, academia, and civil rights became acutely conscious of disenfranchisement policies and their human and institutional toll, but the general public remained, then as now, largely unaware that these policies exist. Two recent opinion polls suggest, however, that once people realize that individuals who have served their sentences and fulfilled all the terms of their release can still be stripped of their political rights into perpetuity, they support—by a supermajority, a whopping 80 or 81 percent—the re-enfranchisement of felons who have "paid their dues."[15] Respondents were less generous toward other offenders; only 66 percent—still a clear majority—want voting rights extended to anyone who is still on probation or parole, and a mere 33 percent want them granted to those still behind bars. (A small minority, only 15.9 percent, favors permanent disenfranchisement.)[16]

According to Rutgers professor Milton Heumann, who headed one study, while citizens have little sympathy for the rights and liberties of ex-felons in general, most still support their right to vote: "Americans are deeply committed to the importance of voting—but only for those who have completed not only their sentences but all their post-sentence obligations."[17] Manza, Brooks, and Uggen, who conducted the second study, similarly discovered that members of the public, proud of their country's democratic government and attached to the ideal of universal suffrage, regard permanent disenfranchisement as too harsh a punishment. As a consequence, the researchers concluded, the likelihood is strong that voting rights will in time be extended to most categories of ex-felons.[18]

Reform: The Role of Interest Groups

Aside from the apparent latent support among the public, reformers have another reason for optimism. Interest groups dedicated to easing the plight of ex-felons have, as Marc Mauer said, "just mushroomed."[19] He noted that when his organization, the Sentencing Project, planned its first national symposium on disenfranchisement in 1999, sixty people attended. When it held another conference on the same topic in 2002, some 230 community activists, scholars, and concerned citizens participated.

Many contemporary theorists, most notably Robert Putnam in *Bowling Alone*,[20] lament the decline of active communal involvement in the United States over the past fifty years. The many public interest groups that have crept, burst, and flown (via cyberspace) into the Sentencing Project conferences represent a different trend. These groups range from large, bureaucratized, and well-funded organizations like Common Cause and the League of Women Voters to small, seat-of-the-pants enterprises that as often as not meet in someone's kitchen. Some finance full-time lobbyists, hold nationwide conferences, and routinely address major media outlets. Others e-mail one another and tack flyers on telephone poles. Many participants aren't even aligned with organizations, but are one-person outfits that send out newsletters and political exhortations to like-minded people whom they often "meet" in electronic chat rooms.

Most organizations support the rights of ex-felons as part of a broader agenda that focuses on civil rights, electoral change, or prison reform. Virtually all participants have a website, moreover, and rely heavily (sometimes exclusively) on the Internet, which has become a giant, worldwide bulletin board through which interested parties can share information, trade gossip, publicize their efforts, recruit volunteers, and announce upcoming events. Anyone accessing one Internet site will discover ten related links, each of which, in turn, yields ten or fifteen more, suggesting that there are both above-ground and subterranean networks "out there" preaching, politicking, and parading for reform.

Major Players

Among the groups championing the rights of former prisoners, none is more influential than the Sentencing Project (SP)—a nonprofit organization incorporated in 1986 that engages in research and advocacy on behalf of prisoners.[21] Its tireless director, Marc Mauer, puts in twenty-hour days testifying before Congress, state legislatures, and any other assembly that seeks his counsel.

Many groups committed to racial justice, such as Human Rights Watch, the American Civil Liberties Union (ACLU), the Association of Community Organizations for Reform (ACORN), the Lawyers' Committee for Civil Rights under Law, and the National Association for the Advancement of Colored People (NAACP) also engage in litigation, and some of their efforts have already paid off.[22] For example, as a result of a lawsuit brought by the Florida ACLU in 2001, state authorities now comply with their statutory obligation to assist felons nearing release with clemency applications.

Among litigators, the Brennan Center for Justice at New York University School of Law is one of the most innovative. It was established in 1995 to honor the humanitarian ideals of the late Supreme Court Justice William Brennan. Staff attorneys, with assistance from law school students, file suits throughout the country challenging what they consider discriminatory electoral policies. In a recent class-action suit, for instance, they argued that Florida's disenfranchisement law violates both constitutional and statutory law.[23] While the attorneys have not yet won their case, in December 2003 they came closer to doing so when the Eleventh Circuit Court of Appeals instructed a lower tribunal to reconsider the arguments raised in their brief (see Chapter 9).[24]

Smaller Players

Small grassroots organizations have also sprung up throughout the country, devoted to causes at least marginally related to re-enfranchisement. One is the Southwest Voter Registration Education Project (SVREP), which works with Latino communities across the Southwest in an effort to engage them in the political process.[25] The group's motto is *Su Voto Es Su Voz* (your vote is your voice). The Prison and Jail Project, based in southwestern Georgia, is another; one of its directors, John Cole Vodicka, describes in its newsletter how he and his cohorts have been harassed, threatened, incarcerated, and "roughed up" by law enforcement officials because they have sought better treatment for convicted felons in and out of prison.[26]

Newer alliances, some more radical, others more "offbeat," than their comparatively staid precursors, are also speaking out. Although many of these organizations, such as "Rock the Vote" or "Black Youth Vote," started off agitating for voting rights in general, they began focusing on disenfranchisement policies in particular once their members realized the extent to which these policies target young adults and people of color.[27]

Nevada gave rise in 1994 to a feisty coalition of "traditionally under-represented groups" called PLAN (Progressive Leadership Alliance of Nevada). As PLAN says on its web page, it "pushes a progressive agenda," and in particular advocates the rights of ex-felons. The organization works in concert with any like-minded activists it can recruit and in collaboration with key legislators and state administrators. With "their eyes on the prize," members have even befriended old nemeses. ("In the mid-1980s," an organizer wrote in PLAN's newsletter, "one of our coalition partners used to arrest me and my Citizen Alert cohorts at Nevada bombing ranges. Now both of our groups work on issues of mutual concern.")[28] The alliance's efforts have succeeded: In 2003 the state's Republican governor, Kenny Guinn, signed a bill that automatically restores voting rights to citizens convicted of first-time nonviolent offenses once they complete the terms of their probation and parole.[29]

Another group, CURE (Citizens for the Rehabilitation of Errants), is composed of prisoners, former prisoners, and anyone else concerned about criminal justice reform. Like many of its counterparts, it came into being more by happenstance than design. Eating breakfast together in 1972, Charles and Pauline Sullivan lamented that some of their neighbors could not afford to visit east Texas, where family members were imprisoned; some had not seen a parent, child, or spouse for more than ten years. They resolved on the spot to raise the money, lease a bus, and drive these neighbors themselves.[30]

One bus soon became a fleet, and the once-docile visitors soon became politicized, as inmates related horrific stories about life behind steel doors. In time these erstwhile "innocents" became the nucleus of an advocacy movement, and today members of CURE can take much of the credit for persuading Texas legislators to eliminate the two-year waiting period imposed on ex-felons before they could vote.[31]

Internet Groups

Many upstart organizations lack even a kitchen table where they can hash out issues over coffee and doughnuts. They are "virtual" organizations, where latter-day Tom Paines can distribute their opinions through the accessible and egalitarian world of cyberspace. Common Dreams, for instance, is a national nonprofit citizens' association, founded in 1997, that promotes a raft of progressive ideas, including rights for ex-felons. It explains on its website's home page that it is "committed to being on the cutting-edge of using the internet as a political organizing tool—and creating new models for internet activism."[32]

On his website, Benjamin T. Greenberg itemizes reasons for re-enfranchising ex-felons: "Among the most 'compelling' reason to do so 'is the embarrassment of charging citizens in a democracy with committing the act of voting.' "[33] Another cyberspace entrepreneur one-ups the competition by offering what the site calls "Felon Disenfranchisement Animation." Access it, and one discovers interactive news and messages for "nonviolent drug offenders who have lost their voting rights because of a drug felony conviction."[34]

It was only a matter of time before ex-felons as a class would have their own website: VotingExCons.com. In large, bold letters its home page proclaims, "As an Ex-felon, you are a member of a fast-growing and powerful special interest group ... and as such you are at the edge of a *golden opportunity to influence public policy*—and the most powerful tool we have is our *RIGHT TO VOTE*." "We've accepted responsibility, done the time," the broadside continues, "and the majority of us have returned to society as law-abiding and gainfully employed citizens. *We have rights to a say in the laws that govern us.*"[35]

Opposition Groups

The disenfranchisement reform movement, however, is by no means the consensual voice of the nation. There are tens of thousands of people "out there" who oppose any effort to restore voting rights to ex-felons. They are less vocal than their ideological opponents, however—not only because their position is increasingly at odds with public opinion but also because they are confident that substantive reform is nowhere in sight. They seldom see the need to engage in group activity focused on this particular issue, moreover, since their opposition to felon re-enfranchisement is part of a larger conservative agenda that influences public opinion through a sophisticated network of pundits, think tanks, journals, and talk shows. The websites maintained by conservative organizations and publications—among them the Federalist Society, the Heritage Foundation, Focus on Family, the Moral Majority, the *National Review*, the *Washington Times*, and many others—provide numerous editorials, letters to the editor, and columns denouncing re-enfranchisement[36] (which they say "rewards criminality" and "cheapens the vote of law-abiding Americans").[37]

Influential and well-financed lobbying groups representing corrections departments, police, and prosecutors also tend to oppose reform. They wield considerable influence, not only with Republican officeholders but also with the public at large.[38] Finally, victims rights' groups are active in every state; whenever a legislative body is considering a proposal to restore voting rights to parolees, say, or nonviolent first offenders, someone who has lost a brother, an only son, or a wife is there to remind lawmakers that their loved one "can never vote again." After their testimony—often tearful, eloquent, and difficult to discount—it's hard for any subsequent speakers to make a case for re-enfranchisement.[39]

Lessons Reformers Learn

These geographically dispersed and enormously varied groups form the nucleus of an incipient civil rights movement that so far is working mainly under the radar. These groups may be idealistic, but whatever reform they've achieved has come from observing the hardheaded rules of practical politics, including the value of a "deal."

An article in the July 2000 issue of Demos's *Democracy Dispatches* describes how such a deal was struck between two ordinarily antagonistic caucuses in the Alabama House of Representatives: Republicans and black Democrats. Together they crafted two bills—one, as long sought by conservatives as it had been resisted by blacks, would require people to produce identification before they could vote. The second, popular among African Americans but anathema to Republicans, would restore the suffrage to former prisoners once they had completed their probation and parole.[40] This compromise also illustrates the "half-a-loaf" principle, another imperative of successful negotiating. The voter ID/felon disenfranchisement bills were acceptable—barely—to both Republicans and the black caucus, although, as one legislator observed, "The bills aren't exactly what either camp wanted, but it's a compromise, and that's what politics is all about."[41]

Alabama's Republican governor, Bob Riley, ultimately signed the identification mandate of this carefully nurtured deal, but on June 24, 2003, he vetoed the re-enfranchisement provision.[42] Therein lies another lesson in practical politics: It's not over till it's over, and even then don't be too sure.

If successful activists know nothing else, they understand the importance of coalitions. Movements dedicated solely to the voting rights of ex-prisoners will create barely a ripple. Let them band together with feminists, gay and lesbian movements, social justice consortiums, committees to preserve the manatee and reform Medicare, and the ripple becomes, if not a tsunami, at least a good-sized current.

In May 2001 Connecticut governor John Rowland signed a bill extending voting rights to some 36,000 probationers, thereby signaling the end of a campaign that provides a case study of successful coalition-building.[43] Marc Rapoport, a former Connecticut attorney general and the founder of Demos, was among those spearheading this campaign. He and fellow activists recruited support from every group that smiled their way, including the NAACP, prisoners' rights movements, Common Cause, and others. "You name it," he said, all "came together with a single, strong progressive voice."[44]

While activists should of course keep their eyes on the ultimate prize, they should not scorn small, "doable" reforms. If their dreams came true, Congress, acceding to its better nature, would simply outlaw felony disenfranchisement, or the Supreme Court would declare the practice unconstitutional "root and branch." Since neither scenario is likely, progressives have little choice but to seek scattered, incremental improvements—like the one Professor Nora Demleitner suggested in a recent law review article.

Legislatures, she said, should vest judges with discretion to determine whether, and for how long, individuals convicted of a crime should forfeit their franchise. Under current practice, the revocation occurs automatically, regardless of whether defendants are convicted of heinous or relatively minor offenses, whether they are first-time offenders, youths, or hard-core recidivists. In a reformed system, if judges determined that particular felons should lose their votes, they would be able to factor the forfeiture into the sentence and announce their decision in open court. As it is now, trial judges—no less than the accused themselves—are often unaware that convictions even trigger disenfranchisement.[45]

Problems Reformers Face, or Why Bad Things Happen to "Good" Groups

Being well-meaning and socially conscious doesn't mean that the gods necessarily smile on movement activists. In attempting to forge successful coalitions, they may discover that other public interest groups—presumably their natural allies—sometimes shy away from them. These groups often fear that by identifying too closely with ex-felons they might offend the mainstream constituents they depend upon for financial and political support. They are also reluctant to sacrifice political capital on behalf of a group whose rights, while not unimportant, are not among their top priorities.[46] (In the 1960s and '70s women's groups faced a similar dilemma: They supported the rights of gays and lesbians in principle, but they worried that by publicly championing their cause they might forfeit broad public appeal.)[47]

A coalition of progressive organizations, cited by Elizabeth Simson as a case in point, recently lobbied Congress for electoral reform. In apprising lawmakers of the many groups that would benefit from this reform, the coalition pointedly omitted any reference to former prisoners. The reason? While its members, to a person, personally supported re-enfranchisement, they feared that any reference to ex-felons would alienate congressional moderates.[48]

Those toiling on behalf of ex-prisoners still find coalition members, however timid, easier to deal with than their own constituents, a singularly uncooperative lot. As anyone who has ever worked with former inmates will attest, coaxing them into any kind of movement is, in a word, *challenging*. If this movement involves voting reform, the challenge is compounded, as many ex-offenders are profoundly alienated from the electoral process. Moreover, while those agitating on behalf of African Americans, say, or the elderly, can usually count on their robust support, those battling for ex-felons can expect outright resistance from many of their beneficiaries. And, again in contrast to many other disempowered groups, felons—at least in the abstract—are an unappealing class, unlikely to pull on the public's heartstrings (let alone its purse strings).

Neither can reform-minded groups expect much support from elected officials. After all, what's in it for them? After the Republican-dominated Florida legislature refused to pass a re-enfranchisement bill, Florida House speaker Tom Feeney offered a candid explanation: "It's not a big issue to me in terms of rectifying the situation," he said. "I wouldn't go out of my way to bump an education reform bill or a growth-management or a cut-the-cost-of-prescription-drugs bill so we could have automatic restoration of felons' voting rights."[49] What's more, he concluded, "People in my district don't think that the problem we had was insufficient numbers of ex-felons qualified to vote." Even if lawmakers *did* go out on a limb, chances are ex-prisoners won't vote for them anyway (or contribute a nickel to their re-election campaigns.) Worse, there are likely political costs. Let elected officials do anything to help out a convicted embezzler or a one-time street thug; by nightfall their political adversaries will be labeling them "soft on crime."

If groups portray a proposal, then, as one designed to benefit prisoners, it automatically becomes suspect. If they portray it as a measure intended to advance democratic principles, though, it may acquire legitimacy, even nobility. As Professor William Boone pointed out during a Ford/Carter Commission panel, all successful reform policy must first be grounded in a philosophy that idealizes full electoral participation. Even sternly conservative lawmakers are disinclined to oppose measures identified as advancing American ideals.[50]

Reformers, then, should characterize their movement as one dedicated to the formation of "a more perfect union." Since its founding America has pursued this ideal, time and again eliminating civic, racial, and penal barriers in response to what the judiciary calls "evolving standards of justice." In 1993, for example, the Supreme Court held that executing the mentally retarded was no longer consistent with these "evolving standards," although from colonial times until the day of this ruling tribunals had consistently upheld the practice. Indeed, during its current term the Court may disallow another centuries-old practice—the execution of youth as young as eighteen—on the same ground, i.e., that inflicting capital punishment on those too young to appreciate the gravity of their actions no longer comports with "evolving standards of justice." Reformers should argue, similarly, that another long-term practice, the disenfranchisement of ex-felons, no longer befits a country dedicated to the equal worth of all its citizens.

In this country the tenet that similarly situated people should be treated in the same way is firmly held; indeed, the notion of "privilege" is consummately un-American. When the Supreme Court threw out the states' death penalty statutes in 1973, it did so not because it considered capital punishment per se unconstitutional but because the statutes as then written inflicted the sanction in "wanton and freakish" ways.[51] Whether or not two people whose crimes were essentially the same received the ultimate punishment was, at bottom, dependent upon variables that were utterly capricious.

So it is with disenfranchisement. No rhyme or reason determines who, among otherwise indistinguishable citizens, forfeits their vote. Deprivation of this precious right is triggered solely by the vagaries of geography, the skill of legal counsel, the peculiarities of respective state laws. Reformers should accordingly borrow a page from the Supreme Court's 1973 ruling and emphasize the "wanton and freakish" ways in which fellow citizens are stripped of their franchise.

Finally, activists should couple America's ideals with its self-interest by stressing the extent to which re-empowering ex-felons would enhance America's international standing. Just as eagerness to curry favor with Third World people encouraged this country's leaders in the 1950s to speak out against de jure segregation,[52] presumably today's public officials would be less eager to support disenfranchisement laws if they fully comprehended how racist such policies are considered by other progressive nations.

Shrewd reformers know, above all else, that they must avoid any action that even hints of partisanship, lest they alienate conservatives and, more important, sully what should be a principled cause. Besides, most are familiar enough with the vagaries of partisanship to know that while newly enfranchised felons are today more likely to vote for Democratic than Republican candidates, like any other voting cohort their allegiance can shift over time.[53]

Finally, many activists have concluded that Congress will probably sidestep indefinitely the politically fraught issue of felon re-enfranchisement, and so, by default, they are now working for change within the various states.

7 State Reforms

Although reformers intent upon re-enfranchising ex-felons are focusing on state legislators rather than Congress, they are doing so with some trepidation. After all, in the area of civil rights, states have checkered histories indeed. Still, these reformers are betting that if any meaningful change occurs it will come from Albany, say, or Sacramento, Olympia or Hartford.

As a spokesman for the influential public interest group Common Cause explained: "While it appears that federal financial support and guidance will be necessary to achieve needed change, the heavy lifting on many of the election reforms ... must be done at the state level. I believe it is unlikely that elections will be federalized in a wholesale fashion, and I am not convinced that it is necessary or appropriate."[1]

Indeed, in a federal system, it is fitting (and, arguably, more democratic) that whenever feasible, change should stem from local initiative and reflect local consensus. Throughout American history, individual states, for all their foibles, have pioneered many critical reforms that in time have been adopted by the country as a whole. Several states granted women the franchise, for instance, before the Nineteenth Amendment extended it to their sisters nationwide. Wisconsin, similarly, instituted unemployment compensation, and California, air-pollution controls, well before Congress nationalized these measures. States are shaking up the status quo right now: Massachusetts is performing gay marriages, and Vermont has legalized civil unions between same-sex couples.

So far, however, progress on re-enfranchisement has been negligible. Some pundits predicted that after the 2000 presidential election states would be outdoing one another in their eagerness to pass voting reforms—a forecast that seemed even more likely to materialize once Congress handed them some $3.8 billion to upgrade their election procedures.[2] Yet, for a variety of self-serving, philosophical, fiscal, and above all partisan reasons, they haven't done so. Individuals arriving at the polls on November 2, 2004, often discovered new, automated voting machines or benefited from a new policy permitting them to cast provisional ballots if their credentials were challenged. Yet they often encountered other problems, particularly if they resided in minority or poor jurisdictions, and most ex-felons intent upon voting soon realized that few of the barriers confronting them in the 2000 race had been dismantled.

While substantive changes were fewer than predicted, they were not nonexistent. New Mexico, in particular, instituted meaningful reform. Since 1911 it had been one of only nine states that disenfranchised ex-prisoners for life. In 2001, however, Governor Gary Johnson signed a measure extending the franchise to felons who have completed their sentences and the terms of their release.[3]

Texas, Kentucky, Missouri, Nebraska, Delaware, Arkansas, and Nevada rank among the "modest reformers" (in some cases they adopted their changes before the 2000 election). They now require correction officials to provide convicted felons, on a timely basis, with application forms and instructions for reactivating their voting rights.[4] Texas and Nevada have also reduced the period one-time offenders must wait, upon completion of their sentences, probation, or parole, before becoming eligible to apply for the restoration of the franchise (see Table 2 in Chapter 1).[5]

Connecticut now extends the franchise to people on probation, so it should also be categorized as a "modest reformer." So should Wyoming, New Mexico, and Maryland, since they now permit nonviolent ex-felons, who were previously disenfranchised for life, to apply for the restoration of their voting rights at a prescribed time after completing their sentences.[6]

New York State also merits an "honorable mention." In 2003 its State Board of Elections (in response to prodding from advocacy groups) notified local affiliates that "everyone who presents themselves to register ... is presumed to be eligible and should be registered." Such a notice should not have been necessary, since anyone in the state who has served his or her maximum sentence or been discharged from parole is automatically entitled to vote, but an investigation revealed that more than half of the state's sixty-two election boards demanded that ex-felons produce various forms of documentation—some of which do not even exist—before they would register them.[7]

From a reformer's perspective, some states have slid backward. Kansas withdrew voting rights from probationers. Citizens in both Utah and Massachusetts—until recently two of only four states that allowed incarcerated prisoners to vote—endorsed ballot initiatives repealing this privilege—in Utah by a record-setting 80 percent.[8] Meanwhile Colorado and Oregon, which have long withheld the franchise from anyone who breaks state law, as of 2000 also retracted it from citizens who break federal laws.[9] (Colorado, while it was at it, also disqualified federal parolees.)[10] (See Table 2 in Chapter 1.)

Virginia has both given and taken away, so it ranks among the "mixed bags." Nonviolent offenders may seek re-enfranchisement three years after completing their sentences, instead of the five or seven years they were previously required to wait, and thanks to the efforts of the state's democratic governor, Mark Warner, former prisoners set on reclaiming the franchise need jump through fewer hoops. Yet Virginia also expanded the definition of a violent felony to include, among many other offenses, burglary, prostitution, obstruction of justice, and personal trespass by computer—thereby snatching the fruits of reform from many past and future offenders.[11]

State Reform: Case Studies

Reform efforts in a few states merit particular examination, either because they illustrate the value of coalition building, strategizing, and mutual back scratching, or because their ultimate failure demonstrates the obstacles activists face in attempting to convince entrenched and partisan powers that helping out ex-felons is the right thing to do.

Florida

In 1999, 6.24 percent of Florida's voting-age population was disenfranchised.[12] At the same time, almost 14 percent of black adults were barred from the polls,[13] the vast majority of whom had been sentenced to probation and never incarcerated (see Table 4 in Chapter 1). They were divested of their voting rights nonetheless, prompting a spokesman for the state branch of the American Civil Liberties Union (ACLU) to conclude that disenfranchisement is "the overriding civil rights problem in the state."[14]

Governor Jeb Bush apparently disagrees; as he wrote in a letter to the *Sarasota Herald-Tribune,* "any person, black or white, who could not legally vote in the last election due to their status as a felon could have retained their right to vote by simply not committing a felony in the first place."[15] He nevertheless appointed a task force on election reform to investigate "all questions" raised by the 2000 presidential race, including the state's refusal to let ex-prisoners vote.

In its report the task force identified felon disenfranchisement as "critical" and referred the issue to the legislature.[16] When state lawmakers subsequently passed the Florida Election Reform Act in May 2001, however, they apparently didn't consider the issue "critical" enough: Although at least six separate re-enfranchisement bills had been introduced, ranging from one providing for the automatic restoration of voting rights to one proposing only modest adjustments, not one made it out of committee.[17]

The question all along, said Jamie Fellner, a member of the New York–based Human Rights Watch, was whether the state's Republican leaders would "do the right thing even if it is not going to benefit them as a partisan issue."[18] Florida Republicans did *not* do the right thing, but according to John Cosgrove, the second-ranking Democrat in the state's lower house, neither did the Democrats. The Republicans are less inclined than the Democrats to do anything, he said, but "you probably are going to see a cautious approach to this, even among most Democrats." Cosgrove noted that Florida's present system "is cumbersome and in need of change," but whether it ever receives this change "could be a real test as to whether compassionate conservatism works in the marketplace. It's the right thing to do. The problem is that some politicians don't think it's the political thing to do."[19]

Florida's ex-felons are minimally better off today than they were in 2000, notwithstanding legislative inaction, because of a lawsuit won by the ACLU.[20] As a result of the 2001 suit, which is discussed in Chapter 4, the Florida Department of Corrections (DOC) agreed to comply with its statutory obligation to assist inmates in preparing their clemency applications before their scheduled release.

Maryland

Until recently few states treated their ex-felons more stingily than Maryland. Although first-time offenders could apply for the restoration of voting rights once they had completed their sentences, individuals convicted of a second felony were disenfranchised for life. Under the new law, enacted in 2002, twice-convicted nonviolent offenders can reclaim their franchise three years after completing their sentences and paying any fines and restitution they might owe.[21] (Individuals whose second offense involves violence can never retrieve their political rights.)

This reform came about through the hard work of the Maryland Voting Rights Restoration Coalition, which evolved from an informal caucus focusing mainly on minority concerns into a signal force encompassing more than fifty organizations, big and small, established and ad hoc. Members included feminists, the League of Women Voters, ex-offender collectives, the Green Party, the Association of Community Organizations for Reform Now (ACORN), and a consortium of two hundred churches.[22]

From the outset coalition leaders portrayed their movement less as one committed to the welfare of ex-prisoners than as one dedicated to promoting the ideals Martin Luther King had enshrined. Members of the black and Puerto Rican caucus countered arguments levied by conservative tough-on-crime colleagues by equating franchise restrictions with the poll taxes and literacy tests that for generations had muted the voices of minority citizens. As state legislator Kerry Hill said, Maryland lawmakers "can correct a glaring injustice—that more than 135,000 of its sons and daughters, and more than one in six African-American males, are not welcome at the table of democracy because they have a criminal record."[23]

The Maryland legislature passed the re-enfranchisement bill none too soon: it had come before the body four times in the past (the preceding year it had been defeated in a senate subcommittee by a single vote). Opposition forces had become skillful saboteurs, learning how to delay votes indefinitely and to attach "killer" amendments (like the one to establish "an irrevocable trust" that would allow the family of a murder victim to vote on behalf of the dead person for as long as the killer himself could vote).[24]

The coalition, however, outmaneuvered the saboteurs. When hearings began in March 2002, it employed what in retrospect was an inspired strategy: On the assumption that most lawmakers regard ex-felons as cold-blooded predators, its members gave them a "human face" by asking several to testify about the ways disenfranchisement affected them and their families. As State Senator Delores Kelley later recalled, "I was struck at how many [among those testifying] were clergy people, schoolteachers, social workers, drug addiction counselors. They are paying taxes, they are rearing families, they are pillars of society. But because of youthful indiscretions, they cannot vote."[25]

One witness, a three-time "loser" named Archie Hill, is today a job-retention specialist for recently discharged prisoners. After the hearing, several legislators admitted being particularly moved by his statement, which he concluded with these words: "There's really no limit on what it takes for an individual to change .... Redemption doesn't have a time on it."[26]

The coalition lobbied and lobbied some more, targeting in particular those legislators identified as "key." It also confronted head on the two arguments most frequently invoked by opponents— i.e., that the bill was "soft on crime" and that it rewarded felons who by rights "should pay for their crimes for the rest of their lives."[27] Coalition members responded by emphasizing the injustice of punishing individuals who had "served their time" and now wanted to assume the responsibilities of citizenship. "If you have met all conditions of the sentence, you shouldn't wear a scarlet letter for life," said Senator Kelly. "What we want is for [former offenders] to be vested in the community, to take ownership of public issues, to pay their taxes, to work, to care about making the world better. To tell them all they cannot vote is not the best way to do it."[28] Members also pointed out that many ex-felons had been convicted of drug charges, and since the state had failed to deal with the drug epidemic, especially in poor and minority Baltimore neighborhoods, it should by rights shoulder some of the responsibility.[29]

The Maryland Senate ultimately voted 25 to 20 for the bill, but only after reformers did what most successful reformers do: compromise. As introduced, both the house and senate bills restored the vote to anyone who had completed his sentence, whatever his crime or recidivist record. In order to garner the necessary support, however, they had to make two concessions: Second-time offenders whose crimes involved violence were declared ineligible for re-enfranchisement altogether, and even those whose second conviction did not involve violence must wait three years after release to regain their vote.[30] (If a good "compromise" is one satisfactory to neither side, this one is stellar. While conservatives charged that it still let thugs "off easy," many of its proponents, particularly members of the clergy, believed it failed to reflect "the Judeo-Christian principle of redemption.")[31]

Marvin L. "Doc" Cheatham Sr., the mastermind behind the coalition's winning strategy, cited some reasons for its eventual success: It created a large, inclusive consortium rather than one identified with any single constituency; it transformed ex-felons in the public's mind from faceless sociopaths into human beings capable of turning their lives around; it not only lobbied "up a storm" but lobbied judiciously; and, finally, it capitalized on a political climate that, in the aftermath of the 2000 presidential election, was primed for change.[32]

And the coalition had money. Not a lot, but enough to pay for full-time organizers, produce mass mailings, bus in former prisoners to testify, and even treat an occasional legislator to an afternoon latte.

Delaware

Ex-felons in Delaware are at least nominally better off than they were before June 2000, when lawmakers repealed a state provision, in effect since the early 1800s, that had disenfranchised convicted malefactors for life. Legislators substituted for this relic a new law allowing felons to apply for restoration of the franchise five years after completing their sentences, provided that they had paid their outstanding fines and restitution and were not convicted of murder, manslaughter, sex offenses, or violations of the public trust.[33]

An alliance formed in 1990, the Delaware Center for Justice, struggled long and against great odds to ease the plight of ex-felons; to its members even this relatively humble reform represented a victory. Besides, humble or not, it allowed more than six thousand former prisoners to regain their voting rights in time for the 2000 presidential election.[34]

In seeking change the center had confronted not only the same obstacles other organizations with similar aims confront but an additional barrier: James Vaughn. A state senate regulation stipulates that no bill can be released to the floor of the chamber unless the chair of the authorizing committee agrees. Since Senator Vaughn was chair of the Corrections Committee, the disenfranchisement bill was in his bailiwick, and for a full ten years he single-handedly prevented its discharge.[35]

Alliance members finally took to heart the old adage, "if you can't beat 'em, join 'em." They approached Senator Vaughn, hands open, and asked how they could gain his approval. They could do so, he responded, by guaranteeing that ex-felons would never regain their suffrage unless and until they had paid every last cent of money they owed in fines and restitution. At the alliance's urging the state senate convened a task force composed of influential state officials, and Vaughn promised that if it could contrive a way to ensure that ex-felons had "paid their debts," he would release the bill. (According to Janet Leban, executive director of the alliance, the senator assumed that the task force "would come up empty-handed.")[36]

While the task force labored, the alliance kept busy garnering favorable newspaper editorials, urging Senator Vaughn's constituents to contact him, amassing signatures on petitions, and recruiting to its cause one public interest group after another. "In the end," Leban said, "virtually the entire state was involved" in promoting the bill, including both Republicans and Democrats.[37]

In time the task force defied the skeptics by producing a viable system, one that used the Department of Corrections' database to track felons and thereby ascertain if and when they had paid their outstanding debts. Beaten at his own game, Senator Vaughn released the bill to the floor of the legislature, where it passed by a large margin.

How did the alliance succeed? Through hard work, of course, and wise strategy, but also, Leban concedes, because Delaware is "atypical." The issue of "ex-felons rights" never became ensnared in a "soft-on-crime" dialogue; advocates faced no large or organized opposition, and polls revealed that 75 to 80 percent of the state's citizens supported reform.[38]

Massachusetts

Inmates in Massachusetts learned the hard way that forming a political action committee (PAC) was not smart politics. Until November 7, 2001, when the electorate retracted this privilege, they had resided in one of only four states then allowing incarcerated prisoners to vote—a tradition the Bay State had observed since prerevolutionary times.[39]

The move to disenfranchise Massachusetts inmates started when the state's elected officials "got wind" that Norfolk County prisoners had formed a PAC—the first in the nation—to agitate for desired reforms and in particular to protest the planned transfer of many of them to facilities in Texas. The PAC, headed by Joe Labriola, was "days away" from being registered with the state Office of Campaign and Political Finance.[40]

During an interview conducted before the PAC was outlawed, Labriola explained that his organization would recruit its members from the state's eleven thousand inmates and their families and would be capable of influencing as many as fifty thousand votes statewide. The PAC would engage in direct mailings, phone calls, and, like its civilian counterparts, endorse prospective officeholders and contribute to their coffers. (Labriola conceded that few candidates would deem it a political "plus" to have the prisoners' backing, and as a consequence his PAC might not disclose the names of those it supported—a practice that would itself probably be illegal.)[41]

Labriola and a fellow inmate were emboldened to organize a PAC, he said, because politicians had made "political hay excoriating prisoners and drafting draconian laws on punishment" that further penalized them, while doing next to nothing to reduce crime. A PAC, moreover, would enable offenders to influence political debates on issues involving criminal justice.[42] A strong political organization, according to Labriola, would also be a vehicle for change. Rather than achieving reform through lethal confrontations with officials—the way inmates had done in 1971 during the deadly riot at New York's Attica prison—his group would rely on the power of the ballot. "In the '70s, we thought we could make change with violence," he observed. "Our whole point now is to make prisoners understand that we can make changes by using the vote."[43]

Some citizens who supported Labriola's efforts maintained that by allowing inmates to vote and join a PAC the state would encourage civic engagement, which in turn would reduce recidivism. Participation in a political action committee, moreover, was precisely the kind of activity the first amendment was adopted to protect. In a letter to the editor one Bay State resident took issue with those who asserted that because "we're talking about prisoners ... it's OK to take away their democratic rights. But rights are not about popularity." "Often in cases of free speech and political participation, exercising democratic rights can be downright unpopular."[44]

Massachusetts officials scoffed at such claims, maintaining that a lobbying organization would allow prisoners to exercise inappropriate and deleterious influence over state policies. (As one jokester observed, if the twenty-four thousand inmates in the state's prison facilities voted as a bloc, they would have almost as much muscle as the Massachusetts Republican Party.)

Upon learning of the proposed PAC, Interim Governor Paul Celluci immediately issued two executive orders, one prohibiting inmates from engaging in any political fund-raising and another forbidding them to either organize a PAC or possess PAC-related material.[45] He then filed a referendum proposal asking "whether the state Constitution should be amended to prevent convicted felons from voting while they are serving time in prison."[46] When he launched this campaign his effort seemed quixotic, since a proposed amendment can be adopted only if it is approved by legislators in two successive sessions and then endorsed by voters in a statewide referendum. (Some Democrats groused that the whole campaign was a political ploy designed to insert an issue on the November ballot calculated to lure to the polls voters who were most likely to support Republican candidate George W. Bush.)[47]

The state legislature not only passed the constitutional amendment by comfortable majorities two years in a row, but Massachusetts voters also approved it by a whopping two-to-one margin.[48] That a disenfranchisement proposal was roundly supported in what is arguably the most liberal state in the union suggests, if nothing else, that reformers face an uphill climb.

Washington

Washington State is an enigma. In many ways it is a bastion of liberalism, yet, as Sandeep Kaushik has observed, the way it treats ex-felons "has more in common with many Southern states still straining under the legacy of Jim Crow laws which stripped many blacks of their voting rights—than with the rest of the country."[49] Washington disenfranchises more than 20 percent of its African American males (some put the figure as high as 24 percent).[50] Only seven states have higher rates.

Washington's laws are also among the country's least forgiving. Everyone convicted of a felony automatically loses the right to vote. Offenders who committed their crimes before July 1984 are permanently disenfranchised, while persons convicted after that date are barred only until they complete their sentences, including parole and probation, and pay all attendant fines. At that point they will be granted a formal discharge by the Department of Corrections (DOC).[51]

Insisting that everyone pay their "legal financial obligations" before qualifying for re-enfranchisement sounds like a reasonable condition, and indeed most states have such a requirement. After all, shouldn't people pay their debts? Isn't doing so a mark of responsibility? The answer is "yes, but ... " A "legal financial obligation," which is a monetary debt the sentencing court imposes, can be considerable, including the costs of incarceration, docket and filing fees, payment due court-appointed lawyers, restitution, and penalty assessments, as well as interest compounded at an annual rate of 12 percent.[52]

The sentencing court determines the amount prisoners owe, moreover, without any reference to the severity of their crimes. A car thief, say, or someone who cashes a bad check can incur higher debt obligations than a professional triggerman. Worse, ex-prisoners are allotted ten years in which to pay their debts, but if they fail to do so by the end of this period, or if the Washington DOC determines in the meanwhile that they are unlikely to do so, they are "terminated" from further supervision.[53] This means that they are effectively disenfranchised for the rest of their lives, since there is no procedure by which they can at that point reclaim their rights. Between 1996 and

2000, according to the Washington ACLU, three times as many ex-felons were terminated (26,000) as discharged (9,000).[54]

The Sentencing Project calculated in a 1998 report that 151,500 Washingtonians were at that time permanently or temporarily disenfranchised, representing 3.7 percent of the state's total voting population (compared to 1.5 percent nationally).[55] Nearly half of those were former prisoners who had completed the terms of their imprisonment, parole, and probation, and only outstanding debts prevented them from regaining their suffrage.[56] The financial restitution requirement, then, is effectively a poll tax—and a poll tax that disproportionately affects not just African Americans but poor people in general. As Paul Marvy of the Defender Association has pointed out, many prisoners can never pay their fines, what with sky-high interest rates and decent jobs hard to come by for people with felony convictions.[57]

During the 2002 legislative session lawmakers introduced a bill that, if passed, would have enabled ex-felons to regain the franchise once they had completed their punishment, even if they still had outstanding debts.[58] The bill never made it out of committee. A similar bill has recently been introduced that, like its predecessor, has the strong backing of progressive organizations throughout the state. According to Democrats, who constitute the bulk of the bill's supporters, re-enfranchisement is not a maneuver to supplement their party's ranks but a chance to ensure "that an individual's right to vote, the most important role and responsibility one has as a citizen, is not conditioned on one's economic status." Still, as Republican legislator Ida Ballasiotes observed, GOP lawmakers are much less inclined than Democrats to favor the measure. "Do you think they're really dying to vote?" she asked. "We're not talking about a lot of money here, and a decade is a long time to pay it off." She predicted that the Republican caucus "would think that it would only be appropriate for people to repay their debts" before regaining the right to vote.[59]

Have Reforms "Paid Off"?

Did ex-felons, by virtue of recent reforms, vote in greater percentages in the 2004 election than in earlier contests? Analysts are still examining voting data, but the answer is probably not. This is partly because liberalization efforts in some states may have been offset by restrictive action in others: Probationers now eligible to vote in Connecticut, for example, may be countered by federal parolees no longer able to cast votes in Colorado or probationers now barred from the polls in Kansas. What influenced races in 2004, as in past contests, was not reform but its absence—i.e., the millions of ex-felons still prohibited from voting may have facilitated Republican victories in some close races.

That more substantive change has not occurred in the past four years is not in itself particularly worrisome, since electoral restructuring often proceeds at a snail's pace. But what advocates fear is that the "Big M"—the all-important momentum—will slow, perhaps even dissipate, before enough disenfranchisement laws can either be repealed or liberalized to make a real difference in 2006, or 2008, or 2012.

8 Voting: Constitutional and Civic Concerns

Reformers have focused on the states—where progress is necessarily incremental—only because they've concluded that Congress, which alone is capable of enacting large-scale and uniform change, is unable or unwilling to do so. Suppose Congress proved them wrong by passing a law permitting ex-felons to vote in federal elections. Would this be an unqualified good, or by empowering ex-felons might lawmakers be encouraging participation from the very people least likely to vote in the public interest? Does Congress even have the constitutional authority to institute comprehensive electoral reform?

Surprisingly, a Constitution dedicated to a government "of the people and by the people" nowhere establishes a universal right to vote. The Supreme Court recently affirmed this fact when it agreed with a lower tribunal that the six hundred thousand citizens of the District of Columbia have no constitutional right to voting representation in Congress: "The equal protection clause does not protect the right of all citizens to vote," the district court said, "but rather the right of all *qualified* citizens to vote."[1]

The United States prides itself on being the modern world's first democracy. By failing to guarantee the right to vote, however, it is able to deny many of its citizens what the revolutionary patriot Thomas Paine called "the primary right by which all other rights are protected"—the franchise. "To remove this right," he wrote, "is to reduce a man to slavery, for slavery consists in being subject to the will of another."[2]

By not guaranteeing all citizens the franchise, the United States distinguishes itself from at least 135 other countries, including almost every other liberal democracy, and aligns itself with countries whose commitment to progressive values is less evident, such as Azerbaijan,

Chechnya, Jordan, Libya, and Pakistan.[3] Moreover, by its failure explicitly to guarantee the suffrage, this country may even be flouting the United Nations' International Covenant on Civil and Political Rights (a possibility explored in Chapter 10).

While the absence of a constitutional right is anomalous in the twenty-first century's generally progressive climate, however, it would have been unremarkable in the early years of the American Republic, when only white men of property could cast a ballot, or even as late as 1885, when the Supreme Court made clear that it still regarded the franchise more as a privilege than as a right. "It would be quite competent," Justice Matthews declared, "for the sovereign power to declare that no one but a married person shall be entitled to vote."[4]

Yet this cavalier attitude has not prevailed, and by 1964 the same tribunal could accurately say that "history has been a continuing expansion of the scope of the right of suffrage in this country."[5] State conventions in the 1820s and 1830s set the expansion in motion. Then, one by one, came constitutional amendments that accelerated the process: the Fifteenth Amendment in 1870 guaranteed ex-slaves the right to vote; the Nineteenth Amendment in 1920 extended the franchise to women, and the Twenty-Sixth Amendment in 1972 gave it to citizens eighteen and older. The Twenty-Third Amendment granted even residents of the District of Columbia the right to choose presidential electors, and the Twenty-Fourth Amendment relieved voters of poll taxes.

Even with these amendments, as recently as 1965 whole swaths of the American electorate were effectively prohibited from casting a ballot. In an effort to address that national shame, Congress in 1965 enacted the enormously important Voting Rights Act, discussed at length in the following chapter, which prohibits states and their subdivisions from adopting or maintaining electoral practices, such as grandfather clauses and literacy tests, that have the effect of "diluting" minority votes. Since the passage of the Voting Rights Act, other federal mandates have also extended rights to citizens with disabilities and limited proficiency in English.[6]

In a halting and centuries-long process, then, Americans have come to embrace the ideal of universal suffrage, with one exception: They continue to tolerate and even encourage laws prohibiting ex-felons from exercising their political rights. Two authorities conclude, in fact, that "rising incarceration rates may constitute a unique 'democratic reversal,' leading away from the universal trend towards franchise extension and the spread of democratic governance."[7]

Constitutional Considerations and Political Realities

If Congress attempted to halt this "democratic reversal" by passing a statute re-enfranchising at least some ex-felons, the statute would, of course, be subject to judicial review, and whether federal courts would uphold it is anything but certain. Someone examining their relevant rulings—on voting rights in general, say, or on state versus federal authority to establish electoral qualifications—could as easily conclude one way as the other.

Until the mid-1960s federal courts assumed that states were largely free to condition the franchise any way they saw fit. In a series of cases beginning in the early 1960s, however, the Supreme Court acknowledged that since "the right to exercise the franchise in a free and unimpaired manner is preservative of other basic civil and political rights, any challenged infringement of the right of citizens to vote must be carefully and meticulously scrutinized."[8]

Accordingly, in the 1964 case *Reynolds v. Sims* the Court proclaimed voting a "fundamental right."[9] This designation carries more than symbolic weight, because once a right is considered "fundamental," courts subject any restrictions imposed upon it to the demanding *strict scrutiny* test. Under this test the state bears the burden of proving that its restriction is absolutely necessary to the furtherance of a compelling interest, that it is as narrowly tailored as possible, and that there are no less burdensome ways to achieve its interests.[10]

All things being equal, state policies denying ex-felons the franchise would be repudiated summarily and emphatically under this test, since the Fourteenth Amendment guarantees in strong language "equal protection of the laws" to all persons. Barring ex-felons from casting a ballot, then, would be no more acceptable than barring college dropouts or divorcees. All things are *not* equal, however. Section 2 of the Fourteenth Amendment, a consequential though frequently disregarded reservation, allows states to remove voting privileges from anyone who has participated in "rebellion or other crime."[11] In a 1972 ruling the Supreme Court declared that by virtue of Section 2, states are constitutionally permitted to disenfranchise felons.[12] (This ruling is analyzed in Chapter 9.)

Because the Fourteenth Amendment was passed, as the Supreme Court noted, "with a special intent to protect the blacks from discrimination against them,"[13] it is surely questionable whether those who drafted Section 2 intended it to become a vehicle by which so many former slaves, and their descendants, would forfeit the basic right of citizenship. The Court nevertheless continues to insulate disenfranchisement statutes from strict scrutiny review.

Judges don't exempt them from review altogether, however. When provisions denying ex-felons the vote are challenged on equal protection grounds, they examine them under the *rational relationship* standard, which is as lenient as strict scrutiny is harsh.[14] Courts use this alternative criterion to assess the constitutionality of statutory schemes that don't impinge upon fundamental, or even "sensitive," rights. The test is intended to be an accommodating one, reflecting the judiciary's understanding that, in a democracy, relatively unaccountable federal judges should accord the people's elected representatives considerable deference.

Even when courts use the gentle rational relationship test, however, they impose some constraints. They don't require the government to use the wisest or most effective means available to further its ends, but they won't permit it to use means that are patently unrelated or invidious. Neither will they allow it to discriminate among similarly situated people in willy-nilly, senseless ways. In a notable 1942 case, *Skinner v. Oklahoma,* for instance, the Supreme Court struck down a state law authorizing the sterilization of felons who had been convicted of "larceny," but not those found guilty of "embezzlement."[15] The Court concluded that the differentiation made no sense because "the inheritability of criminal traits does not follow the 'neat legal distinctions which the law has marked between the two offenses.' "[16]

What about laws denying voting rights to former prisoners? Would they pass the rational relationship test? The distinction many states draw between misdemeanors, which do not result in disenfranchisement, and felonies, which do, is arguably as illogical as the one Oklahoma drew between larceny and embezzlement. Yet, despite this serious infirmity, do laws excluding ex-felons at least satisfy the rational relationship's "means/end" requirement?

States frequently justify these laws by claiming that they protect the electoral process from people who may have an antisocial agenda or be predisposed to engage in fraudulent activity—by stuffing the ballot box, for example. The question then becomes: Are classificatory schemes prohibiting ex-felons from voting at least minimally related to these admittedly legitimate goals?

Yes, claim their proponents, moving from constitutional principles to an analysis of voting behavior. Former prisoners are indeed apt to abuse the electoral process—by casting ballots as a bloc to "hazard the welfare of the communities, if not of the state itself,"[17] or by banding together to prevent those who put them behind bars from winning re-election. As Alabama senator Jeff Sessions explained, when asked why he opposed the repeal of disenfranchisement laws: "As a prosecutor for 15 years, I wonder how those people I helped put in the slammer feel about me. I do not care about them voting on my election."[18]

The courts have traditionally accepted this logic, as evidenced by Judge Henry Friendly's celebrated and oft-quoted opinion:

> It can scarcely be deemed unreasonable for a state to decide that perpetrators of serious crime shall not take part in electing the legislators who make the laws, the executives who enforce these, the prosecutors who must try them for further violations, or the judges who are to consider their cases. This is especially so when account is taken of the heavy incidence of recidivism and the prevalence of organized crime.... A contention that the equal protection clause requires New York to allow convicted Mafiosi to vote for district attorneys or judges would not only be without merit but as obviously so as anything can be.[19]

Yet Senator Sessions's reasoning is as suspect as Judge Friendly's. Ex-felons are too few in number and generally too preoccupied with immediate concerns to sway any election, and there's not a whit of evidence that they have ever done so. Nor is there reason to believe that they vote as a coherent bloc, or support judges, defense attorneys, or anyone else who is "pro-crime."

Prisoner-rights activist Marc Mauer, testifying before Congress in 1999, addressed the argument raised by some lawmakers that felons or ex-felons, if allowed to vote, would constitute "a criminal's voting block or criminal lobby." For example, he said, "you might have burglars coming together who want to lower the penalty for burglary." What does this oft-cited allegation mean? Mauer asked.

> If you had a group of burglars in your community who wanted to accomplish this goal, you would first have to find a candidate running on a platform that calls for lowering the penalties for burglary, then find 51 percent of the electorate that wanted to vote for that candidate, and then have that candidate convince his or her fellow legislators to also lower the penalties for burglary. This does not seem to me to be a terrible threat.[20]

Certainly the government is obliged to ensure honest elections, but achieving this goal by prohibiting ex-felons from voting makes as much sense as attempting to discourage fraud by denying driving licenses to former pickpockets. There is no rational connection between the crime and the penalty. If disenfranchisement provisions were reviewed under the strict scrutiny test, they would collapse unceremoniously. They have been sustained under the rational relationship test, but less because they encourage honest elections than because courts using this standard will uphold practically any statutory scheme that is not flatly absurd.

Proposed Legislation on Disenfranchisement

Congress has passed several significant statutes in the last half-century extending or strengthening the suffrage—including the all-important Voting Rights Act of 1965. It has not yet enacted a statute broadening the rights of ex-felons, though not for lack of effort on the part of individual members. A major proposal comes repeatedly from Representative John Conyers, Democrat of Michigan. Providing some predictability in a largely random universe, he has introduced the Civic Participation and Rehabilitation Act at the beginning of each legislative session since 1994. It provides that "the right of an individual who is a citizen of the United States to vote in any election for Federal office shall not be denied or abridged because that individual has been convicted of a criminal offense unless such individual is serving a felony sentence in a correctional institution or facility at the time of the election."[21]

Conyers, the ranking minority member of the House Judiciary Committee, justifies his bill as "a narrowly crafted effort to expand voting rights for ex-felons, while protecting state prerogatives to generally establish voting qualifications." Although states would retain full authority to determine who could vote in any nonfederal election, his bill would eliminate the profound "discrepancies in state laws" that determine whether or under what conditions ex-felons can vote, which "leads to an unfair disparity and unequal participation in Federal elections based solely on where a person lives."[22]

The 2003 proposal, like its predecessors, was supported by a galaxy of groups concerned with voting and civil rights, including the NAACP, ACLU, National Council of Churches, National Urban League, Human Rights Watch, and Lawyers' Committee for Civil Rights. Still, it never made it to the floor of the House.

Neither did a joint resolution sponsored by Representative Jesse Jackson Jr. proposing a constitutional amendment guaranteeing every American citizen eighteen or older the right to vote. Since the proposal did not mention "ex-felons," and provided federal and state governments with some latitude to impose restrictions for the express purpose of ensuring "efficient and honest elections," many reformers thought it might succeed where more specifically worded legislation had failed. Jackson's proposal, however, never acquired a single co-sponsor. None of the other bills that address felony disenfranchisement—each somewhat different in its details—has fared any better, although a Senate bill bears mention because, unlike its House counterparts, it at least gathered steam.[23]

On February 14, 2002, members of the U.S. Senate were taken by surprise. While they were considering the Help America Vote Act (HAVA), a comprehensive election-reform bill introduced by Christopher Dodd, two of Dodd's colleagues—Democrat Harry Reid of Nevada and Republican Arlen Specter of Pennsylvania—introduced what may have been the first felony re-enfranchisement bill with bipartisan sponsorship.[24]

Reid, like Conyers in the House, stressed the bill's narrow scope:

It does not extend voting rights to prisoners. Some States do that. I don't believe in that. It does not extend voting rights to ex-felons on parole, even though 18 states do that.

It does not extend voting rights to ex-felons on probation, even though some States do that. This legislation simply restores the right to vote to those individuals who have completely served their sentences, including probation and parole.

The legislation, moreover, would apply only to Federal elections.[25]

Both Reid and Specter were former district attorneys, and both emphasized their "tough-on-crime" credentials. As Reid said:

I want to make sure that not lost in this debate is the fact that criminal activity is wrong and must be punished and punished severely. I am for the death penalty . . . . Sufficient and appropriate sentences should be imposed upon those who violate our laws. We should not, however, disenfranchise those who have fully completed their prescribed sentences . . . . We have a saying in this country: If you do the crime, you have to do the time. I agree with that. But if you do the time, and do it completely, why should you have to do more time?[26]

The Senate quickly defeated the proposed amendment, 63-31. Christopher Dodd, an influential Democrat and at the time the chair of the Senate Judiciary Committee, supported the amendment, yet he voted against it. Why? "Not because I disagree with what [Senator Reid] is trying to do ... but I think this is not the right place for us to be dealing with that idea."[27] Given its controversial nature, Dodd feared that its inclusion would jeopardize his entire bill.

The senator was probably right. No bill proposing to ease voting restrictions on ex-felons has ever been introduced in either house of Congress without triggering a fusillade of objections from lawmakers, who assert that the absence of uniformity among states' disenfranchisement statutes, far from being a liability, reflects the "benign diversity" that a federal system is designed to promote. This is a subsidiary point, however: Legislative opponents object primarily to disenfranchisement provisions for a reason that will be explored later in this chapter—i.e., that the states alone, as distinct from Congress, have the constitutional authority to determine their own voter qualifications.

HAVA, the comprehensive electoral reform bill Christopher Dodd shepherded through the Senate, became law two years after the chaotic presidential election of 2000. It authorized $3.86 billion to upgrade voting equipment, improve election administration and poll-worker training, provide the disabled with access to voting machines, and furnish those whose names don't appear on registration lists with provisional ballots.[28]

By virtue of this new legislation, said Senator Dodd, "the right to cast a ballot is never again going to be denied to anyone in America who shows up at a polling place." The senator was mistaken: Among its many provisions, HAVA nowhere addresses the needs of ex-felons; come the next election, as a result, in many states an entire class of people will again be denied its "right to cast a ballot."[29]

Does Congress Have the Authority to Re-enfranchise Ex-Felons?

If Congress *were* inclined to pass a law re-enfranchising ex-felons, does it have the constitutional authority to do so? That depends upon whom one asks, and whether its reforms would affect state or federal elections—or both or neither.

The Fourteenth Amendment, arguably, vests Congress with ample power, and it is discussed in Chapter 9. So, too, does the Fifteenth Amendment, which provides that the "right of citizens of the United States to vote shall not be denied or abridged by the United States or by any State on account of race, color, or previous condition of servitude." Section 5 of this amendment grants Congress "power to enforce this article by appropriate legislation," and when lawmakers passed the Voting Rights Act in 1965 they accordingly cited the Fifteenth Amendment as authority for the statute's many provisions that protect and facilitate voting by racial minorities.[30]

It seems logical that Congress could also cite the Fifteenth Amendment if it decided to outlaw disenfranchisement policies on the ground that they disproportionately penalize racial minorities. Yet it is unlikely to do so, and there's a reason why: According to recent federal court decisions, Congress has no authority under this Civil War amendment to outlaw such policies, whatever their impact, in the absence of proof that they were enacted with the express purpose of fostering invidious discrimination. Even if a particular statute was drafted, adopted, maintained, and even reenacted for racially discriminatory reasons, proving as much can be daunting. Accordingly, a re-enfranchisement statute might be less susceptible to judicial attack if it were justified on the basis of Article I, Section 4 of the Constitution, the "elections clause."

This clause, which grants Congress supervisory power over federal contests, provides that "the Times, Places and Manner of holding Elections for Senators and Representatives, shall be prescribed in each State by the Legislature thereof, but the Congress may at any time by Law make or alter such Regulation, except as to the Places of chusing Senators." This apparently straightforward grant of power, however, is complicated by the language of Article I, Section 2, the qualifications clause, which reads: "The House of Representatives shall be composed of Members chosen every second Year by the People of the several States, and the Electors in each State shall have the Qualifications requisite for Electors of the most numerous Branch of the State Legislature." Since courts have interpreted the term "House of Representatives" to embrace all federal offices, Section 4 could be interpreted to vest states with sole authority to determine which of their residents are eligible to vote.[31]

How, then, to reconcile the two clauses? Who really has the power to determine whether ex-felons can vote—Congress or the individual states? In rulings that have occasionally been inconsistent or ambiguous, the Supreme Court *apparently* has suggested that while Congress's power to regulate *state* contests is sharply limited, its authority to establish eligibility standards for *federal* elections is more extensive. Indeed, it stands to reason that Congress, generally empowered to establish uniformity in affairs that affect the country as a whole, should be able to regularize procedures for nationwide elections. As Congressman John Tierney observed after the 2000 contest, "[t]he serious problems that manifested themselves in the most recent federal election were not limited to any one state, and those problems will not be solved except through a national mandate for change."[32]

States that disenfranchise ex-felons prevent tens of thousands of United States citizens from voting in federal elections. By unilaterally deciding who can and cannot vote, moreover, they create a system in which an individual's right to exercise the constituent act of citizenship ends up depending upon the accident of geography—as Representative Conyers noted when he introduced his Civic Participation and Rehabilitation Act in 1999. Finally, states can skew the outcomes of federal elections by manipulating the demographics of their voter pools (and indeed researchers have documented the extent to which disenfranchising states have already biased the results of several senatorial and even presidential elections. For discussion, see Chapter 11).

Congress alone can overcome the obstructionist and parochial interests that historically have prevented individual states from democratizing their voting procedures. While it was debating the Voting Rights Act in 1965, several witnesses asserted that without federal intervention few states would eliminate the various schemes they relied on to discourage African Americans from voting.[33] In the absence of federal prodding, at least some states will similarly guard their disenfranchisement statutes as jealously as they once did their poll taxes and grandfather clauses.

Yet no matter how strong the arguments for uniform election procedures, they are basically irrelevant if the nation's highest Court concludes that the power to determine voting qualifications rests with the states alone. Such a conclusion seems unlikely, however, because as far back as 1880 the Supreme Court declared that the "make or alter" language of the elections clause should be construed broadly:

> [If Congress] chooses to interfere, there is nothing in the words to prevent its doing so, either wholly or partially. On the contrary, their necessary implication is that it may do either. It may either make the regulations, or it may alter them. If it only alters, leaving, as manifest convenience requires, the general organization of the polls to the State, there results a necessary co-operation of the two governments in regulating the subject. But no repugnance in the system of regulations can arise thence; for the power of Congress over the subject is paramount. It may be exercised as and when Congress sees fit to exercise it. When exercised, the action of Congress, so far as it extends and conflicts with the regulations of the State, necessarily supersedes them.[34]

As recently as 2001 the Court interpreted the phrase "Manner of holding Elections" with similar expansiveness: "in our commonsense view that term encompasses matters like 'notices, registration, supervision of voting, protection of voters, prevention of fraud and corrupt practices, counting of votes, duties of inspectors and canvassers, and making and publication of election returns.'"[35]

Elsewhere the Court has asserted that the "comprehensive words" of the elections clause "embrace authority to provide a complete code for congressional elections." In a 1997 ruling it also noted that while this clause assumes that states themselves will enact appropriate regulations, it

> is a default provision; it invests the States with responsibility for the mechanics of congressional elections, but only so far as Congress declines to pre-empt state legislative choices. Thus it is well settled that the Elections Clause grants Congress the power to override state regulations by establishing uniform rules for federal elections, binding on the States. The regulations made by Congress are paramount to those made by the State legislature; and if they conflict therewith, the latter, so far as the conflict extends, ceases to be operative.[36]

While these rulings establish that Congress has near-plenary authority to regulate the *what*, *when*, and *where* of federal elections, less clear is whether it has the power to regulate the *who*—who is eligible to cast a ballot in national contests. The Supreme Court addressed this question in a 1986 case, concluding that, "far from being a device to limit the federal suffrage, the Qualifications Clause was intended by the Framers to prevent the mischief which would arise if state voters found themselves disqualified from participating in federal elections."[37]

Gillian Metzger, a law professor and authority on election law, interprets Article I, Section 2 to mean that while the states clearly have the right to determine voting qualifications, nothing in its language prohibits Congress from altering these qualifications, "particularly in the case of a state's exclusive voting regulations." The qualifications clause, she says, does not prevent Congress from altering the eligibility standards for federal electors, but only imposes an outer limit on both Congress and the states. It vests states with broad power to regulate federal elections but at the same time authorizes Congress to preempt state regulations; neither body, however, can exclude anyone eligible to vote in state elections for "the most numerous branch of the state legislature" from participating in national elections.[38]

If Congress may indeed determine who can vote in federal elections, then logically it could also permit ex-felons to participate, a conclusion reinforced by the Court's statement, in *Tashjian v. Republican Party* (1986), that identical voter qualifications are not required in federal and state elections.[39] This conclusion is buttressed by the Court's holding in a 1941 case, *United States v. Classic*, in which it intimated that Congress's powers under the elections clause were extensive enough to preempt states' prerogatives under the qualifications clause: "While, in a loose sense, the right to vote for representatives in Congress is sometimes spoken of as a right derived from the states ... this statement is true only in the sense that the states are authorized by the Constitution, to legislate on the subject as provided by §2 of Article I, to the extent that Congress has not restricted state action by the exercise of its powers to regulate elections under §4."[40]

Few authorities, however, believe that Congress could directly alter voter qualifications that states themselves have established for their own elections—other than to prevent invidious discrimination that is specifically prohibited by the Fourteenth and Fifteenth Amendments. Their views find support in the circumstances surrounding the implementation of the 1993 National Voter Registration Act (the so-called Motor Voter Act), which permits citizens to register when they conduct business with their local Motor Vehicle Department.[41]

Virtually every party to the act assumed that while Congress was entitled to use this venue to register federal electors, it could not presume to grant registrants the simultaneous right to participate in statewide contests. That is the prerogative of the states themselves. (After the Motor Voter Act passed, many states dutifully made eligibility co-extensive; others balked, however, creating no little confusion among the many citizens who were told, upon showing up at the polls, that they could cast a ballot for a presidential but not a gubernatorial candidate.)[42]

The Seventh Circuit Court of Appeals upheld the Motor Voter Act in 1995, but, notably, only because the law "does not purport to [directly] alter the qualifications" in federal or state elections.

Federal power under the elections clause, the court emphasized, "was subject in the first place to the reservation to the states of the power to fix the qualifications for votes for Senators and Representatives."[43] The ruling is thus a burr in the shoes of legislators intent upon reforming disenfranchisement policies, particularly since the Seventh Circuit also made clear that while the Motor Voter Law falls under the "Time, Place, and Manner of Elections," legislation extending eligibility to voters themselves would concern *who* can register to vote.

Many prominent conservatives have insisted that the federal government has no power to determine voter qualifications in either federal or state elections, period. Echoing the Seventh Circuit's logic in the Motor Voter case, former assistant attorney general Viet Dinh professed that while Congress has the authority to establish the time, place, and manner of congressional elections, and to safeguard the privileges and immunities of national citizenship, its powers "do not extend to prescribing voter qualification." Article I, he maintained, expressly differentiates between the "qualifications" of voters in House elections, stipulated in Section 2, which must be the same as the qualifications for voters for the most numerous body in the state legislature, and the "Times, Places and Manner" of such elections that is addressed in Article I, Section 4. To vest Congress with authority to regulate voter qualifications, he said, the justification in Section 4 must overcome "the explicit language of the Qualifications Clause."[44]

Roger Clegg, a leading conservative analyst, agrees with Viet Dinh and cites as support for their shared conclusion *The Federalist, No. 60*, in which Alexander Hamilton said, in reference to the elections clause, that the national government's "authority would be expressly restricted to the regulation of the *times*, the *places*, and the *manner* of elections. The qualifications of the persons who may choose or may be chosen ... are defined and fixed in the constitution; and are unalterable by any legislature."[45]

Whether or not Congress could end disenfranchisement, even if it wanted to, is thus uncertain. Throughout American history Congress has significantly broadened the franchise by banning literacy tests in federal elections, for instance, and at-large voting schemes that effectively deny representation to blacks. The Supreme Court sanctioned these bans but made clear that it was doing so only because they targeted practices that historically "have been rooted in intentional discrimination."

As a consequence, even assuming that the elections clause authorizes Congress to extend voting rights to ex-felons in federal elections, it would still have to clear the same high hurdle that anyone relying on the Fifteenth Amendment must clear: It must prove purposeful discrimination. Amassing such proof is a formidable undertaking, requiring legislators to investigate the history surrounding a particular law, unearth incriminating statements made by its drafters, and compile copious statistics documenting the way it has been implemented.

Disenfranchised citizens can't rely on Congress, then, which lacks the will and possibly even the constitutional authority to be of much help. Neither can they rely on the judiciary. As we shall see in the next chapter, while federal courts have been stalwart in their defense of voting rights in the abstract, they have generally looked kindly upon state policies that prohibit ex-felons from casting a ballot.

9 Constitutional Challenges and the Voting Rights Act

When plaintiffs challenge disenfranchisement policies in court, they can avail themselves of several constitutional and statutory weapons, including the equal protection clause of the Fourteenth Amendment and the 1965 Voting Rights Act.

The Equal Protection Clause

The equal protection clause, Section 1 of the Fourteenth Amendment, provides that no state may "deny to any person within its jurisdiction the equal protection of the laws." Whenever plaintiffs have argued that disenfranchisement provisions violate this clause by unduly burdening racial minorities, however, they have generally been rebuffed by the courts. In fact, while the judiciary now safeguards the voting rights of virtually every other class of citizens, it withholds similar protection from ex-felons. Its reticence dates back at least to the late nineteenth century, when the Supreme Court concluded that both a state and a territorial law denying the suffrage to convicted felons were not "open to any constitutional ... objection."[1]

From 1900 until 1974 the Supreme Court issued no written opinions dealing with felon disenfranchisement, but it summarily affirmed two lower court decisions validating the practice, and frequently noted *in dicta* that states could legitimately prohibit ex-prisoners from casting a ballot. In a 1974 case the Court cited "residence requirements, age, [and] previous criminal record" as "obvious examples of ... factors which a State may take into consideration in determining the qualifications of voters."[2]

Lower courts have been comparably amenable to disenfranchisement statutes. According to the influential Second Circuit Court of Appeals, in an oft-quoted 1967 ruling, "a man who breaks the laws he has authorized his agent to make for his own governance could fairly have been thought to have abandoned the right to participate in further administering the compact."[3]

In the 1970s a few public interest groups, galvanized by the recent struggles for civil rights and universal suffrage, began campaigning for people with felony records. They considered disenfranchisement not only undemocratic but also flatly at odds with the goal of rehabilitation to which penologists were then dedicated. Between 1960 and 1998 fifteen states consequently enacted (largely modest) reforms (see Chapter 2), and a lower court occasionally penned a sympathetic ruling.

In *Otsuka v. Hite*, a notable 1966 case, two conscientious objectors imprisoned during World War II sought the restoration of their voting rights, which had been denied them under a California statute disenfranchising anyone convicted of an infamous crime—a rubric interpreted to embrace all felonies. The state's supreme court concluded that plaintiffs' refusal, on religious grounds, to serve in the armed forces was not so "infamous" a crime as to render the men "morally corrupt and dishonest." The phrase "infamous crimes," said the court, should be applied only to those whose actions could "reasonably be deemed to constitute a threat to the integrity of the elective process."[4]

When California's new policy was challenged, the state's high court subjected it to the *strict scrutiny* standard of review—a noteworthy step because until then no tribunal had suggested that felons merited such solicitude. Although combating electoral fraud was indeed a "compelling interest," as the court had acknowledged in *Otsuka*, it asked whether so drastic a remedy as disenfranchisement was "necessary in the sense that it is the least burdensome means available to achieve that goal."[5] According to one wag, "seeking honest elections by stripping the vote from ex-felons is the equivalent of using a mine sweeper to clean out a fish bowl,"[6] and the court apparently agreed. It concluded that the statute penalized far too many people who posed no threat to the integrity of the electoral system.

In a 1970 case, *Stephens v. Yeomans*, a New Jersey district court held that the state's disenfranchisement laws must comport with the equal protection clause, and thus must bear a rational relationship to the achievement of a permissible state goal. The court accepted New

Jersey's ostensible goal: to ensure and preserve the purity of the state electoral process. But, it said, there was no logical nexus between the crimes prompting vote loss and the protection of the ballot box. Moreover, there was a "remarkable contrast" in the way different classes of crime were treated. Embezzlers and most defrauders, for instance, including persons convicted of income-tax fraud, retained their voting rights. Anyone convicted of larceny, however, did not. Thieves lost their vote, but recipients of stolen property kept theirs. Such "randomness," the court concluded, appeared altogether "irrational and inconsistent," and it accordingly invalidated the statute on the grounds that it did not meet the "exacting standard of precision required by the equal protection clause for a selective distribution of the franchise."[7]

In 1972 the Ninth Circuit Court of Appeals was similarly perplexed by a Washington State law that denied the franchise to certain classes of unpardoned ex-offenders:

> Courts have been hard pressed to define the state interest served by laws disenfranchising persons convicted of crimes.... Search for modern reasons to sustain the old governmental disenfranchisement prerogative has usually ended with a general pronouncement that a state has an interest in preventing persons who have been convicted of serious crimes from participation in the electoral process or a quasi-metaphysical invocation that the interest is preservation of the "purity of the ballot box."[8]

Ramirez v. Brown (1973) was the culmination of the brief reign of judicial liberalism.[9] In response to the California Supreme Court's 1965 ruling that the crimes spurring disenfranchisement were unrelated to the integrity of the electoral process, the state attempted to rationalize its policy. (Under the new scheme anyone operating a motor vehicle with a faulty muffler could forfeit her vote, and while skeptics might question how this offense relates to fair elections, the historian Alexander Keyssar thinks it made perfect sense for a state besieged by smog and utterly dependent upon the automobile to deny voting rights to such malefactors.)[10]

It is no longer necessary to engage in wholesale disenfranchisement in order to prevent election fraud, the California tribunal asserted. Instead, it said, this worthy goal could be achieved, and in a way that least burdens the right of suffrage, by enforcing laws regulating the voting process and punishing its misuse. Moreover, while "it may have been feasible in 1850 to influence the outcome of an election by rounding up the impecunious and the thirsty, furnishing them with free liquor, pre-marked ballots, and transportation to the polls," doing so in this day and age, if possible at all, "would require the coordinated skills of a vast squadron of computer technicians."[11]

The Supreme Court Steps In

Ramirez v. Brown, a persuasive and well-reasoned case, was also short-lived. The U.S. Supreme Court overruled it the following year in *Richardson v. Ramirez.* Justice William Rehnquist, speaking for a six-member majority, declared that disenfranchisement statutes are exempt from the stringent standards of scrutiny ordinarily applied to voting restrictions, and under the more appropriate rationality test the California provision was clearly constitutional.

Such statutes are exempt, Rehnquist argued, by virtue of the express language in Section 2 of the Fourteenth Amendment, which provides in part:

> [W]hen the right to vote at any election for the choice of electors for President and Vice-President of the United States, Representatives in Congress, the Executive and Judicial officers of a State, or the members of the Legislature thereof, is denied to any of the male inhabitants of such State … or in any way abridged, *except for participation in rebellion, or other crime*, the basis of representation therein shall be reduced in the proportion which the number of such male citizens shall bear to the whole number of male citizens twenty-one years of age in such State. (Emphasis added.)

By exempting "participation in rebellion, or other crime" from the provision reducing representation, Justice Rehnquist argued, the framers who drafted Section 2 expressly sanctioned criminal disenfranchisement. Moreover, although Section 1 of the same amendment does indeed prohibit any state from denying "to any person within its jurisdiction the equal protection of the laws," it "could not have been meant to bar outright a form of disenfranchisement which was expressly exempted from the less drastic sanction of reduced representation which Section 2 imposed for other forms of disenfranchisement."[12] An influential circuit court judge, Henry Friendly, had also adopted this reasoning in a 1967 case: "The framers of the Amendment ... could hardly have intended the general language of Section 1 to outlaw a discrimination which Section 2 expressly allowed without the penalty of reduced representation." Since Section 2 grants states an "affirmative sanction" to restrict the voting rights of ex-offenders, policies denying them the suffrage differ from "other state limitations on the franchise which have been held invalid under the Equal Protection Clause."[13]

Justice Rehnquist acknowledged that disenfranchising former prisoners was an outmoded notion "characteristic of mid-Nineteenth Century thought," and that a "more modern view"[14] of the issue, emphasizing the importance of rehabilitation, might lead to a different policy. Enacting a different policy, however, was the legislature's and not the judiciary's prerogative.

In a dissenting opinion, Justice Thurgood Marshall, writing also for Justices William O. Douglas and William Brennan, accused the majority of basing its decision on an "unsound historical analysis which already has been rejected by this Court." Section 2, in Marshall's interpretation, "was not intended to exempt felons from equal protection coverage"; on the contrary, it was created as a special remedy to combat the disenfranchisement of African Americans when "an explicit grant of suffrage to Negroes was thought politically unpalatable at the time." Southern states were put to a choice, Marshall concluded: "enfranchise Negro voters or lose congressional representation."[15]

Moreover, Justice Marshall asserted, simply "because Congress chose to exempt one form of electoral discrimination from the reduction-of-representation remedy provided by Section 2 does not necessarily imply congressional approval of this disenfranchisement," and, he concluded, "such discriminations thus are not forever immunized from evolving standards of equal protection scrutiny."[16] (Judicial scholar Gary Reback had earlier made the same argument: "[R]ather than specifically permitting a state to disenfranchise ex-felons, Section 2 merely indicates that if a state chose to disenfranchise ex-felons, it would not be penalized [by a reduction in representation] under Section 2.")[17]

By apparently legitimizing the unrestricted use of disenfranchisement laws, the Court in *Richardson* suggested that a state might disenfranchise a citizen convicted of jaywalking, or one who "lacks good
character."[18] In fact, although Section 2 refers broadly to "treason and
other crimes," when the southern states were readmitted into the
Union after the Civil War, the phrase was understood to mean "such
crimes as are now felonies at common law."[19] At the time, such
"common law felonies" were specific and relatively few. This is quib-
bling, however: The important question is what the 39th Congress
had in mind when it drafted Section 2 of the Fourteenth Amendment.

As the Court conceded in *Richardson*, "the legislative history
bearing on the meaning of the relevant language ... is scant indeed."[20] From what little there is, however, judicial scholars have
reached very different conclusions. Some are convinced that the
39th Congress did indeed authorize felony disenfranchisement.
David E. Rosenbaum, for one, finds that at the time the Fourteenth
Amendment was adopted, twenty-nine states had constitutional
provisions either prohibiting, or authorizing the legislatures to
prohibit, anyone convicted of felonies or infamous crimes from exercising the franchise.[21] John W. Burgess also pointed out in 1907
that before a former confederate state could free itself from military
rule it was required to grant universal suffrage to all males "not
disenfranchised ... for felony at common law."[22]

Yet Justice Rehnquist's claim that the express language of
Section 2 "compelled the conclusion" that disenfranchisement laws
are countenanced by the equal protection clause has many challengers in addition to Justice Marshall. According to David Shapiro,
"[t]here is not a word in the Fourteenth Amendment suggesting
that the exemptions in Section Two's formula are in any way a
barrier to the judicial application of Section One in voting rights
cases, whether or not they involve the rights of ex-convicts."[23]
William W. Van Alstyne similarly reasons that "it seems quite im-
possible to conclude that there was a clear and deliberate understanding in the House that Section 2 expressly recognized the states'
power to deny or abridge the right to vote."[24] George Fletcher
maintains, finally, that Section 2 had one purpose: to eradicate what
he calls "the stain" in Article I of the original Constitution, which
had sanctioned racial inequality in its provision that apportionment

of representatives would be based on the number of free persons, "excluding Indians not taxed" and "three-fifths of all other persons."[25]

Justice Rehnquist himself acknowledged that the most compelling argument against the Supreme Court's interpretation was offered by the tribunal itself in a 1927 opinion: The Fourteenth Amendment, he wrote, "while it applies to all, was passed ... with a special intent to protect the blacks from discrimination against them. It is thus illogical to assume its drafters intended to thwart the Amendment's very *raison d'etre* by sanctioning policies that from their inception have stripped the premiere right of citizenship from an unconscionably high number of black citizens."[26]

Recent Developments

In the years since *Richardson* was decided, a lower court has occasionally attempted to soften its edges, although none has challenged its conclusion that Section 2 of the Fourteenth Amendment expressly sanctions criminal disenfranchisement. In *Shepherd v. Trevino,* decided four years after *Richardson,* felons found guilty of federal crimes claimed that Texas violated the equal protection clause by restoring voting rights only to former prisoners convicted of *state* offenses. The Fifth Circuit Court of Appeals was not persuaded, holding that the "classifications created by the Texas system bear a rational relationship to the state's interest in limiting the franchise to responsible voters."[27] (The court explained that ex-felons, "like insane persons, have raised questions about their ability to vote responsibly." It neglected to explain why this reasoning applied to those convicted of federal crimes but not of state offenses.)

Only once in its history has the Supreme Court invalidated a disenfranchisement provision. This occurred in a 1985 case, *Hunter v. Underwood,* which I discuss below, and involved a section of the Alabama constitution that was so flagrantly racist that even the Court's most conservative members joined the opinion striking it down.

One other case bears noting. In 1995 a district court concluded in *McLaughlin v. City of Canton* that Mississippi had not offered a compelling reason why it was necessary to disenfranchise ex-felons convicted of misdemeanors as well as those convicted of felonies.

Since Section 2 of the Fourteenth Amendment applies only to "felonies," the court reasoned, a measure stripping voting rights from individuals convicted of less serious offenses must be examined with the same stringent scrutiny that courts apply to any other voting restrictions.[28]

These rulings suggest, then, that courts will not tolerate disenfranchisement statutes that are blatantly racist, or, at least in some jurisdictions, that apply to people convicted of crimes minor enough to be labeled "misdemeanors." The Court's ruling in *Richardson v. Ramirez* still stands, however, a few branches trimmed, but its roots still firm.

According to the Supreme Court, Section 1 of the Fourteenth Amendment, forbidding a state to "deny to any person within its jurisdiction the equal protection of the laws," prohibits only government policies that are *intentionally* discriminatory, and as a result disenfranchisement policies have withstood challenge as long as there is no incontrovertible proof they were racially motivated. The Supreme Court invalidated an Alabama statute in *Hunter v. Underwood* because there was indeed such proof, but in most cases plaintiffs have difficulty compiling a paper trail anywhere near as damning as the one introduced in that case. However, if the equal protection clause were interpreted to forbid governmental policies that are discriminatory *in practice* as well as in intent, disenfranchisement laws would topple like a house of cards.

Disenfranchisement policies would also topple if courts subjected them to the rigorous strict scrutiny test, under which governmental measures must be absolutely necessary to the furtherance of a compelling governmental aim. As I discussed in the previous chapter, the courts invoke this rigorous standard whenever they examine government measures that affect fundamental rights, such as voting. They invoke it under another set of circumstances, as well—whenever they assess governmental measures affecting what they call "discrete and insular minorities" or, variously, "suspect classes." Racial and ethnic minorities are considered "suspect classes," as are resident aliens and certain other groups whose members lack the wherewithal necessary to defend themselves through the political process, and who, as a consequence, are easy targets for a thoughtless or even vengeful majority.

Most "suspect classes" possess, in addition to minimal political clout, "immutable biological characteristics," such as skin color, that bear no relationship whatsoever to their intelligence or capabilities. Finally, they have usually suffered a history of unfair treatment, prompting the Court to assume that punitive policies directed at them are often more reflexive than reasoned.

Laws disenfranchising ex-convicts should qualify for strict scrutiny on two independent grounds: They deprive a vulnerable class of people of a fundamental right, and they penalize a group that, in most respects, represents the quintessential "discrete and insular minority" scorned by the public and bereft of anything approaching political clout. (As one editorialist pointed out, "If you don't vote, you don't even have any say on when the trash man is going to pick up the garbage.")[29]

The Voting Rights Act

Attorneys challenging disenfranchisement laws frequently maintain that by disproportionately burdening racial minorities these laws violate the 1965 Voting Rights Act (VRA). Although this remarkable act has accomplished wonders in its forty years, as a vehicle for assisting ex-felons it has yet to reach its potential.

Theoretically the VRA should not have been necessary, because Congress is authorized by the Fifteenth Amendment to prevent racially discriminatory electoral practices. Yet during Reconstruction and the prolonged Jim Crow era that followed, this amendment did not prevent states from concocting one ploy after another to prevent blacks from exercising their dearly won franchise—poll taxes, literacy tests, grandfather clauses, egregious gerrymandering, white primaries, harassment, economic reprisals, and out-and-out violence.[30]

Congress invalidated many of these stratagems, but such is human inventiveness that as soon as one was banned states instituted new, often more subtle ways to discourage African Americans from voting. "Pitchfork" Ben Tillman, a South Carolina senator who spearheaded a ruthless campaign against black suffrage, boasted about the legislature's ingenuity: "We have done our level best. We have scratched our heads to find out how we could eliminate every last one of them. We stuffed ballot boxes. We shot them. We are not ashamed of it."[31]

Eventually Congress exchanged its slingshot for a more effective legislative weapon. As the Supreme Court observed in 1966, "[a]fter enduring nearly a century of systematic resistance to the Fifteenth Amendment," in 1965 lawmakers decided "to shift the advantage of time and inertia from the perpetrators of the evil to its victims."[32] In response to both the mounting sophistication with which states were barring minorities from the polls and the futility of attacking discriminatory ploys on a case-by-case basis, Congress passed the Voting Rights Act.[33]

The act was intended to remedy what the Supreme Court had called the "insidious and pervasive evil" of racial discrimination in this country's electoral system.[34] Accordingly, Section 2 of the act prohibits any practices or voting qualifications, such as literacy tests, that deny or abridge a citizen's right to vote on account of race or color, particularly practices that, while neutral on their face, are inequitable in operation.[35] Since the VRA is intended, as the Supreme Court said, "to rid the country of racial discrimination in voting," it should therefore be construed as having "the broadest possible scope."[36]

When President Johnson signed the act in August 1965, he called it "a triumph for freedom as huge as any victory that has ever been won on any battlefield."[37] Indeed, some forty years later it remains the most successful civil rights legislation ever enacted by the United States Congress. Since 1972, when the Supreme Court essentially immunized disenfranchisement laws from attack on equal protection grounds, the VRA has also been the tool most frequently wielded by activists attempting to dismantle these laws.

Section 5, the heart of the VRA, mandates that any change in election law—be it as minor as moving a polling place or as major as redrawing legislative districts—must be preapproved, either by the U.S. Justice Department or by the federal district court in the District of Columbia, to ensure that no change renders minority group members "worse off" with respect "to their opportunity to exercise the electoral franchise effectively."[38]

For seven years the Supreme Court used a "results-oriented" approach, thereby interpreting the act with the liberality Congress intended. Then, however, it issued the first of several restrictive rulings that have hobbled an act intended by its framers to have "the broadest possible scope."[39] The first of these rulings occurred in a

1980 case, *Bolden v. City of Mobile*.[40] Black voters had challenged the at-large election of officers to the Mobile, Alabama, city commission. In response, the Court held that plaintiffs must do more than show that this electoral scheme was diluting their voting strength: They must establish, as well, that the scheme had a discriminatory *purpose*. By so ruling it thrust a major roadblock before anyone challenging disenfranchisement policies, since proving intent is almost always extremely difficult: The origins of long-standing practices may be long forgotten, and lawmakers drafting new policies know enough to keep silent about unsavory motives.

The *Bolden* ruling had one redeeming feature: It spurred Congress to amend the VRA in 1982 by strengthening Section 2 and explicitly outlawing any scheme that resulted in vote dilution, whatever the motives underlying the scheme.[41] In contrast to "vote denial," dilution occurs, as the Supreme Court explained in a 1986 case, when a particular act or policy weakens the overall voting strength of the minority community. It takes place if, based on "the totality of the circumstances," plaintiffs are able to show that the political process leading to nomination or election in the state or political subdivision is "not equally open to participation by members of a class of citizens protected by [the act] in that its members have less opportunity than other members of the electorate to participate in the political process and to elect representatives of their choice."[42]

In this case, *Thornburg v. Gingles,* the Court suggested ways that anyone attempting to establish vote dilution might document their claims. Although it did not specifically address claims made on behalf of ex-felons, its advice has nevertheless benefited plaintiffs who allege that disenfranchisement laws inordinately penalize racial minorities. Since the Court encouraged challengers to provide reviewing judges with statistical data whenever appropriate, for instance, these plaintiffs have accordingly introduced figures comparing disenfranchisement rates in a given jurisdiction between minorities and whites of voting age.

The Court also advised plaintiffs to document the ways in which whites and minorities have been variously targeted and treated by government authorities, particularly in the area of voting rights, and to alert presiding judges to the "lingering effects of discrimination in socioeconomic areas such as education, employment, and health

[that] thwart effective black participation in the political process."[43] Lawyers challenging disenfranchisement laws have interpreted "lingering effects" to encompass "psychological barriers," in the form of a "lack of a habit of voting derived from years of exclusion from voting, fear, deference to whites, and apathy," and "institutional obstacles" in the form of inadequate voter registration and procedure information, inconvenient registration locations and hours, and the "scarcity of black registration officials, especially in the South."[44]

Finally, in response to the Court's recommendation in *Thornburg v. Gingles* that plaintiffs address opposing arguments "head on," they have attempted to rebut the state's claim that disenfranchisement laws promote important social or criminological objectives by emphasizing the abundant research suggesting such laws actually impede, rather than advance, these objectives.[45]

The first challenge to a disenfranchisement statute under the amended VRA occurred in a 1986 case, *Wesley v. Collins,* which arose when a black ex-Marine challenged a Tennessee law that prohibited him from voting while he was serving a suspended sentence. This law, he claimed, "progressively dilute[s] the black vote thereby impeding the equal opportunity of blacks to participate in the political process."[46]

In an attempt to establish vote dilution using a "totality of the circumstances" defense, the plaintiff noted that Tennessee's longstanding discrimination against blacks was "marked by limited access to and segregation in the provision of health care, housing and education, and by sustained efforts to prevent blacks from registering to vote." As a result of this centuries-old discrimination and the debilitating socioeconomic inequities it spawned, blacks have a "significantly higher rate of felony conviction" than whites.[47]

Plaintiffs pointed out that in Tennessee, whereas there was one white felon for every thousand white citizens, there was one black felon for every hundred black citizens.[48] As a consequence, African Americans make up a disproportionate number of those prohibited from voting—a phenomenon that diminishes their electoral strength and represents the "crowning blow" in the chain reaction set in motion by the initial discrimination.

The Sixth Circuit Court of Appeals, hearing *Wesley v. Collins* on appeal, acknowledged that the disputed statute did indeed penalize blacks disproportionately, and that it operated in a social context "characterized by a history of discrimination against blacks at the polls." The court nevertheless dismissed the case on the grounds that plaintiffs failed to establish "a causal connection" between the indicators of historically rooted discrimination and the disenfranchisement law—a proof the court insisted was required by the VRA.[49]

The court undertook a cursory examination of the statute's discriminatory forebears and their "lingering effects" before determining that the current version bears no "taint of historically-rooted discrimination." Historical discrimination, it said, could not, "in the manner of original sin, condemn action that is not in itself unlawful." Felons had been disenfranchised, the court concluded, "because they chose to commit crimes, not because of their race."[50]

The Sixth Circuit's ruling was misguided. By demanding proof that a disputed electoral practice was motivated by racial discrimination, this court reintroduced the "intent" requirement that Congress enacted the 1982 amendments expressly to disavow. Legislators made clear at the time that "disproportionate education, employment, income level and living conditions arising from past discrimination tend to depress minority political participation." Once plaintiffs establish the presence of these conditions, they "need not prove any further causal nexus between their disparate socioeconomic status and the depressed level of political participation."[51]

By citing abundant evidence of historic discrimination and minority vote dilution, plaintiffs easily established the "totality of circumstances" necessary to demonstrate a violation of the VRA. Indeed, in the VRA's legislative history the Senate emphasized that "even a consistently applied practice premised on a racially neutral policy would not negate a plaintiff's showing through other factors that the challenged practice denies minorities fair access to the process."[52]

Unhelpful as *Wesley v. Collins* was to their cause, reformers found a 1996 ruling issued by the Second Circuit Court of Appeals even worse. In this case, *Baker v. Pataki*, the majority suggested that it was "not unmistakably clear" that Congress intended the VRA's "results" test even to apply to disenfranchisement statutes.[53] The court thus concluded that, despite compelling evidence that New York penalizes black and Hispanic felons far out of proportion to their numbers, the state is still free to disenfranchise them in any way it desires, as long as it does not discriminate explicitly on the basis of race.[54]

Reformers, deflated after the *Wesley* and *Pataki* rulings, are again "cautiously optimistic." For one thing, they can now avail themselves of new documentary evidence, yielded by two recent studies, detailing both the vast disparity in disenfranchisement rates between blacks and whites and the systemic racial bias that in many states infects virtually every facet of the criminal justice system.[55] For another, since these earlier cases, they have enjoyed two appellate court victories—and however partial and tentative these victories may ultimately be, they still buoy hopes that eventual success is possible.

Of the two appellate victories, the more carefully watched is *Johnson v. Bush,* not only because the public interest groups that filed this suit, in September 2000, devised an impressively sophisticated legal strategy, but also because such influential legal authorities as former deputy attorney general Eric Holder and former solicitor general Seth Waxman submitted *amici* briefs on their behalf.[56] (Conspicuously missing from their list of supporters, however, is the formidable Department of Justice, which is siding with Florida.)

In designing their strategy, plaintiffs had to maneuver around two substantial roadblocks previously discussed: the Supreme Court's 1974 *Richardson v. Ramirez* ruling that laws stripping voting rights from convicted felons are not inherently unconstitutional because Section 2 of the Fourteenth Amendment expressly sanctions such laws; and the Sixth Circuit's holding in *Wesley v. Collins* that in order to establish a violation of the VRA, challengers must demonstrate discriminatory intent.

In an effort to clear these hurdles, plaintiffs filed several different claims, including one used for the first time in disenfranchisement suits—that the state violates the Fourteenth and Twenty-Fourth Amendments and Section 6 of the VRA by refusing to restore voting rights to ex-felons who still owe restitution. This requirement is effectively a poll tax, plaintiffs assert, in that it discourages the poor from exercising their basic right of citizenship.[57] Plaintiffs also charged that Florida's disputed law, which strips blacks of voting rights at more than twice the rate of whites, violates the Fourteenth Amendment's equal protection clause because it was "initially adopted to discriminate against African American voters and continues to have a discriminatory impact."[58] Florida countered that the original statute was part of a "venerable tradition" and noted that its challenged provision first appeared in an antebellum constitution adopted at a time when only whites could vote.[59] Moreover, the state averred, even if the provision had been *adopted* nearly 150 years ago for discriminatory reasons, that did not mean that legislators had similar motives when they *reenacted* it in 1968. In language reprising that used in *Wesley*, Florida argued against condemning "a potentially legitimate practice ... on the basis of some sort of original racial sin."[60]

The plaintiffs' third claim focused on the "arbitrary, irrational, and excessive" character of the challenged statute. Its provisions, they argued, disempower anyone convicted of a felony, regardless of the nature of a particular offense or the circumstances surrounding its commission; they target every ex-felon, moreover, not just those whose crimes relate to the electoral process, such as voting fraud, or "strike at the heart of government," such as treason. Finally, far from promoting any legitimate penal interest, "lifetime exclusion from voting gravely disserves the State's overwhelming interest in rehabilitating the offender and re-integrating him into civil society."

Plaintiffs asserted, in conclusion, that the state's disenfranchisement laws violate the VRA because under their sway "African-Americans have less opportunity than other members of the electorate to participate in the political process and to elect representatives of their choice."[61]

In an opinion announced on July 17, 2003, U.S. District Judge James Lawrence King rejected outright every claim plaintiffs raised, essentially finding them too flimsy even to warrant a trial. Although Florida's disenfranchisement statute was racially motivated in 1868, he contended that plaintiffs had offered no evidence that its 1968 reincarnation was similarly inspired. In fact, said the judge, the 1968 legislature "significantly deliberated and substantively revised" the 1868 law without "racial animus." Rather than falling victim to a biased state law, then, plaintiffs "disenfranchised themselves by committing a felony."[62]

The judge's peremptory dismissal was ill considered and his thinking facile. By sanctioning a reenacted disenfranchisement statute as long as its drafters left no racist footprints, he effectively reassured legislators that they can enact any manner of discriminatory scheme as long as they camouflage their true motives. Judge King never asked why Florida lawmakers, in reenacting the statute, failed to confront, much less disavow, either the 1868 law's discriminatory purpose or its baleful consequences. Neither did he ask what governmental interests the 1968 statute was intended to serve.[63]

Even more seriously, Judge King never conducted the "searching practical evaluation of the 'past and present reality' " that Congress mandated when it amended the VRA. Instead, he apparently agreed with the defendants that Florida washed its hands of all responsibility for the inequities spawned by its Confederate–era disenfranchisement statute once it adopted a better-packaged successor. (As Jeffrey Solochek asks, "does reenacting a law automatically reset the constitutional clock?")[64]

The judge ignored the extent to which historical discrimination "is relevant," as the Supreme Court observed in 1982, "to drawing an inference of purposeful discrimination, particularly ... where the evidence shows that discriminatory practices were commonly utilized, that they were abandoned when enjoined by courts, or made illegal by civil rights legislation, and that they were replaced by laws and practices which, though neutral on their face, serve to maintain the status quo."[65]

Had Judge King investigated the legacy of historical discrimination, he would have discovered the extent to which the 1868 law—which he conceded was enacted with racist intent—fostered social and economic inequities that still "linger," so much so that even today African Americans, as a class, suffer from inferior education, housing, and health care, enjoy far fewer employment and professional opportunities than whites, and have considerably less opportunity to participate in the electoral process.[66]

Judge King, moreover, noted but totally disregarded a Supreme Court case decided just months earlier that should have influenced his ruling. In this case, *Hunter v. Underwood,* Chief Justice Rehnquist, speaking for a unanimous court, struck down Alabama's disenfranchisement statute on the basis of abundant evidence that it had been adopted in 1901 largely to prevent blacks from exercising their newly acquired voting rights.[67] Although the Court in *Hunter* based its decision on the equal protection clause, its reasoning is as applicable to cases involving the VRA.

Section 182 of the Alabama statute authorized the disenfranchisement of any person convicted of a "crime ... involving moral turpitude." The state claimed that the statute was racially neutral, since it targeted whites as well as blacks. The chief justice scoffed at such logic. Although the disputed provision was indeed nondiscriminatory on its face, since its adoption ten times as many blacks as whites had lost their voting rights. There was abundant evidence, moreover, that the crimes triggering disenfranchisement—such as vagrancy, adultery, and wife beating—were infractions that members of the 1901 Alabama constitutional convention assumed blacks were more likely than whites to commit.[68]

Further, under administrative interpretations of the provision, some nonfelony offenses—such as presenting a worthless check and petty larceny—resulted in the forfeiture of the franchise, while more serious misdemeanors—such as second-degree manslaughter, assault on a police officer, and mailing pornography—did not. According to Chief Justice Rehnquist, among those who participated in the 1901 convention the "zeal for white supremacy [had run] rampant." The disputed provision, then, directly countermanded the Fourteenth Amendment because it represented a bald attempt "to disenfranchise practically all of the African Americans."[69]

Earlier, the Sixth Circuit Court of Appeals had acknowledged *Hunter v. Underwood,* and had even observed that if the lower court had not dismissed plaintiff's claim for discovery he might have established that the motives for Tennessee's post-Reconstruction statute were as pernicious as the ones underlying Alabama's. When the plaintiff in *Wesley* subsequently sought access to government documents, however, to demonstrate a parallel, the appellate tribunal dismissed his request as "a fishing expedition for unspecified evidence."[70] Judge King similarly sidestepped this Supreme Court decision. In both cases, then, an important precedent directly relevant to ex-felon disenfranchisement was simply ignored.

On December 19, 2003, the decision in *Johnson v. Bush* to deny plaintiffs a trial was reversed by a three-judge panel of the Ninth Circuit Court of Appeals. As a result, Judge King may not have the last word, after all, because now plaintiffs have another chance to assert the compelling claims he dismissed out of hand.

Reformers were also heartened when, on July 23, 2003, the Eleventh Circuit Court of Appeals reversed a district court in Washington State, for essentially the same reasons the Ninth Circuit overruled Judge King. Although the higher tribunal in *Farrakhan v. Locke* voiced no opinion on the merits of plaintiffs' argument, it faulted the lower court for—significantly—misunderstanding Section 2 of the VRA's "totality of the circumstances" test, which "requires courts to consider how a challenged voting practice interacts with external factors such as 'social and historical conditions' to result in denial of the right to vote on account of race or color."[71]

What's more, the court declared, "evidence of discrimination within the criminal justice system can be relevant to a Section 2 analysis," and plaintiffs had presented "compelling" statistical data that the state's criminal justice system was riddled with racial discrimination. Blacks, for example, make up about 3 percent of Washington's population but account for 37 percent of those prohibited from voting. The Ninth Circuit remanded the case, instructing the lower court to conduct a "searching investigation."[72] (On February 24, 2004, it denied the state's request for an *en banc* rehearing.)[73]

Regardless of what this "searching investigation" yields, the Ninth Circuit's opinion revives hope that disenfranchisement suits might indeed be won under the Voting Rights Act, provided that plaintiffs are able to mount a well-documented offense and judges are willing to take their cue from the Eleventh Circuit and examine the "totality of the circumstances" that foster and sustain policies that deny ex-felons their suffrage.

10 Cruel and Unusual Punishment and International Law

Given that opponents of disenfranchisement policies have had only limited success attacking them on equal protection or statutory grounds, perhaps it is time they take a risk. They might assert that such policies violate the cruel and unusual punishment clause of the Constitution's Eighth Amendment, for example. While such a strategy is worth pursuing, it is admittedly problematic: Laws denying ex-felons their voting rights for long periods, or even for life, are unquestionably harsh, but they must be "cruel" in the constitutional sense before they violate the Eighth Amendment.

What, then, did those who drafted this amendment have in mind when they used the ambiguous and somewhat open-ended phrase "cruel and unusual punishment"? According to Justice Antonin Scalia, the term was intended only to prevent the government from subjecting anyone to barbaric forms of punishment;[1] if he is correct, then the phrase lacks any contemporary vitality. Justice Thurgood Marshall maintained, however, that the "cruel and unusual punishment" clause, understood in its historical context, prohibits excessive fines and excessive bail: *the entire thrust of the Eighth Amendment is… against that which is excessive*" (emphasis added).[2]

Many scholars, agreeing with Justice Marshall, believe that the clause reflects a cardinal principle of American jurisprudence—i.e., that punishment should be at least roughly commensurate with the crime and the moral culpability of the offender. Otherwise, as Douglas Tims observes, "the line between justifiable vindication and outrageous revenge" is crossed.[3]

This notion of "proportionality" emerged early in Western thought. The ancient Greeks recognized it, and Aristotle declared that an incommensurate sentence, whether to the advantage or disadvantage of the offender, is the very essence of injustice. In Jewish thought, God, or Yahweh, honored the principle of proportionality by giving Moses the *lex talionis* (*talio* being the Latin of "equivalent" or "equal"), which prescribes a maximum limit on punishment and requires that it fit the crime. Hence the passage from Exodus: "If a man injures his neighbor, what he has done must be done to him: broken limb for broken limb, eye for eye, tooth for tooth. As the injury inflicted, so must be the injury suffered" (Exod. 21:22–25). This principle is articulated again in the Book of Leviticus ("You shall do no injustice in judgment," Lev. 19:15). As early as 900 A.D. the concept of *lex talionis* was codified in England, and it remained part of the common law either since the Magna Carta in 1215, as some historians claim, or the Bill of Rights in 1688, as others aver.

Exactly what "cruel and unusual punishment" meant in English common law arouses debate even today between so-called traditionalists, who contend that the term refers exclusively to excessive cruelty; and so-called nontraditionalists, who insist that it was intended to forbid not only barbarous punishments but also those disproportionate to the crime. The differing positions of Justices Scalia and Marshall reflect this long-standing dispute.

The text of the U.S. Constitution's Eighth Amendment is almost identical to its precursor in the English Bill of Rights, and American scholars debate its meaning as adamantly as their British counterparts do, although today most concede that, whatever its original intent, the clause as it has evolved now prohibits sentences that are egregiously excessive.[4]

Between 1789 and 1910, however, with one partial exception, American judges assumed that the words addressed only modes of punishment. The slight exception occurred in an 1892 dissenting opinion by Justice Stephen Field, who considered a fifty-four-year sentence imposed on a defendant for repeatedly selling liquor without authorization a violation of the cruel and unusual punishment clause. This clause, Field wrote, prohibits in addition to torture, "all punishments which by their excessive length or severity are greatly disproportionate to the offences charged."[5]

Justice Field's vindication came eighteen years later, when in *Weems v. United States* the Supreme Court found the defendant's punishment "cruel in its excess of imprisonment and [the penalty] which accompanies and follows imprisonment." It also rejected the contention that the Eighth Amendment was only intended to outlaw the "forms of abuse that went out of practice with the Stuarts." "The framers were men of action, practical and sagacious," said the Court, and surely "it must have come to them that there could be exercises of cruelty by laws other than those which inflicted bodily pain or mutilation."[6]

What constituted "cruel and unusual punishment," the Court ruled in *Weems*, was not a concept frozen in time but rather one to be assessed, at least to some extent, according to evolving circumstances. "Time works changes" and "brings into existence new conditions and purposes. Therefore a principle to be vital must be capable of wider application than the mischief which gave it birth." "This is particularly true of Constitutions."[7]

In 1962 the Court invalidated on Eighth Amendment grounds a California law making it a crime to be addicted to narcotics. A state, said the Court, may not punish an individual for being "mentally ill, or a leper, or ... afflicted with a venereal disease or having any similar physical illnesses." Echoing the logic used in *Weems*, the Court held that the cruel and unusual punishment clause must be continually revitalized "in the light of contemporary human knowledge."[8]

Finally, Justice Byron White explained in a 1989 plurality opinion that the government also violates the Eighth Amendment if it imposes a sentence that "makes no measurable contribution to acceptable goals of punishment and hence is nothing more than the purposeless and needless imposition of pain and suffering."[9] In scores of other cases judges have reiterated the principle that punishment must fulfill a legitimate penal purpose, including "deterrence, rehabilitation, retribution, and denunciation."[10]

These rulings established not only that the Eighth Amendment contains a proportionality principle, but also that the meaning of cruel and unusual punishment is not "frozen in time"; it is a "progressive" concept and "may acquire meaning as public opinion becomes enlightened by a humane justice."[11] Elsewhere the Court said that the clause "takes its meaning from the evolving standards of decency that mark the progress of a maturing society."[12]

Applying the "evolving standards" doctrine, the Court continues to outlaw practices that, while not barbaric, nevertheless sear the "enlightened conscience." In a 1993 case, for instance, it granted an inmate standing to challenge prison authorities who, he said, refused to remove him from a cell that also housed a man who smoked five packs of cigarettes a day. "Contemporary standards of decency require no less," the Court explained.[13] "Although accidental or inadvertent failure to provide adequate medical care to a prisoner would not violate the Eighth Amendment," "deliberate indifference to serious medical needs of prisoners" does, because it constitutes the "unnecessary and wanton infliction of pain contrary to contemporary standards of decency."[14]

How do judges determine "contemporary standards of decency"? Many consult legal precedents, history, and even international practices. To determine whether there was a national consensus against executing juveniles, for instance, members of the Supreme Court assayed "the views that have been expressed by ... other nations that share our Anglo-American heritage, and by the leading members of the Western European community." They also considered jury decisions and the way similarly situated offenders were treated, both within the same jurisdiction and among different jurisdictions.[15]

In a 2002 case, *Atkins v. Virginia*, the Supreme Court held that the Eighth Amendment's cruel and unusual punishment clause prohibits states from executing anyone who is mentally retarded. The Court thereby reversed an opinion handed down just thirteen years earlier in which it had concluded exactly the opposite. In that earlier opinion, Justice John Paul Stevens argued, only Maryland and Georgia banned the execution of the mentally retarded, and as a consequence there was "insufficient evidence of a national consensus."[16] By 2002, fully eighteen of the thirty-eight states that permitted executions exempted the retarded—indicating, he said, "widespread judgment about the relative culpability" of retarded offenders.[17]

"It is not so much the number of these states that is significant," Justice Stevens wrote, "but the consistency of the direction of the change." Although national surveys show that a majority of Americans support the death penalty, a 2002 Gallup poll indicated that 82 percent of Americans believe that no one should be executed who lacks the mental capacity to appreciate the nature of his or her actions.[18] Perhaps in tacit recognition of this poll, the Court in

Atkins concluded that "the practice ... has become unusual, and it is fair to say that a national consensus has developed against it."

Following the lead of *Atkins*, the Supreme Court might conclude that disenfranchising ex-felons no longer comports with contemporary values, either, given the number of states and countries that no longer engage in this practice, and that more than 80 percent of Americans believe that felons who have "paid their debts" in full should have their voting rights reinstated. Yet the Court's pronouncements in a different line of cases, involving "enhanced" sentences, suggest that "evolving standards" analysis may extend only to situations involving capital punishment.

Since 1980 the Supreme Court has heard several challenges to so-called "three-strikes" laws that impose long or even lifetime sentences on repeat offenders.[19] The first of these cases, *Rummel v. Estelle*, involved a defendant, convicted previously of several nonviolent felonies, who was given a life term for fraudulently obtaining $120.75. Chief Justice Rehnquist, writing for the majority, noted in a much-quoted footnote that "a proportionality principle [might] come into play ... if a legislature made overtime parking a felony punishable by life imprisonment," but indicated that anything less draconian raises no constitutional objections. He implied, moreover, that courts might even violate principles of federalism and separation of powers if they presumed to review the scope of permissible punishments.[20]

Three years later, in *Solem v. Helm*, the Court heard a second challenge to a recidivist statute, although in an apparent about-face it concluded that since the Eighth Amendment prohibits "sentences that are disproportionate to the crime committed," the proportionality principle was applicable to noncapital as well as capital offenses.

Justice Powell, writing for the majority, emphasized that proportionality review does not mean unfettered discretion. Rather, proportionality can be assessed by reference to the same objective criteria the Court relied upon in *Weems, Trop v. Dulles, Robinson v. California*, and the death penalty cases—i.e., the gravity of the offense and the harshness of the penalty, and the sentences imposed on other criminals in both the same and in other jurisdictions. Guided by these "objective criteria," Powell concluded that the defendant's "sentence is significantly disproportionate to his crime, and is therefore prohibited by the Eighth Amendment."[21]

Solem v. Helm's three-step proportionality review was not long for this world. Eight years later, in *Harmelin v. Michigan,* a plurality found nothing amiss in a life sentence without parole for someone convicted of possessing 672 grams of cocaine and declared that inter- and intrajurisdictional review would be appropriate only in "rare" cases.[22]

In 2003 the Supreme Court heard two other cases—*Ewing v. California* and *Lockyer v. Andrade*—in which defendants argued that the sentences they received under California's "three-strikes" law violated the Eighth Amendment. The Court concluded that neither sentence qualified as an occasion "rare" enough to justify proportionality review—even though one defendant received twenty-five years to life for stealing golf clubs and the other fifty years to life for heisting $150 worth of videos.[23]

According to Justice O'Connor, who spoke for the plurality in both cases, the Court should conduct an intra- and interjurisdictional review only if the penalty is found to be "grossly disproportionate" to the offense. The defendants' sentences were long, she conceded, but given their criminal histories not incommensurate with "the gravity of [their] offenses."[24] Both were justified, moreover, by the state's interest in public safety.

Justice O'Connor explained that the Court's decision was guided, in part, by its respect for the principles of federalism: "We do not sit as a super-legislature to second-guess [the legislature's] policy choices. It is enough that the state of California has a reasonable basis for believing that dramatically enhanced sentences for habitual felons advances the goals of its criminal justice system in any substantial way."[25]

Justice Stevens, in a dissenting opinion, pointed out that "[t]he Eighth Amendment succinctly prohibits 'excessive' sanctions," and that the Court, "[f]aithful to the Amendment's text," has always exercised its duty to decide whether fines are too high, bail unreasonable, or the death penalty excessive under the circumstances.[26] It "would be anomalous indeed,"[27] to conclude that while the Eighth Amendment mandates proportionality review in the context of bail and fines, it does not do so in the context of other forms of punishment, such as imprisonment.

The absence of clear-cut rules, moreover, does not disqualify judges from exercising their discretion in determining the outside parameters of sentencing authority, Stevens wrote. After all, judges are "constantly called upon to draw ... lines in a variety of contexts,"[28] and to exercise their judgment whenever they interpret any of the Constitution's broadly phrased protections. The vague and open-ended due process clause, for instance, obligates the Court to use proportionality review in determining, on a case-by-case basis, whether punitive damage awards are unreasonable.[29] The Sixth Amendment, to cite another example, guarantees criminal defendants the right to a speedy trial, and accordingly judges must determine, again on a case-by-case basis, whether a particular delay is or is not constitutional.[30]

Justice Stevens's logic left most of his colleagues unpersuaded. They apparently believe that in noncapital cases no sentence will constitute cruel and unusual punishment—at least no sentence short of life imprisonment for overtime parking. This conviction, in tandem with its deference to legislative prerogatives, suggests that the Court is unlikely to invalidate disenfranchisement statutes, either. This is not a foregone conclusion, however, because for all the similarities between laws penalizing recidivists, on the one hand, and ex-felons, on the other, there are also significant distinctions. The former, at least arguably, promote legitimate penal objectives, whereas the latter do not.[31] Recidivist laws are gaining in popularity, moreover, indicating that they comport with community values, whereas penalties imposed upon citizens who have fulfilled the terms of their sentences are steadily losing favor with the public.

Are Disenfranchisement Statutes "Cruel and Unusual"?

Eighth Amendment jurisprudence is presently inconsistent, contradictory, and muddled. That said, courts still agree on a few basic principles: The cruel and unusual punishment clause prohibits sanctions that, in addition to being torturous or degrading, serve no legitimate penal or nonpenal ends, that are inflicted solely on the basis of an individual's status, and, finally, that affront "evolving standards of decency."

Felon disenfranchisement laws violate many of these core principles. They serve no valid governmental objectives (as I pointed out in Chapter 3). They promote no penal objectives, unless one considers "stigmatization" a legitimate goal of the criminal justice system. States contend that such laws further nonpenal ends by "preserving the purity of the ballot box" or reinforcing the social contract by penalizing those who breach its terms, but only in the most attenuated sense is either goal advanced by denying political rights to citizens who have paid their debts. But even if disenfranchisement *did* further these ends in some incremental way, they would still be unconstitutionally excessive in that both goals could be furthered in ways that are less burdensome and more effective. Shorn of lofty rationalizations, the only real reason to disenfranchise ex-felons is this: They are bad people, not "one of us," and the government may punish them any way it sees fit.

Disenfranchisement is an excessive penalty, certainly when applied to the vast majority of former prisoners whose crimes are relatively "small-time." It is also an arbitrary one, inflicted on ex-felons without regard to either their crime or their moral culpability, regardless of whether they committed homicide or, in California, conspired to operate a motor vehicle without a muffler.

When states prohibit ex-felons from voting, moreover, they are essentially penalizing them for their status, and, as the Court has frequently noted, central to the American system of justice is the principle that "criminal penalties may not be inflicted upon a person for being in a condition he is powerless to change."[32] Individuals of course determine whether or not they will engage in crime; once they have been duly punished for this crime, however, they attain a status over which they have no control, and inflicting further punishment on them at this point flouts the doctrine the Court established in *Robinson*.

Finally, a sentence is unconstitutional if it offends contemporary moral standards. According to an appellate court in a notable 1967 case, the large number of states that prohibit ex-felons from voting demonstrates that the practice does not affront "evolving standards of decency."[33] Yet standards change. At one time the Supreme Court upheld the death penalty for mentally retarded criminals. Then, as we have seen, it reversed itself in *Atkins v. Virginia*, recognizing that the practice "has become unusual, and it is fair to say that a national consensus has developed against it."

In time the same logic might persuade the Court to outlaw disenfranchisement statutes. When such statutes were upheld in

1973, fully forty-two states denied ex-felons the suffrage for life. In 2005, only eight states do.[34] Today, moreover, the trend among most other progressive and humane countries is to extend voting rights not only to former prisoners but to people who are still behind bars, which indicates that disenfranchisement no longer comports with "evolving standards of decency" in these countries.

International Law

Even if America's disenfranchisement policies withstand constitutional and statutory attack, resourceful plaintiffs could argue that they are arguably inconsistent with fundamental tenets of international law. They are only *arguably* inconsistent because, while many international law documents proclaim the importance of universal suffrage, their language is so vague that interpretive bodies are often unsure whether a particular restriction is permissible.

Article 25 of the International Covenant on Civil and Political Rights (ICCPR), for instance, provides that every citizen has the right to vote and that this right may not be subject to "unreasonable restrictions."[35] The UN Human Rights Committee, which reviews adherence to the ICCPR, has stated further that since Article 25 "lies at the core of democratic government based on the consent of the people," any restrictions on the right to vote must be on grounds that are "objective and reasonable."[36] Do felony disenfranchisement laws, then, constitute "reasonable restrictions?"[37]

Article 25's framers considered limitations based on age, minimum residency, and mental capacity "reasonable."[38] (During the drafting stage, the American delegate also argued that the exclusion of illiterates in the United States was a "legitimate" restriction.)[39] The UN drafters devoted scant attention to disenfranchisement provisions, however, presumably because at the time the ICCPR was adopted few countries practiced electoral democracy, and even the ones that did imposed restrictions—on the participation of women, for instance, or ethnic groups—that by today's standards would be unacceptable.

In regard to prisoner disenfranchisement, the Human Rights Committee indicated some support for the practice. In one case, the committee wrote that even though the covenant "implies a recognition of the principle of universal suffrage ... this right is neither absolute nor without limitations but subject to such restrictions which are not arbitrary and which do not affect the expression of the opinion of the people in the choice of the legislature."[40] It went on to say, in the same case, that it did not consider the disenfranchisement of prisoners per se to violate the covenant: "A large number of State Parties to the Convention have adopted legislation whereby the right to vote of a prisoner serving a term of imprisonment of a specific duration is suspended in certain cases, even beyond the duration of the sentence." (Such restrictions, it explained, are based in notions of *dishonor* that accompany certain convictions for an established period, and such notions "may be taken into consideration by legislation in respect of the exercise of political rights.")[41]

Still, the committee has been troubled by practices it deems excessive. In 1995, for instance, it determined that "laws depriving persons of their voting right for periods of up to ten years may be a disproportionate restriction of the rights protected by Article 25,"[42] and, a year later, that "[i]f conviction for an offence is the basis for suspending the right to vote, the period of such suspension should be proportionate to the offence and the sentence."[43]

According to renowned international law authority Karl Josef Partsch, the committee is inordinately reticent. Article 25, properly interpreted, would prohibit signatories from depriving prisoners of their voting rights under any circumstances, he says, unless such a penalty has "been pronounced by a judge for a certain time, in connection with punishment for some particular offense, for instance those connected with elections or for high treason."[44]

The Human Rights Committee, even at its most cautious, would surely conclude that many U.S. laws violate Article 25—certainly those disenfranchising ex-prisoners for life, or for offenses that by any reasonable standard are minor. The authors of *Losing the Vote* assert further that a "strong argument can also be made on similar grounds that laws depriving all persons of the right to vote while in prison, on probation or on parole—regardless of the underlying offense—are also inconsistent with Article 25."[45]

In this country people of color lose the franchise at severely disproportionate rates. On this basis, the United States may also be violating the principles of nondiscrimination enshrined in both Article 25 of the ICCPR and the Convention on the Elimination of All Forms of Racial Discrimination (CERD).[46] CERD, which was ratified in 1994, requires signatories to guarantee, "without distinction as to race, color, or national or ethnic origin.... Political rights, in particular the right to participate in elections—to vote and to stand for election—on the basis of universal and equal suffrage."[47] When the United States became a party to the ICCPR, it agreed that its provisions would be binding on the states as well as on the federal government.[48]

A signatory violates CERD, notably, if its practices have "the purpose or effect" of restricting rights on the basis of race, regardless of whether there is any proof it intended to discriminate.[49] The convention could thus arm opponents of felon disenfranchisement with a powerful weapon were it not for one thing: The United States refuses to make the convention self-executing, meaning that until Congress enacts legislation rendering it domestically enforceable, CERD has no legal effect in this country.

A United Nations Perspective

The issue of prisoner and ex-felon enfranchisement has also been considered by the world's most universal body, the UN General Assembly. It has urged its members to respect the right of imprisoned people, although its entreaties are theoretically unnecessary since member states pledge to respect these rights upon becoming signatories to any of the major international covenants dealing with social and political rights. In a recent statement of principle, which carries no legal weight but has considerable moral force, the General Assembly expressed the increasing disfavor with which the international community looks upon felon disenfranchisement when it urged all nations to commit by this resolution to take all measures necessary to implement universal and equal suffrage in their respective countries, including prompt adoption of such domestic legislation as may be necessary to effectively ensure this fundamental human right for all disenfranchised persons of every status in life, including prisoners and ex-prisoners, in accordance with international human rights obligations and the general welfare of all peoples.[50]

In March 2004 a noteworthy if underreported development took place in Strasbourg, France. The European Court of Human Rights (ECHR) declared that by indiscriminately disenfranchising incarcerated felons, the United Kingdom violated Article 3 of the First Protocol of the European Convention.[51] Article 3 reads: "The High Contracting Parties undertake to hold free elections at reasonable intervals by secret ballot, under conditions which will ensure the free expression of the opinion of the people in the choice of the legislature." The ECHR stopped short of outlawing all disenfranchisement provisions but concluded that to be permissible they must accomplish something the UK policy notably failed to do—i.e., advance important governmental interests.[52]

While this ruling has immediate consequences for the European Convention's thirteen other signatories who still prohibit prisoners from voting,[53] it will, of course, have no direct impact on the United States other than to underscore the disfavor with which the international community increasingly regards its disenfranchisement policies.

Plaintiffs bent on demolishing disenfranchisement laws can assail them on Eighth Amendment grounds, arguing that they are "cruel" in both the commonly understood and constitutional senses of the word, and also "unusual," given the number of states and foreign countries that no longer penalize ex-felons. So far this argument has left the Supreme Court unconvinced, but that could change as, in time, a majority of justices came to accept another proposition the Court has long disputed—i.e., that it is unconstitutional to execute the mentally retarded.

Finally, if more conventional approaches fail, plaintiffs can mount an offense based on international law. At the moment this strategy seems fanciful, but proclamations by the United Nations and decisions by international tribunals condemning disenfranchisement make it harder for individual states to justify the practice, and harder still for the Supreme Court to argue that it "comports with evolving standards of justice."

Whether plaintiffs rely on equal protection or the Voting Rights Act (as discussed in the previous chapter), the Eighth Amendment or international law, one thing is certain: Without sustained judicial pressure, few public officials will tamper with policies disenfranchising former convicts. As we shall see in the next chapter, they suspect that vote-wielding ex-felons might imperil the status quo in which they thrive, and many are prepared to use every legal and political means at their disposal to prevent them from doing so.

11 The Political Consequences of Disenfranchisement

Disenfranchisement is not, at its core, about philosophy, electoral integrity, criminology, or judicial interpretation. It is about politics and power. Accordingly, there is one reason, beyond all others, why disenfranchisement laws stay on the books: Incumbents are convinced that they preserve the political status quo from which they themselves are benefiting.

They are correct only in part. In many respects ex-felons are sufficiently indistinguishable from the electorate at large in voting turnout, civic attitudes, and policy preferences, that most of the time their re-enfranchisement would scarcely disturb the partisan waters.

The Ex-Felon as Voter

In an effort to assess the voting behavior of erstwhile prisoners, and at the same time to convey some of the political voices "muted through disfranchisement," Jeff Manza and Christopher Uggen recently conducted a series of in-depth interviews with individuals serving sentences inside and outside prison.[1] They also examined survey data in order to compare the political views of arrested persons and inmates with those of nonoffenders. Some of their findings are unremarkable: Former prisoners, as a class, regard government with less confidence and public officials with less trust than do members of the general population (171). Present and former convicts in general are poorly educated and possess below-average citizenship norms, resulting in high levels of political apathy and rendering them, as the authors say, a "low-information group" (168). Predictably, they are less interested in politics and less likely to engage in political activity than are people without felony convictions. Individuals who engage in civic activity, moreover, usually possess a strong sense of political efficacy—that is, confidence they can influence public officials or public policy, that in some unquantifiable way "they count." Men and women with criminal convictions, not surprisingly, report considerably less faith in their ability to effect political change (175).

Fewer than 10 percent of ex-felons bother to vote, although once such sociodemographic factors as educational level, marital status, employment history, race, and gender are taken into account, the gap in turnout between them and the public at large diminishes "dramatically" (177). That relatively few ex-felons vote may not mean that they devalue the franchise but only that they have more urgent survival needs (193). In fact, the authors conclude, for many former prisoners disenfranchisement is a "salient" issue: "The denial of voting rights is perceived as 'another loss to add to the pile' ... disenfranchisement carries a powerful sting for those citizens convicted of crimes" (193).

Although all of the felons interviewed knew they would be unable to vote for a period of time, few were sure how long their ineligibility would last. Many ex-felons assume that they are not entitled to vote even after their political rights have been restored, and the authors note the possibility that this misperception, coupled with hesitancy to inquire about their status, "may extend the impact of voting restrictions far beyond a formal period of legal disfranchisement" (184).

Despite their subjects' low civic involvement, the authors were impressed by the ways in which some people behind bars reflect upon their role in the polity, their civic duties and obligations. According to one prisoner, "No [I have never voted] ... but after being incarcerated and having that time to reflect on all the issues, I see how important it really can be" (182). Manza and Uggen conclude that, under some circumstances, "incarceration actually stimulates political consciousness" (169). This makes sense, of course, considering that prisoners—perhaps for the first time in their lives— have an opportunity to acquire an education, read, ruminate, and occasionally even engage in communal action. As Malcolm X said in his autobiography, "where else but in a prison could I have attacked my ignorance by being able to study intensely sometimes as much as fifteen hours a day?"[2]

Manza and Uggen found, significantly, that far from voting against the public welfare, convicted felons don't even vote in ways that sharply distinguish them from other members of the electorate. Like everybody else, they worry about issues that affect them personally—education, health care, new federal time limits on the receipt of public assistance. Many, however, are also troubled by phenomena that transcend their immediate needs—inequality in American life, for instance, deficiencies in the criminal justice system, and especially what they consider "irrational" laws and public policies (including disenfranchisement) (185–88).

Respondents' views, the authors observed, were nuanced and often unpredictable: While many favored changes in public policy, the changes they recommended were not necessarily more permissive than ones endorsed by a majority of the electorate. Some argued against leniency for their fellow inmates, and one was actively lobbying for harsher laws against child pornography. Many prisoners support the very laws they broke!

Some disenfranchisement advocates fear, not unreasonably, that restoring voting rights to former prisoners would inevitably benefit the Democratic Party. They might be surprised to learn that, while respondents were indeed more likely than nonfelons to identify themselves as Democrats or political independents, there was among them a "healthy sampling" of support for George Bush (188). (According to one twenty-four-year-old prisoner, "Since this incarceration I'm kind of anticriminal. And he [Bush] did some good stuff in Texas.") Besides, voting cohorts tend to be fickle—just ask the disappointed Democrats who thought their party would receive a long-term boost after the Twenty-Sixth Amendment extended the franchise to eighteen-year-olds.[3]

Political Repercussions

That ex-felons tend to vote pretty much like everyone else does not mean that their re-enfranchisement would not have political repercussions. For one thing, the urban areas from which so many come, and to which so many return, would gain more clout. As it is now, these straitened communities, politically weak to begin with, suffer a "double whammy." When their residents are incarcerated and then stripped of their votes, they suffer not only the loss of their potential ballots but also the loss of population and the governmental benefits calculated on the basis of population. Their diminished influence, perversely, enhances the clout of conservative rural communities, where the bulk of prisons are located, since the U.S. Census counts inmates as residents of the region where they are incarcerated.[4] (In New York State, to cite one example, fully 90 percent of prisoners are housed in upstate facilities, yet the vast majority of them come from just seven poor, largely minority enclaves in New York City.)[5]

Jeffrey Manza and Christopher Uggen, whose interviews with ex-felons are cited above, have analyzed additional repercussions. In their seminal study, the two sociologists concluded that with more than 2 percent of the electorate currently unable to vote because of a past or current felony conviction, "there are good reasons to be concerned that rising rates of criminal punishment affect communities by influencing political outcomes in a highly competitive, two-party system."[6]

According to Manza and Uggen, disenfranchisement laws might have provided the scratch hit that allowed George W. Bush to score a disputed winning run in the 2000 contest for the White House. While he lost the popular vote nationwide in the 2000 presidential race, he won it in Florida by a razor-thin margin, capturing Florida's electoral votes and, in a stranger-than-fiction twist, gained the presidency.[7] (Later in this chapter, I will examine the way the state's disenfranchisement laws contributed to George Bush's ultimate victory.)

As Manza and Uggen point out, Florida disenfranchises roughly 887,000 ex-convicts, the vast majority of whom—given their race and socioeconomic status—would vote Democratic. While they note that many factors could have affected the outcome of the 2000 election, they conclude that the participation of even a fraction of these former convicts would have enabled Bush's Democratic rival, Al Gore, to overcome Bush's Florida margin (537 in the final count) and capture the state's electoral votes. Then, the authors conclude, the results of the last presidential election "almost certainly would have been reversed."[8]

What about other elections—how many of them would have turned out differently if even some ex-felons had been allowed to participate? To answer this question, Manza and Uggen analyzed elections going back to the 1960s, comparing the net Democratic votes to the margins of victory in races won by Republicans. They extrapolated felons' voter turnout and voting preferences from that of similar demographic populations, allowing for the fact that felons are even less likely to vote than nonfelons with similar characteristics.[9]

As the authors point out, "[w]e don't have any measures that capture defiance, marginalization, or isolation from the social norms of citizenship." They can, however, "crudely simulate" ex-convicts' likely turnout and preferences by employing a so-called "independent partisan identity," which voting analysts ascribe to citizens claiming no partisan preferences and who, partly as a result, are least likely to participate in elections. Using this simulation, they estimate that roughly one-third of ex-felons allowed to vote would do so in presidential elections, and that of this number between 70 and 90 percent would support Democratic candidates.[10]

Manza and Uggen, using what they emphasize is an extremely conservative estimate of ex-felon turnout, conclude that barring ex-felons from the polls has had a "profound effect" on the political configuration in the United States.[11] This effect may be particularly felt in mayoral, House, and state legislative districts, since individuals who end up with criminal convictions are disproportionately drawn from relatively impoverished urban areas.

Disenfranchisement policies have occasionally influenced the outcome of U.S. Senate elections, as well. While the participation of ex-felons would have reversed the outcomes of only a handful of the more than four hundred such elections that have taken place between 1970 and 1998, Democrats nevertheless would have defeated conservative Republicans in at least six key contests and thus controlled the Senate from 1986 until 2000 or 2002. Democratic leadership might have salvaged more of the programs favored by President Clinton, and to some extent countered the partisan vitriol that passed for public debate during his second term.

Manza and Uggen point out, moreover, that in every presidential and Senate election from 1972 to 2000, disenfranchisement policies have provided "a small but clear advantage to Republican candidates."[12] Democrats themselves are partly to blame for this phenomenon. By accepting and even promoting harsh criminal justice policies since the 1970s, they succeeded in eliminating "crime" as a wedge issue that for at least forty years has benefited Republicans. In so doing, however, Democrats struck a Faustian bargain: Abetted by these law-and-order policies, between 4 and 5 million felons and ex-felons cannot vote. Manza and Uggen surmise that it is "possible, though not proven, that these losses in voter eligibility may have caused significant vote losses for the Democratic Party in recent elections."[13]

Their research has already borne fruit: In March 2001 New Mexico replaced its lifetime ban on ex-felon voting with a new law automatically re-enfranchising felons once they complete their prison terms, probation, and parole. One among several reasons why this reform effort succeeded is that every Democratic member of the state legislature received a copy of Manza and Uggen's report, at the time still in progress, citing the key elections Democrats would have won had ex-felons been allowed to cast ballots.

Obstacles to Reform

For reform-minded individuals, the windows of opportunity may never again be opened as wide as they were after the 2000 presidential election. The public learned from that debacle not only that ballots could be lost or miscounted, but also that in many states anyone with a felony conviction can't vote. A variety of interest groups sprang up or refocused their energies to protest this exclusion, and perhaps as a result of their educational efforts the general public now overwhelmingly rejects the notion that felons should be denied the franchise once their time has been served.[14]

Well before the 2000 election most legal professionals and penologists had come to regard disenfranchisement policies as punitive and counterproductive. The bipartisan National Commission on Federal Election Reform, headed by former presidents Jimmy Carter and Gerald Ford, came to the same conclusion. Noting that the 2000 race "shook Americans' faith in the legitimacy of the democratic process," it recommended measures to restore this faith, including re-enfranchising ex-convicts.[15]

Yet, as we have seen, Congress continues to squelch any proposal that would extend voting rights to ex-felons in federal elections, and even after the international brouhaha occasioned by the 2000 election, only a few states—Florida, notably, not among them— have made any effort to liberalize their disenfranchisement statutes in any meaningful way. Despite the many voices urging large-scale reform, then, it's not about to happen.

There are several reasons for this inaction. The beneficiaries of reform, the people whose political rights will be restored, can't vote, and politicians who champion their cause gain little but a reputation for being "soft on crime." Efforts on behalf of former convicts, moreover, lack the drama, the good-versus-bad cast of characters, and what columnist Katharine Seelye calls the "bloodletting" of the civil rights struggle.[16] Discrimination is now more subtle, and it is levied against people for whom the public feels none of the sympathy it felt for the black children, say, who were spat upon and cursed by angry white mobs when they attempted to integrate southern schools.

The main reason reform has hit a brick wall, however, is the one noted above: Many politicians and influential interest groups fear that the enfranchisement of ex-felons would threaten the overall balance of power. Former president Carter acknowledged as much during a commission meeting: "A safe and secure Congressional seat or House seat in the Legislature is a very valuable thing, and to open up the Pandora's box for new registrants is not always an easy thing to sell."[17]

Republicans are understandably reluctant to repeal disenfranchisement laws, convinced as they are that former prisoners constitute Democrats' natural constituency. (As conservative columnist Evan Gahr recently quipped, "Will the jailhouse become a Democratic mainstay, like labor union conventions, feminist gatherings, and Buddhist temples? Talk about political prisoners.")[18] Yet President Carter said he "was surprised to find that some of the most liberal Democrats in the Congress" were among those who opposed reform.[19] He shouldn't have been surprised, because incumbents, whatever their party, are threatened by any move to widen the franchise. Former convicts, after all, might support challengers in a Democratic primary whom they consider more "progressive."[20] According to congressional authority Thomas Mann, because legislators are reluctant to support any measure that could imperil their prospects for re-election, they "would likely block any broad reform package."[21]

There are abundant moral, philosophical, and even practical reasons for repealing disenfranchisement laws. Yet laws penalizing ex-felons remain resistant to change because they serve the interests of the political establishment—a fact dramatically illustrated by the way in which Republican operatives finessed their candidate's victory in the 2000 presidential election, at least in part, by purging ex-felons from the voting rosters. Their maneuvers also underscore the impact that a single state's disenfranchisement policies can have on the country at large.

The Florida Fiasco

On November 7, 2000, close to six hundred thousand ex-felons were prohibited from casting a ballot in the Sunshine State.[22] Well aware that former prisoners vote disproportionately for Democratic candidates, top-ranking Republican officials were determined to prevent any of them—even those who had been re-enfranchised in other states—from blocking George W. Bush's victory in the state. Katherine Harris, then serving as both the Florida secretary of state and Bush's Florida campaign chair, and Jeb Bush, the candidate's brother and governor of the state, commanded an ex-felon "purge" that investigative reporter Gregory Palast described as being "so quiet, subtle, and intricate, that if not for Bush's 500-vote eyelash margin of victory... the chance of [its] discovery would have been vanishingly small."[23]

This purge surely ranks among the country's most successful political coups. In separate accounts both Palast and John Lantigua, a reporter for the *Miami Herald*, chronicled its conception and dexterous execution. It began in November 1998, when Katherine Harris, complying with a law enacted by the Republican-dominated state legislature, paid a private company $4 million to expunge from the state's voting rolls duplicate registrations, people who had died, and felons. In time the company, Database Technologies, Inc. (DBT) produced a "scrub list" of Florida residents who could be struck from the rolls. The list, as Gregory Palast documents, was wildly inaccurate. Among those slated for purging, for instance, were individuals whose conviction dates were cited as sometime in the future. DBT itself, forced to rely on the state's Byzantine record keeping, voiced concern that many names would be erroneously deleted.[24]

Many names were indeed mistakenly expunged. DBT intended to strike the names of anyone whose name, date of birth, and social security numbers matched those of a known felon. The problem was that Florida records *some*, but not all, social security numbers. Not to worry, the firm was told: It should go ahead and eliminate anyone whose vital statistics closely matched those of a known felon. Accordingly, Lantigua reports, the firm focused on people who *might* have been deceased, or *might* have been listed twice, or *might* be "possible felons."[25]

Both Palast and Lantigua quote company directors who said they assumed that the list would be "verified" by county election officials. Yet, considering that DBT had come up with a list of fifty-eight thousand "possible" felons who had been registered to vote, these directors must have ascribed prodigious talents to the already overtaxed county election officials if they expected them to find the necessary time and resources to confirm that every one of these fifty-eight thousand people had been properly removed from the rolls. Election officials, predictably, were overwhelmed by the scope of their assignment. As a result, Palast says, investigators who analyzed available figures concluded that at least 15 percent of those cited as felons had been wrongly identified.[26]

In May 2000, using a list provided by DBT, Harris's office also ordered counties to strike from eligibility lists any former inmates who had moved to Florida after their voting rights had been restored by other states. Harris was well aware that purging these people was unconstitutional, Palast asserts. Only two years earlier the state's court of appeals had ruled unanimously, in an important and well-publicized case, that election officials could not require a man convicted in Connecticut twenty-five years earlier "to ask [Florida] to restore his civil rights. They were never lost here." Felons who have regained their vote in another state "arrive as any other citizen, with full rights of citizenship," because the Constitution's "full faith and credit clause" commands every state to accept the legal rulings of the forty-nine other states.[27]

At a meeting in the summer of 1998, Florida's county elections officials discussed at length the court of appeals decision. As Palast recounts, Chuck Smith, a systems administrator with Hillsborough County, said he was therefore surprised when Katherine Harris's office directed local officials at this meeting to expunge the name of every felon from out of state who was identified by DBT. The Hillsborough office refused to comply until it received written instructions, duly sent in a letter dated September 18, 2000. The governor's office of executive clemency ordered the county to instruct former inmates who were attempting to register that they were ineligible to vote until Florida itself restored their political rights, expressly including those who had been re-enfranchised by another state.

How many former inmates were improperly forbidden to register? Palast estimates that "[p]eople from other states who've arrived in Florida with a felony conviction in their past number clearly over 50,000 and likely over 100,000." He calculates that 80 percent arrived with their voting rights intact.[28]

The purge effectively blindsided African Americans. On the basis of nationwide conviction rates, David Bositis, senior research associate at the Washington, D.C.–based Joint Center for Political and Economic Studies, concluded that they accounted for 46 percent of the ex-felons who were wrongly disenfranchised in Florida.[29] Figures provided by Florida election officials validate this estimate; 54 percent of the voters in Hillsborough County targeted by the "scrub" were African American, in a county where blacks make up 11 percent of the voting population. In Miami-Dade, where blacks make up 20 percent of the population, fully 66 percent (3,794) of those struck from the rolls were black. Lantigua quotes Florida civil rights veteran Elmore Bryant: "They done got us. They had themselves a game and we had no game."[30]

George W. Bush won the popular vote in Florida by a mere 537 votes out of more than 5.8 million cast, and hence every one of the state's pivotal electoral votes. In their preliminary analysis of the 2000 election, Manza and Uggen concluded that "the Republican electoral college majority ... would have been reversed, even if only ex-felons were granted the right to vote."[31] According to their calculations, based in part on the fact that George Bush captured only 6 percent of the black vote in Florida, Vice President Al Gore would have won the state by anywhere from a 10,000 to an 85,000-vote margin.[32]

John Lantigua confirmed their findings. After reviewing both state and nationwide statistics and past voting records, he estimated that roughly 10 percent of Florida's former prisoners would have cast ballots in the November election if they had been eligible—although in a highly contested contest like that year's presidential race, and given the NAACP's energetic voter-turnout drive, the percentage might have been greater. Even using the most conservative estimates, Lantigua calculated that twenty thousand former inmates would have turned out to vote if they had been permitted to do so. And, based on race and economic factors, he concluded that 75 percent of their ballots would have been cast for Al Gore.[33]

While most other countries looked upon the machinations in Florida with a mixture of bemusement and disbelief, the most progressive among them also reacted with consternation and even outrage. As we shall see in the next chapter, most of these countries repudiated disenfranchisement policies long ago, and that American states would continue excluding fellow citizens, especially those who had "done their time," struck them as unfair and punitive.

12 Thinking the Unthinkable

Sarah Walton, the former president of Maine's League of Women Voters, explains why her state has historically allowed inmates to vote: "In the midst of America's movement toward independence, back when Maine was a part of Massachusetts, the writers of the state constitution were all too aware of the state's ability to silence dissent with incarceration. Therefore, in the democracy they created, those incarcerated retained their right to participate in our self-government despite their loss of physical liberty. When Maine became a state, its constitution also allowed Maine citizens who were in prison to vote.

"And why shouldn't they?" Walton continued. "Inmates in Maine prisons are still human beings and Maine citizens, many with family and property. Their obligations as Maine taxpayers do not cease while they are in prison. Stripping prisoners of the right to vote will not deter crime, provide restitution to victims, nor promote rehabilitation. In fact, especially for those few who do exercise the right to vote, this move to take away their right to vote would only serve to further alienate and isolate these prisoners, the vast majority of whom will ultimately return to our communities."[1]

There is still the possibility that the United States could "silence dissent with incarceration," despite its generally commendable record, especially in eras as fraught with anxiety as the present. Alone among the fifty states, nevertheless, only Maine and neighboring Vermont extend the franchise to people in prison. Until recently Utah and Massachusetts did so as well, but they retracted this right in 1998 and 2000, respectively. So, while the number of foreign countries that allow incarcerated felons to vote grows by the year, in this country the opposite trend prevails.

According to a survey conducted in 2001 by the Prison Reform Trust, fully thirty nations, including countries as diverse as Israel, Japan, Kenya, Peru, Zimbabwe, and Macedonia, extend voting rights to prisoners as well as ex-felons.[2] (Not that all these countries are necessarily worth emulating, their generosity to erstwhile offenders notwithstanding; while Bosnia, Iran, and Serbia, for instance, allow prisoners to vote, judging by their human rights records they accord them few other basic rights.)

In 2000 South Africa's highest court extended the franchise to people behind bars, proclaiming that "the universality of the franchise" is important both for nationhood and democracy.[3] Two years later Canada's highest tribunal similarly held that under the country's Charter of Rights and Freedoms, even incarcerated prisoners are entitled to their franchise. According to Canadian Chief Justice Beverly McLachlin, "[t]he right to vote is fundamental in our democracy" and can be "set aside only if the government demonstrates a compelling reason for doing so."

"The government's novel political theory that would permit elected representatives to disenfranchise a segment of the population," McLachlin continued, "finds no place in a democracy built upon principles of inclusiveness, equality, and citizen participation."[4]

The United States—the "self-proclaimed democracy" to which Chief Justice McLachlin referred—ordinarily marches in step with other liberal democracies (sometimes even leading the parade). Yet in this country rare is the public official who would so much as whisper in private that incarcerated felons deserve the franchise, and indeed, even public interest groups most dedicated to prisoners' rights and electoral reform would never risk their credibility by suggesting out loud that anyone still behind bars is entitled to vote.

Nineteen-term congressman John Conyers is reputedly fearless, but when he periodically introduces a re-enfranchisement bill, he too makes sure to stress that its provisions apply only to those who have fully completed their sentences. Like anyone else committed to re-enfranchisement, Conyers knows that there is no surer way to sabotage this goal than to recommend the political empowerment of incarcerated prisoners.[5]

Of course inmates, by virtue of the harm they've inflicted on society, forfeit many of the privileges they enjoyed in civilian life. They are still entitled to most constitutional safeguards, however—due process, freedom from cruel and unusual punishment, first amendment rights to petition the courts and to worship as they see fit. They cannot travel, assemble, or "read girlie magazines,"[6] because these restrictions, far from being gratuitous, are necessary to maintain a prison facility's order and security. But why aren't prisoners as entitled to their franchise as they are to most reading material or their religious observances? According to Martin Narey, the head of Britain's prison service, inmate voting "poses no problems" at all, and indeed, jurisdictions that allow prisoners to vote report no security breaches, disorder, or fraudulent electoral activity.[7]

Some objections are clearly political in character. Residents of rural areas adjacent to correctional facilities understandably fear that if inmates were enfranchised they might sway local elections, perhaps by voting in concert for issues these residents oppose. Stanford law professor Pamela Karlan echoes their concern: "Imagine the occupants of a large, maximum-security penitentiary voting as a bloc and essentially running the small town in which their prison's located."[8] Yet there is no evidence that prisoners have ever influenced, let alone determined, the outcome of local contests. If they *were* bent on doing so, however, there's a simple solution: Emulate Maine and Vermont, which allow offenders to cast mail-in absentee ballots in the jurisdiction where they lived prior to their incarceration.

As the UN General Assembly declared in the nonbinding resolution excerpted below, permitting prisoners to vote by direct or absentee ballots would also "grant them a voice with which to protest the horrific conditions that often characterize prison life." This is critical because, as the General Assembly observed, "the institutional environment in prisons may render them likely repositories of human rights abuses unlikely to occur elsewhere, such as wrongful detention, torture, cruel and inhuman treatment, denial of medical care, and other abuses of governmental authority."[9]

In Britain, where the enfranchisement of prisoners is vigorously debated, both incarcerated offenders and social activists have echoed the UN's sentiments. According to one inmate there whose comments were widely publicized, "The ban on prisoners voting means MPs [Members of Parliament] do not have to pay attention to prisons and the issues raised by prisoners. This leads to issues such as the poor state of health care for prisoners being neglected. While I accept that criminals must be punished, I cannot accept that it is just for me to die in custody, or to be denied the democratic rights of others in society: to vote my MP in or out and to represent me in Parliament."[10]

The Prison Reform Trust, an organization that prepares inmates for release, found that many MPs with a prison in their district had never visited the facility; one was unaware that a riot had occurred at his local jail two days earlier. The organization concluded in a May 2001 memorandum that with "no votes at stake on making imprisonment humane and purposeful, the quality of debate about prisoner disenfranchisement is unlikely to improve."[11]

In the resolution quoted above, the General Assembly also called attention to the vast overrepresentation of racial and ethnic minorities in many prison populations. Denying prisoners the franchise, therefore, "results not only in their exclusion as a class from the right to vote, but also may result in the dilution or canceling out of the voting strength of entire racial or ethnic minorities in a given State or political subdivision."[12]

Joseph "Jazz" Hayden made the same point at a New York City press conference. Describing himself as "one of the 1.4 million African-American men who are disenfranchised," he urged Americans "to take care of some unfinished business." While the civil rights movement was a great success, he said, "when it came to the right to vote, the movement stopped at the prison walls." The consequences, he said, have been devastating for this country's minority population.[13]

Indeed. Since people of color make up at least 63 percent of those behind prison walls in the United States, as long as inmates can't vote, racial minorities on both sides of these walls will continue to experience the neglect, scapegoating, and even abuse to which disempowered groups are vulnerable.[14] In 2000, Canada's Supreme Court recognized this phenomenon when it observed that aboriginals, that country's own most vulnerable members, are incarcerated at rates far exceeding their proportion of the population.[15] Depriving prisoners of the franchise, it concluded, would only compound their travails.

Since its founding, the United States has marched steadily toward the democratic ideal of universal suffrage, over time extending the franchise to those without property, African American males, women, and youth as young as eighteen. It has adopted "motor voter" laws and absentee and bilingual ballots, and eliminated poll taxes and malapportioned districts. In light of this progress, its continuing disenfranchisement of ex-felons constitutes a unique "democratic reversal."[16]

How, then, can the practice be justified? In past decades courts defended disenfranchisement on the ground that it preserves the "purity of the ballot box." This justification, never persuasive, is today more feeble than ever; as the California Supreme Court noted in *Ramirez v. Brown*, even if ex-offenders were prone to election chicanery, "it is difficult to accomplish in the modern era, when sophisticated technology has replaced open-access ballot boxes and backroom head counts."[17]

Still, even if convicted felons cannot easily rig an election, many Americans oppose their re-enfranchisement on intuitive if not veri-fiable grounds: They fear that anyone with a criminal conviction is too morally compromised to vote on sensitive issues that affect the general welfare. Todd Gaziano, director of legal studies at the Heritage Foundation, an enormously influential conservative think tank, captures their apprehension: "Felony disenfranchisement makes sense for a lot of reasons," he says, "but in particular because of the way ex-prisoners might vote .... There are critical resource decisions—whether to keep this police chief, whether to get rid of the mayor, whether to post police officers at the schools. There are dozens of decisions like this that come up every year that I believe only citizens and only citizens in good standing should make."[18]

There is no evidence that ex-felons, even if re-enfranchised, are capable of, or interested in, voting *en masse* for candidates who pledge to oust the mayor or prohibit the deployment of police officers in public schools. In fact, researchers have concluded that far from voting against the public welfare, convicted felons don't even vote in ways "that sharply distinguish them from other members of the electorate."[19] Like the rest of us, they worry about their kids, where their next paychecks are coming from, whether Medicaid will cover their dental work.

Ultimately, however, whether or not ex-felons tend to favor marginal over mainstream policies, one candidate over another, begs the larger question: So what if they do? So what if they *do* endorse unconventional platforms—the liberalization of New York State's draconian Rockefeller drug laws, say, or the repeal of California's punitive "three-strikes-and-you're-out" measure? By virtue of their time behind bars, and the insights and firsthand experiences they have acquired, public policy in this country might benefit from their input.

The Supreme Court has characterized the franchise as a "fundamental right," moreover, precisely because it provides critics of the status quo with an opportunity to reform it through democratic channels. Indeed, democracy's vitality depends upon its capacity to "reinvent" itself by remaining responsive to shifting values born of voters' perceived self-interest, personal experiences, and changing alliances. Accordingly, the Court has also declared that "the exercise of [voting] rights so vital to the maintenance of democratic institutions ... cannot be obliterated because of a fear of the political views of a particular group of bona fide residents."[20]

Its ringing declaration notwithstanding, the Supreme Court has nevertheless been willing to squelch the "political views" of ex-felons as long as doing so arguably furthers some legitimate state interest. Although Alexander Keyssar, in his authoritative book *The Right to Vote*, points out that judges have always been "hard put" to define just what interests are actually served by disenfranchisement,[21] most have uncritically accepted proponents' claim that the practice furthers the traditional objectives of the criminal justice system. Rare is the penologist, however, who would seriously argue that stripping the franchise from ex-felons serves either retributive or deterrent functions—still less that it facilitates rehabilitation.

John Stuart Mill recognized almost 150 years ago that it is engagement in the political process, rather than exclusion from it, that discourages recidivism.[22] New research has confirmed his observation: Two-thirds of the ex-felons who are not arrested again within three years of their release—who "desist from crime"—are individuals who, in addition to reuniting with family and securing employment, become "politically active" and vote.[23]

Even if disenfranchisement does not advance penal objectives, its supporters nevertheless find the practice defensible on democracy's own terms. Subjects in a monarchy or dictatorship don't have to be particularly virtuous as long as their leader is capable, according to this way of thinking. In a democracy, by contrast, citizens are sovereign, and as a consequence the regime they govern can thrive only to the extent that they themselves are high-minded and law-abiding.[24]

This argument—which many judges have found persuasive—reflects and conflates two philosophical constructs that have influenced democratic thought since the Enlightenment. The first, the "civic republican" theory, posits that a polity's moral and institutional well-being depends upon the virtue of its citizens. The second, the "social contract" theory, asserts that individuals living freely but perilously in a state of nature agree to exchange some of their liberty for a government that will safeguard their lives and property. A freely chosen sovereign enacts laws that will govern the community, with the understanding that members who violate these laws—who "break the terms of the contract"—renounce their right to participate in communal decision making.

Both theories, at least as they've been interpreted by American courts, are stern and unforgiving. They assume, to begin with, that voting is a privilege accorded only to the "good citizen." Even if the line separating the good from the bad were less blurry, however, a democracy is by definition "government of the people"—the good, the bad, and the in-between. They also assume that lawbreakers are free moral agents who have deliberately chosen to break the rules. They have only themselves to blame, then, when they are shunned by the community. As one judge explained: "Felons are not disenfranchised based on any immutable characteristic, such as race, but on their conscious decision to commit an act for which they assume the risks of detection and punishment."[25]

Yet, as Michael Tonry has observed, "[w]hen some are prevented from full participation by discrimination, disability, or exclusion ... it is difficult to claim that they enjoy the benefits of autonomy that produce obligation."[26] By assuming that anyone with a criminal conviction is mentally defective or inherently untrustworthy, moreover, both theories also foster self-righteous and exclusionary impulses. They suggest that ex-felons are irredeemably flawed individuals, qualitatively so different from their fellow citizens as to forfeit any right to participate in communal affairs.

Although the theoretical as well as the pragmatic reasons for defending disenfranchisement collapse under scrutiny, that does not mean that the practice lacks appeal. On the contrary, by prohibiting ex-felons from voting, politicians curry favor with many constituents; incumbents minimize the number of "disaffected" voters who might jeopardize their re-election; and the public at large reassures itself that criminals are not being "coddled." Yet, in pursuing these dubious goals, the country perpetuates a practice that is wantonly unfair.

Whether or not ex-felons are denied their fundamental right of citizenship depends on wholly fortuitous phenomena—their state of residence, whether their offense is designated a misdemeanor or a felony, whether they have the money necessary to hire a competent attorney or file for clemency. They are rendered political outcasts, automatically upon conviction, without regard to the severity of their crimes or the length of their sentences.

The hundreds of thousands of prisoners who are discharged each year must honor all the obligations of citizenship at the same time that they are denied many of its rights and privileges. Upon release they encounter a wide range of what Jeremy Travis calls "invisible punishments"—restrictions on employment, housing, education, eligibility for social services, mortgages, loans, licenses.[27] Cumulatively these restrictions are devastating to those who bear their brunt.

How unfair, moreover, to deny voting rights to people who have completed their prison terms and the conditions of their probation. Isn't it a principle basic to Judeo-Christian ethics that individuals can atone for their sins and be redeemed? As George Fletcher observes, "the idea that you would pay the debt and be treated as a debtor (felon) forever verges on the macabre."[28]

Yet is it really that "unfair," in the scheme of things, when comparatively few ex-prisoners even vote? Of course it's unfair. Even citizens who rarely cast ballots would be outraged to learn they no longer had the option. Besides, by their own accounts ex-felons do indeed value the franchise, and the rate at which they vote climbs significantly once their more immediate needs are met.[29] The great Nelson Mandela, who spent twenty-seven years behind bars, certainly spoke for many of these former inmates when he said that the most important day of his life was not the day he was released from prison, not even the day he became president of post-apartheid South Africa, but the day he voted for the first time.[30]

Disenfranchisement is noxious as well as unfair: It is creating and perpetuating an underclass—what a report issued by Human Rights Watch called "a huge pool of political outcasts in America"[31]—or what a member of the Open Society Institute called a "shadow society of people who do not participate and have no stake in the society in which we live."[32]

The Supreme Court has consistently disavowed policies that would create or sustain such "shadow societies," not only because such policies often collide with the guarantees of equal protection but also because they spawn alienation and resentment—toxins to the body politic. The Court has accordingly held that "separate but equal" education is inherently unequal and that laws discriminating against illegitimate children are similarly degrading, as are statutes providing males with benefits unavailable to women, or religious minorities with encumbrances not foisted upon mainstream believers. In *Plyler v. Doe* the Court repudiated a Texas statute imposing stiff tuition fees on the children of undocumented aliens in large part because these children, effectively prohibited from acquiring an education, would grow up illiterate, angry, and marginalized.

Policies that render ex-felons voteless, that prevent them from ever regaining their status as respected members of the community, stamp these men and women, in the same way that separate-but-equal laws stamped blacks, "with a badge of inferiority." That ex-felons are disproportionately members of racial and ethnic minorities strengthens the parallel.

Penologists predict that in states with the most restrictive voting laws, as many as 40 percent of black men will be prohibited from voting during some or all of their adult lives.[33] Disenfranchisement, then, is accomplishing what poll taxes and literacy tests, grandfather clauses, white primaries, and racial gerrymandering are no longer able to do. So many people of color have been politically silenced that, according to civil rights leader Jesse Jackson, disenfranchisement has effectively "rolled back" the successes of the civil rights movement.[34]

Disenfranchisement laws harm not only individuals but the communities in which they reside. Upon their release from prison, ex-felons tend to congregate in urban enclaves already debilitated by poverty, unemployment, and crime.[35] Their pariah status siphons off what scant political reserves these neighborhoods have left. Worse, the resulting powerlessness feeds on itself: These communities, unable to win needed funds from the state or federal government, can't rehabilitate their aging voting machines or train their few poll watchers or mount legal challenges against the "fraud squads" who intimidate anyone lined up to cast ballots. The fewer the votes successfully cast or recorded in Homestead, Florida, or Cleveland, Ohio, or Camden, New Jersey, the less attention officeholders need pay to the men, women, and children who inhabit their mean streets.

In ways real if unquantifiable, exclusionary policies harm not just racial minorities but the nation as a whole. They harm it in the same way institutionalized segregation once did—by tarnishing its image among progressive countries throughout the world that look upon state laws prohibiting more than 4.5 million ex-felons from casting a vote as vindictive and racist.

Ironically, it is long-reviled South Africa that now accords even its lowliest members greater respect than the United States accords its own citizens who have broken the law. On April 1, 1999, South Africa's highest court voted unanimously to extend voting rights to prisoners. As Judge Albie Sachs explained when he announced the decision, "[t]he vote of each and every citizen is a badge of dignity and personhood," which is of particular importance, because "in a country of great disparities of wealth and power it declares that whoever we are, whether rich or poor, exalted or disgraced, we all belong to the same democratic South African nation; that our destinies are intertwined in a single interactive polity." Quite literally, he concluded, "everybody counts."[36]

The South African tribunal's noble proclamation was later reaffirmed by the Supreme Court of Canada, and most recently by the European Court of Human Rights when it struck down a British law disenfranchising incarcerated prisoners. Other progressive countries are similarly removing the barriers that separate the "disgraced" from the "exalted." Until it follows their lead, the United States will remain on the wrong side of history and estranged from its own ideals.

Afterword

This book was first inspired by the 2000 presidential election, revealing as it did the magnitude of ex-felon disenfranchisement in the United States and the civic and political ramifications of this phenomenon. Statistical and other analyses suggest that particular electoral contests may have been swayed by the exclusion of Democratic-leaning ex-convicts, leading me to detail the numerous, varied, and committed efforts undertaken during the past five years to extend voting rights. Partisanship aside, the events of 2000 raise vital questions about the equality and dignity of the men and women who, having served their sentences, seek readmission into the community of citizens.

Since the disputed contest of 2000, another presidential election has passed. But this vital question remains: For all this effort, for all the legislative and bureaucratic changes that were consequently instituted, for all the public outrage, commission reports, and official investigations that resulted from the 2000 contest, did ex-felons fare any better the last time around?

Analysts are still parsing the election returns, but the tentative answer is a resounding "yes and no." Yes, because in some states a significant number of ex-felons did indeed benefit from statutory or administrative reforms. And yes, because advocacy groups were on high alert, quick to detect and expose at least the most flagrant attempts to prevent eligible ex-felons from voting.

Among these groups was the Organization for Security and Cooperation. At the invitation of a congressional delegation it sent an international team to monitor the November 2004 election (to the consternation of many both inside and outside government).[1] More than sixty U.S.-based nonprofit groups also participated in a "voter protection coalition," and under its auspices some twenty-five thousand volunteers—including five thousand lawyers—managed hotlines on election day, videotaped poll activities, and challenged dubious procedures in court.[2] Thousands of others registered ex-felons and tutored them in the arcane minutiae of election laws. Activists in Illinois, Louisiana, and South Carolina aired radio spots and established a toll-free hotline to assist former inmates;[3] in Ohio the Fortune Society, working with members of the Racial Fairness Project, placed flyers and registration forms in parole offices and jails.[4]

Yet the answer is also no, because in most states the number of former prisoners eligible to vote in 2004 was not appreciably greater than in 2000—in part because liberalization moves in one state were frequently offset by new restrictions in others. For every newly enfranchised probationer in Connecticut, there was a prisoner in Utah or Massachusetts no longer able to cast a ballot. No, as well, because even in this exquisitely scrutinized election, too many people were still prevented from casting a ballot.

In 2000 Katherine Harris, then serving as both Florida's secretary of state and the campaign director for Republican candidate George W. Bush, subjected her state to widespread derision when the public learned that among the reputed ex-felons she had purged from the rosters were thousands of citizens whose voting rights were still intact. During the 2004 election advocacy groups thus kept a spotlight on Florida in the hope of deterring similar mischief. (They disregarded Jesse Jackson's suggestion, however, that they should "get some yellow tape and put it around the whole state and say it is a crime scene.")[5]

Many political observers actually predicted that Florida's election officials would be on their best behavior in 2004. They were wrong. Perhaps the single most egregious incident involving ex-felons again took place in the Sunshine State. It involved Secretary of State Glenda Hood, a Republican partisan chosen by Governor Jeb Bush to replace Katherine Harris.

Early in 2004 Hood compiled a list of forty-eight thousand ex-felons, and on May 5 she ordered Florida's sixty-seven local election supervisors to expunge their names from voting rosters.[6] Worse, until a court forced her hand, she steadfastly refused to make these names public, thus preventing inaccuracies from being detected. Her list, as it turned out, contained the names of some twenty-two thousand blacks but only sixty-one Hispanics.[7] Why the disparity? Presumably because in Florida many people with a Spanish surname belong to the Republican-leaning Cuban community. The *Miami*

Herald revealed, moreover, that at least 2,119 people did not belong on the secretary's scrub list because their voting rights had been formally restored through the state's clemency process.[8] In the wake of these disclosures Ms. Hood was eventually forced to abandon the flawed list, and so, thanks to alert "watchdogs," the state averted a replay of the 2000 fiasco.

In the weeks following the November election there were more than thirty-eight thousand reports of alleged irregularities.[9] To be sure, many arose from the inevitable pressures of the November 2 election, characterized as it was by record turnout, including throngs of first-time voters whose processing took additional time, by new voting machines still riddled with glitches, and by provisional ballots, available in many states for the first time in 2004, whose use perplexed voters and poll workers alike.

Still, these impediments occurred with dismaying frequency in the poor neighborhoods of so-called "battleground" states—Arkansas, Michigan, Missouri, New Jersey, Pennsylvania, and especially Florida and Ohio. Ex-felons who live in these neighborhoods, including many whose votes have been reinstated, often found themselves entangled in nets designed to snare minorities and poor people in general.

Why minorities and poor people "in general"? Perhaps, to raise a partisan suspicion, because most vote Democratic. There certainly is a disturbing association. It is the minority and Democratic communities that have too few voting machines—particularly ones that don't malfunction, too few technicians to make repairs, too few trained poll workers.[10] Theirs are the communities where would-be voters—at least those with abundant time and stamina—wait in lines that go around the block,[11] or where notorious punch-card ballots are still in use (as they were in many Ohio precincts, their hanging chads accounting for many of the more than ninety thousand votes that were thus rejected).[12]

Ex-felons tend to live in poor communities where polling sites were moved at the last moment,[13] where registration forms and absentee and provisional ballots were rejected or inexplicably disappeared,[14] where prospective voters not able to produce unnecessary identification were turned away,[15] and where others were cowed by so-called "fraud squads" that hovered near ballot boxes challenging their credentials.[16]

Yet partisanship in itself is not the full explanation. Ex-felons were ultimately thwarted as much by the scarcity of reliable advice as by these deliberate maneuvers. As one observer noted, "there is a stunning lack of information and transparency surrounding felon disenfranchisement across the country."[17] Election officials often withheld vital information, or did not understand the law, or required former inmates to produce unnecessary—and even nonexistent—documentation.[18]

Even in states where ex-felons are entitled to vote, upon leaving prison they were rarely so apprised, still less often told how to go about retrieving their franchise. In thirty-six states, moreover, election officials are not even required to notify people when they have been purged from the voting rosters, thereby preventing them from contesting wrongful cancellations. In one recent case, a Minnesota election board notified some thirty-six hundred individuals that their voter registrations had been annulled because of their felony convictions, but neglected to tell them they could re-register upon the completion of their sentences.[19] The Ohio Department of Rehabilitation and Correction, bowing to pressure from the state's Republican secretary of state, no longer tells parolees how they can go about reclaiming the franchise.[20] Thousands of prospective voters who called officials with eligibility-related questions, moreover, were told by staff members at twenty-one out of Ohio's eighty-eight election boards that no one on probation or parole could vote in the November election.[21]

In many states men and women intent upon regaining the franchise must, metaphorically speaking, first climb Mt. Everest. For the first time in 2004, for instance, certain ex-felons in Nevada could apply for the restoration of their voting rights. Few did so, however, because of the formidable paper work involved.[22]

Finally, Florida demonstrated in the 2004 election that even if a state has procedures for reinstating felons' voting rights, and even if felons fully understand these procedures, they are still out of luck, because most clemency applications take years to process.

In response to a court order, Florida reformed its clemency procedures in 2001; in August 2004, however, the First District Court of Appeals concluded that the state's new procedures were inadequate. As Judge Peter D. Webster observed, "It sounds to me like [they are] intended to continue to disenfranchise a number of these felons."[23]

Indeed. The number of Floridians attempting to regain the franchise swells by the day. Yet the clemency board, which meets only rarely, considers only about 134 applications a year.[24] At the same time it has expanded the number of crimes that trigger disenfranchisement, while refusing requests for more staff to process the mounting caseload.[25] This state, which bans more people from the polls than any other, accordingly prevented some forty-three thousand people from voting in the 2004 presidential election,[26] including many who have been waiting years for the privilege, because the clemency board has not found time to schedule their hearings.

In the bitterly contested 2004 election, ex-felons frequently fell victim to unbridled partisanship.[27] In Ohio, for example, just weeks before the registration deadline, the redoubtable secretary of state announced that any applications submitted on paper of less than eighty-pound stock would be rejected—including thousands of forms completed on the twenty-to-twenty-four-pound gauge in everyday use.[28] He later rescinded this directive, but what motivated his initial action? Was it prudence, since thicker paper is unquestionably more durable, or political calculation, since if it had been successfully promulgated, it would have foiled thousands of first-time registrants, including many ex-felons?

Florida's secretary of state similarly attempted to reject thousands of registration forms whose signatories had not checked a box attesting to their citizenship, even though they signed an oath on the same document affirming their status.[29] Why so punctilious? Was Ms. Hood dutifully following the letter of the law or, like her counterpart in Ohio, attempting to eliminate many "problematic" voters?

Both of these maneuvers were attempted by Republican secretaries of state, but it is also true that five bills broadening voting rights for former prisoners were signed into law by Republican governors—including Florida's Jeb Bush. Both parties, in fact, have mixed records when it comes to ex-felons, although, as Robin Templeton, head of the nonpartisan Right to Vote Coalition, points out, when it comes to re-enfranchisement, "[n]either party has championed this issue."[30]

One factor distinguishing the 2004 from the 2000 presidential election was the dearth of public protests in its aftermath. Reformers, moreover, are apparently focusing less on the role played by disenfranchisement than on the consequences of other sorts of electoral chicanery—partly because this chicanery received greater media attention and partly because, even though ex-felons fared almost as badly, nationwide, in the 2004 as in the earlier race, their maltreatment was generally less blatant, more indirect, and less easily documented than in the previous contest. Yet this maltreatment was no less indefensible, its consequences no less baleful, and I, for one, hope that once activists rest up and take stock, they will commit themselves anew to the re-enfranchisement movement. After all, only dedicated and sustained action will secure basic rights for America's last remaining group of second-class citizens.

Notes

Chapter One

1. Christopher Uggen and Jeffrey Manza, "Democratic Contraction? The Political Consequences of Felon Disenfranchisement in the United States," *American Sociological Review* 67 (Dec. 2000): 797, appendix, table A, "Estimates of Number of Disenfranchised Felons by State: Dec. 31, 2000."

2. *Reynolds v. Sims*, 377 U.S. 533, 751 (1964).

3. Hazel Trice Edney, "Denying Ex-Felons the Right to Vote," National Newspaper Publishers Association, Oct. 23, 2002. http://www.blackpressusa.com/news/Article.asp.

4. *McLaughlin v. City of Canton*, 947 F.Supp. 954, 971 (S.D. Miss. 1995).

5. Office of the Pardon Attorney, "Report on Civil Disabilities of Convicted Felons: A State-by-State Survey," quoted in Alec C. Ewald, "'Civil Death': The Ideological Paradox of Criminal Disenfranchisement Laws in the United States," *University of Wisconsin Law Review* 5 (2002): 1045–1138.

6. Sentencing Project, "Felony Laws in the United States," Washington, D.C., 2001, 1, http://www.sentencingproject.org/ (accessed August 12, 2004).

7. Ibid., 19. See also Christopher Uggen and Jeffrey Manza, "The Political Consequences of Felon Disenfranchisement Laws in the United States," paper presented at the annual meeting of the American Sociological Association, Washington, D.C., August 16, 2000; Patricia Allard and Marc Mauer, "Regaining the Vote: An Assessment of Activity Relating to Felon Disenfranchisement Laws," Open Society Institute, 2000, 7, http://www.soros.org/initiatives/justice/articles_publications/publications/regainingthevote_2000(accessed June 15, 2005); Andrew L. Shapiro, "Challenging Criminal Disenfranchisement under the Voting Rights Act: A New Strategy," *Yale Law Journal* 103 (Nov. 1993): 538. See also *United States v. Watson*, 423 U.S. 411, 438–41 (1976) (Marshall, J., dissenting) (felony/misdemeanor distinction often reflects history, not logic); *Rummel v. Estelle* 445 U.S. 263 (1983) ("The most casual review of the various criminal justice systems now in force in the 50 States of the Union shows that the line dividing felony theft from petty larceny, a line usually based on the value of the property taken, varies markedly from one State to another").

8. Quoted in "Prisoners and the Right to Vote," editorial, *America, the National Catholic Weekly*, reprinted by the Fortune Society, http://www.fortunesociety.org/spring 0309.htm (accessed October 10, 2004).

9. Margie Hyslop, "Right to Vote? More States Debate Giving Felons Ballot Access," *Washington Times*, July 14, 2002, 1.

10. "Disenfranchised for Life," *The Economist*, Oct. 24, 1998, 31.

11. Ibid.; Alexander Keyssar, *The Right to Vote: The Contested History of Democracy in the United States* (New York: Basic Books, 2000).

12. Quoted in John Lantigua, "How the GOP Gamed the System in Florida," *The Nation*, April 30, 2001.

13. Elizabeth Simson, "Justice Denied: How Felon Disenfranchisement Laws Undermine American Democracy," Americans for Democratic Action Education Fund, March 2002, 17, available at www.adaction.org/adaction@ix. netcom.com (accessed June 15, 2005).

14. Ibid., 1.

15. Allard and Mauer, "Regaining the Vote," 7.

16. "Restoring Your Right to Vote: Washington," U.S. Department of Justice, Civil Rights Division, December 2000, http://www.usdoj.gov/crt/ voting/misc/faq.htm (accessed June 15, 2005).

17. Simson, "Justice Denied," 20.

18. Allard and Mauer, "Regaining the Vote," 11.

19. Simson, "Justice Denied," 26.

20. Uggen and Manza, "Estimates of Disenfranchised Felons by State," appendix, table B.

21. Ibid. See also House Judiciary Committee, Subcommittee on the Constitution, *Hearing on the Civic Participation and Rehabilitation Act of 1999, HR 906*, 106th Cong., Oct. 21, 1999 (testimony of Hilary O. Shelton, director of the Washington Bureau of the NAACP), 86. http://www.house. gov/judiciary/con1021.htm (accessed July 10, 2005).

22. U.S. Commission on Civil Rights, Staff Report, "Voting Irregularities in Florida during the 2000 Presidential Election," (approved by the commissioners on June 8, 2001), http://news.findlaw.com/hdocs/docs/election2000/ USCCRFLvoterprt60701.pdf (accessed June 15, 2005).

23. Simson, "Justice Denied," 28–29; Duncan Campbell, "It's Divine Justice, Gore Is Told: Drugs Policy Denied Vote to Two Million Blacks," *The Guardian* (Manchester), Nov. 14, 2000, http://www.guardian.co.uk/inter-national/story/397152,00.html (accessed June 15, 2005). See also "They Don't Count," editorial, *Boston Bay-State Banner*, April 8, 2004; Abby Goodnough, "Disenfranchised Florida Felons Struggle to Regain Their Rights," *New York Times*, March 28, 2004, A1.

24. Alice E. Harvey, "Comment: "Ex-Felon Disenfranchisement and Its Influence on the Black Vote: The Need for a Second Look," *University of Pennsylvania Law Review* 142 (1994): 1155; Marc Mauer, "Disenfranchising Felons Hurts Entire Communities," *Focus* (published by the Joint Center for Political and Economic Studies, May–June 2004): 5–6; and Sentencing Project,

"Felony Disenfranchisement in the United States," http://www.sentencing project.org/losing_04.htm (accessed June 15, 2005).

25. Marisa J. Demeo and Steven A. Ochoa, "The Lost Latino Vote: A Preliminary Analysis of Latino Felony Disenfranchisement in Ten States," Mexican American Legal Defense Fund, June 27, 2003, 5; Santa *Fe New Mexican*, Nov. 19, 2000, quoted in Noam Chomsky, "United States: Election 2000," http://www.otherdavos.net/pdf/Chomsky2000.pdf (accessed June 15, 2005).

26. Demeo and Ochoa, "Lost Latino Vote," 5.

27. See Rebecca Perl, "The Last Disenfranchised Class," *The Nation*, Nov. 24, 2003. See also Brandon Rottinghaus III, "Incarceration and Enfranchisement: International Practices, Impact, and Recommendations for Reform," International Foundation for Election Systems (June–July 2003): 14.

28. Rottinghaus, "Incarceration and Enfranchisement."

29. Deborah Sontag, "'Second Israel' Hails First Big Election Triumph," *New York Times*, May 21, 1999, A3.

30. See Marc Mauer, "A Policy Whose Time Has Passed?" *Human Rights* 31 (winter 2004): 17; Jamie Fellner and Marc Mauer, "Disenfranchisement in Other Countries," in *Losing the Vote: The Impact of Felony Disenfranchisement Laws in the United States*, ed. Jamie Fellner and Marc Mauer (Washington, D.C.: Sentencing Project, and New York: Human Rights Watch, 1998), http://www.hrw.org/reports98/vote/usvot98o-04.htm#P112_2733 (accessed June 15, 2005); see also Rottinghaus, "Incarceration and Enfranchisement."

31. Nora V. Demleitner, "Continuing Payment on One's Debt to Society: The German Model of Felon Disenfranchisement as an Alternative," *Minnesota Law Review* 84 (April 2000): 781–82, 799.

32. Ibid., 753.

33. See Rottinghaus, "Incarceration and Enfranchisement."

34. See Jeffrey Manza, Clem Brooks, and Christopher Uggen, "Public Attitudes toward Felon Disenfranchisement in the United States," *Public Opinion Quarterly* 68, no. 2 (2004): 275–86; Brian Pinaire, Milton Heumann, and Laura Bilotta, "Barred from the Vote: Public Attitudes toward the Dis-enfranchisement of Felons," paper presented at the annual meeting of the Northeastern Political Science Association, Philadelphia, Nov. 8–10, 2001.

Chapter Two

1. 351 U.S. 12, 20 (1956) (citing Alexis de Tocqueville) (concurring opinion).

2. See, e.g., Carl Ludwig Von Bar, *A History of Continental Criminal Law* (Boston: Little, Brown, 1916), 37–38; Jason Belmont Conn, "Excerpts from the Partisan Politics of Ex-Felon Disenfranchisement Laws," (senior honors thesis, Cornell University, Department of Government, 2003), http://

www.righttovote.org/upload/resources/157_ufile_conn-fur.pdf (accessed June 15, 2005); Alec Ewald, "Punishing at the Polls: The Case against Disenfranchising Citizens with Felony Convictions," Demos: A Network for Ideas and Action (Nov. 24, 2003): 14–21, http://www.demos-usa.org/pubs/punishing_at_the_polls.pdf (accessed June 15, 2005); George P. Fletcher, "Disenfranchisement as Punishment: Reflections on the Racial Issues of Infamia," *UCLA Law Review* 46 (Aug. 1999): 1895–1907.

3. See sources cited in note 2 above. See also Demleitner, "Continuing Payment on One's Debt to Society," 766.

4. See Demleitner, "Continuing Payment on One's Debt to Society." See also Note, "The Equal Protection Clause as a Limitation on the States' Power to Disenfranchise Those Convicted of a Crime," *Rutgers Law Review* 21 (1967): 310.

5. See Ewald, " 'Civil Death,' " 18.

6. Ibid.

7. Rottinghaus, "Incarceration and Enfranchisement."

8. John J. Miller, "Public Policy: Votes for Felons," *National Review*, April 3, 2000, http://www.findarticles.com/p/articles/mi_m1282/is_6_52/21_60137472. R. R. Preuh would disagree with Clegg's assertion. On the basis of his research, using cross-sectional data on current state disenfranchisement policies, Preuh concludes that the minority population of a state (in terms of percentages) determines, more than any other single factor, whether or not it will have severe disenfranchisement laws. "State Felon Disenfranchisement Policy," *Social Science Quarterly* 82 (Dec. 2001): 733–48.

9. Roger Clegg, "Who Should Vote?" *Texas Review of Law and Policy* 6 (fall 2001): 177.

10. Nicholas Thompson, "Locking Up the Vote: The Disenfranchisement of Former Felons Was the Real Crime in Florida," *Washington Monthly* (Jan.–Feb. 2001), http://www.washingtonmonthly.com/features/2001/010.1/thompson/html (accessed June 16, 2005).

11. Angela Behrens, Chistopher Uggen, and Jeffrey Manza, "Ballot Manipulation and the 'Menace of Negro Domination': Racial Threat and Felon Disenfranchisement in the United States, 1850–2002," *American Journal of Sociology* 109 (Nov. 2003): 559–605.

12. Ibid., 569.

13. For discussion, see Eric Foner, *Reconstruction: America's Unfinished Revolution, 1863-1877* (New York: Harper & Row, 1988), 253–61, 323–24.

14. *Richardson v. Ramirez,* 418 U.S. 24, 52 (1974), quoting *Congressional Globe,* 40th Cong., 2d sess., 1868, 2600.

15. *Ratliff v. Beale,* 74 Miss. 247, 266–67 (1896).

16. Ibid.; Steven Carbó, Ludovic Blain, and Ellen Braune, "Democracy Denied: The Racial History and Impact of Disenfranchisement Laws in the United States," Demos, *Democracy Dispatches* 32 (April 16, 2003): 2, 4–5.

17. Thompson, "Locking Up the Vote."

18. *Ratliff v. Beale,* 74 Miss. 247, 541–42.

19. *Hunter v. Underwood,* 471 U.S. 222, 229 (1985).

20. Shapiro, "Challenging Criminal Disenfranchisement under the Voting Rights Act," 541.

21. Foner, *Reconstruction,* 593–94.

22. "The Right to Vote as Applied to Ex-Felons," *Federal Probation* 45 (March 1981): 14.

23. Marc Mauer, "Race, Poverty, and Felon Disenfranchisement," *Poverty and Race* 11 (July–Aug. 2002): 2, quoting J. Morgan Kousser, *The Shaping of Southern Politics* (New Haven: Yale University Press, 1974).

24. Eric Foner, *Freedom's Lawmakers: A Directory of Black Officeholders during Reconstruction* (New York: Oxford University Press, 1993). See also Howard Itzkowitz and Lauren Oldak, Note, "Restoring Ex-Offender's Right to Vote: Background and Developments," *American Criminal Law Review* 11 (spring 1973): 721–22.

25. Juan Cartagena, Janai Nelson, and Joan Gibbs, "Felons and the Right to Vote," *Gotham Gazette,* Feb. 17, 2003, http://www.gothamgazette.com/article/feature-commentary/20030217/202/285 (accessed June 16, 2005); *Baker v. Pataki,* 85 F.3d 919 (2d Cir. 1996), interest of *amicus curiae,* Brennan Center.

26. Campaign to End Felon Disenfranchisement, "Felons and the Right to Vote."

27. New Jersey Statutes, 19:4-1.F. See Jon Shure and Rashida MacMurray, "Restoring the Right to Vote: Isn't It Time?" (October 2000), http://www.njpp.org/pr_votingrights.html (accessed June 16, 2005). See also Jonathan Schuppe, "Voting Rights Sought for Rehabbed Ex-cons," *Newark Star-Ledger,* Jan. 7, 2004, 16.

28. "Restoring the Ex-Offender's Right to Vote: Background and Developments," *American Criminal Law Review* 11 (spring 1973): 725.

29. Demleitner, "Continuing Payment on One's Debt to Society," 767.

30. Ibid.

31. 64 Cal. 2d 596, 414 P.2d 412, 421 n.10 (Cal. 1966).

32. Demleitner, "Continuing Payment on One's Debt to Society," 789–80.

33. Ibid. See *Davis v. Beason,* 138 U.S. 333, 348 (1890) (sustaining Idaho law denying the franchise to anyone practicing or counseling bigamy or polygamy); *Murphy v. Ramsey,* 114 U.S. 15, 39–45 (1885) (upholding an 1882 congressional statute prohibiting anyone practicing bigamy or polygamy from voting).

Chapter Three

1. Uggen and Manza, "Democratic Contraction?" 777–803. See also Allen J. Beck, "Prisoners in 1999" (NCJ 1834 76) (Washington, D.C.:

Department of Justice, Bureau of Justice Statistics, revised Feb. 8, 2001); "U.S. Prison Population at New High," AP News, April 20, 2000, http://www.a1b2c3.com/drugs/law15.htm.

2. Demleitner, "Continuing Payment on One's Debt to Society," 767.

3. See Chapter 2, note 28, above; see also Elizabeth Simson, "How Felony Disenfranchisement Laws Undermine American Democracy" (Washington, D.C.: Americans for Democratic Action Education Fund, March 2002), 7–10, http://www.adaction.org/lizfullpaper.pdf (accessed June 16, 2005).

4. Sarkaris Avakian, "Racial Disparity among the Incarcerated," *Law, Social Justice, and Global Development Journal* 1 (Nov. 8, 2002), http://www.2.warwick.ac.uk/fac/soc/law/elj/lgd/2000_1/avakian (accessed June 16, 2005).

5. Uggen and Manza, "Democratic Contraction?"

6. Fox Butterfield, "U.S. 'Correctional Population' Hits New High," *New York Times,* July 26, 2004.

7. See Avakian, "Racial Disparity among the Incarcerated."

8. "U.S. Incarceration Rates Reveal Striking Racial Disparities," *Human Rights Watch World Report,* Feb. 27, 2002, http://www.hrw.org/backgrounder/usa/race (accessed June 16, 2005).

9. Ibid.

10. Avakian, "Racial Disparity among the Incarcerated."

11. "Prisoners on the Streets," *The Economist,* May 3, 2001, http://www.economist.co.uk/world/na/displayStory.cfm?story_id (accessed June 16, 2005). See also "U.S. Drug Laws Are Racist," Reuters, Aug. 23, 2001, reprinted at Common Dreams News Center, http://commondreams.org/headlines01/0823-o1.htm (accessed June 16, 2005); see also "A Stigma That Never Fades," *The Economist,* Aug. 8, 2002, http://www.economist.co.uk/world/na/displayStory.cfm?story_id=1270755 (accessed June 16, 2005).

12. I found the letter at http://www.drugpolicy.org/news/raceconf.letter.html; see also Silja J. A. Talvi, "The Color of the Drug War," *Lip* magazine (Oct. 10, 2002), available at Alternet, http://www.alternet.org/drugreporter/14276 (accessed June 16, 2005).

13. See Randall Sheldon, *Controlling the Dangerous Classes: A Critical Introduction to the History of Criminal Justice* (Boston: Allyn and Bacon, 2001).

14. See Leadership Conference on Civil Rights, "Justice on Trial: Racial Disparities in the American Criminal Justice System," http://www.civilrights.org/publications/cj/index.html (accessed May 27, 2005).

15. Mike Males and Dan Macallair, "The Color of Justice: An Analysis of Juvenile Adult Court Transfers in California," Building Blocks for Youth (a consortium of public interest organizations located in Washington, D.C.), http://www.jjpl.org/Publications_JJ_InTheNews/Juvenile Justice Special Reports/BBY/colorofjustice/coj.html (accessed June 16, 2005).

16. Human Rights Watch Backgrounder, "Race and Incarceration in the United States" (Feb. 27, 2002), http://www.hrw.org/backgrounder/usa/race (accessed June 16, 2005).

17. New York State, Division of Criminal Justice Services, "Disparities in Processing Felony Arrests in New York State, 1990–1992" (New York Felony Study, Sept. 1995), v–vi, xi. See also Leadership Conference on Civil Rights, "Justice on Trial."

18. Testimony of Marc Mauer, assistant director, the Sentencing Project, before the Subcommittee on Legislation and National Security and the Subcommittee on Government Information, Justice and Agriculture of the House Government Operations Committee, May 2, 1990.

19. Avakian, "Racial Disparity among the Incarcerated."

20. Thompson, "Locking Up the Vote."

21. See "Voting Rights for Prisoners and Ex-Prisoners in New York," Talking Points for CSS, Jan. 15, 2003, www.cssny.org/pdfs/factsheet.pdf (accessed May 27, 2005).

22. Civil Rights Coalition for the 21st Century, "Criminal Justice," http://www.civilrights.org/research_center/civilrights101/crimjustice.html (accessed May 27, 2005).

23. Fellner and Mauer, *Losing the Vote*, 12–13. See also Table 4 in Chapter 1; "Felon Laws Bar 3.9 Million Americans from Voting," Oct. 22, 1998, http://www.hrw.org/press 98/oct/vote 1022.htm (accessed June 16, 2005).

24. U.S. Department of Justice, Bureau of Justice Statistics, http://www.ojp.usdoj.gov/bjs/ (accessed May 27, 2005). See also Demeo and Ochoa, "Diminished Voting Power in the Latino Community."

25. Sentencing Project, "Felony Disenfranchisement Rates for Women," August 2004, http://www.sentencingproject.org/pdfs/fvr.women.pdf (accessed June 16, 2005).

26. See note 24 above.

27. Ibid. See also Paul Street, "Starve the Racist Prison Beast," *Black Commentator*, Nov. 20, 2003, http://www.blackcommentator.com/65/65_street_ prison.html.

28. See Carrie Conaway, "Doing Well by Doing Time?" *Regional Review*, no. Q4, Federal Reserve Bank of Boston, 20–30.

29. See Marc Mauer and Meda Chesney-Lind, eds., *Invisible Punishment: The Collateral Consequences of Mass Imprisonment* (Washington, D.C.: New Press: 2003).

30. Edney, "Denying Ex-Felons the Right to Vote."

31. Clegg, "Who Should Vote?" 172, 177. See also House Judiciary Committee, Subcommittee on the Constitution, *Hearing on the Civic Participation and Rehabilitation Act of 1999, HR 906*, 106th Cong., 1st sess., Oct. 21, 1999 (testimony of Roger Clegg).

32. Quoted in Frank Phillips, "Lawmakers Push to Ban Inmate Votes, Amendment Would Target Those Convicted of Felonies," *Boston Globe,* June 28, 2000, B1.

33. Quoted in Scot Nakagawa, "Voting Rights Battle in Washington State," spring 2004, http://www.westernprisonproject.org/Publications/Newsletters/JM_Spring_04.pdf (accessed June 16, 2005).

Chapter Four

1. Silja J. A. Talvi, "The Color of the Drug War," Aug. 24, 2002, http://www.lipmagazine.org/articles/feattalvi_205.shtml. See also Legal Action Center, "After Prison."

2. Michael C. Dorf, "Do Symbolic Pardons Do More Harm than Good?" http://www.writ.news.findlaw.com/dorf/20040107.html (accessed January 7, 2004). See also New York State Probation and Correctional Alternatives, http://dpca.state.ny.us/general_faq.htm (accessed June 16, 2005).

3. "Behind Bars, but Still Campaigning," http://www.cbsnews.com/stories/2002/08/01/politics/main S17141.shtml (accessed October 29, 2002); U.S. House of Representatives, "Code of Conduct," http://www.usgovinfo.about.com/blhousecode.htm (accessed June 16, 2005).

4. According to the U.S. Constitution, Article I, Section 2: "No person shall be a Representative who shall not have attained to the Age of twenty five Years, and been seven Years a Citizen of the United States, and who shall not, when elected, *be an Inhabitant of that State in which he shall be chosen*" (emphasis added).

5. "Though Jailed, Could Traficante Run?" http://www.usgovinfo.about.com/library/weekly/aa081402a.htm (accessed June 16, 2005). See also "Convicted Traficante Vows to Run Again," http://www.usgovinfo.about.com/library/weekly/aa04150da.htm (accessed April 15, 2002). Nothing in the Constitution prevents convicted and incarcerated individuals from serving in Congress or even as president, so if the former Ohio representative had been jailed in Ohio and lawfully reelected, he could have attended sessions of the House under a work-release program.

6. "Though Jailed, Could Traficante Run?" See also the Pennsylvania Constitution website, http://www.paconstitution.dug.edu/P.PA_NEWS 2002.html.

7. Pennsylvania Constitution website.

8. See http://www.usdoj.gov/pardon/collateral.consequences.pdf (accessed June 16, 2005). See also "Felon Disenfranchisement: Purging the Minority Vote," *Democracy Now* (a daily radio, TV, and online news program), July 9, 2004, http://www.democracynow.org/article.pl?sid=04/07/09/144240 (accessed June 16, 2005).

9. Edney, "Denying Ex-Felons the Right to Vote."

10. Assembly Committee on Public Safety, "Disenfranchised for Life" (April 21, 2005), http://info.sen.ca.gov/pub/bill/asm/ab_0551-0600/ab_561_cf (accessed June 16, 2005).

11. Kristina Hals, *From Locked Up to Locked Out: Creating and Implementing Post-Release Housing for Ex-Prisoners* (Boston: AIDS Housing Corp., published in collaboration with AIDS Housing of Seattle, Washington, 2003), http://www.aidshousing.org/usr_doc/From_Locked_Up_to_Locked_Out.pdf (accessed June 16, 2005).

12. Jeremy Travis, "Invisible Punishments: An Instrument of Social Exclusion," in Mauer and Chesney-Lind, *Invisible Punishment*, 12, 18.

13. See Drug Policy Alliance, "Barriers to Re-Entry for Convicted Drug Offenders," http://www.lindesmith.org/library/factsheets/barriers/index.cfm (accessed April 2003); see also Anthony C. Thompson, "Navigating the Hidden Obstacles to Ex-Offender Reentry," *Boston College Law Review* 45 (March 2004): 255.

14. Mauer, "Felon Voting Disenfranchisement: A Policy Whose Time Has Passed?" Robert Johnson, former president of the National District Attorneys Association, has suggested that "at times, the collateral consequences of a conviction are so severe that we are unable to deliver a proportionate penalty in the criminal justice system without disproportionate collateral consequences. There must be some reasonable relief mechanism. It is not so much the existence of the consequence, but the lack of the ability of prosecutors and judges to control the whole range of restrictions and punishment imposed on an offender that is the problem. As a prosecutor, you must comprehend this full range of consequences that flow from a crucial conviction. If not, we will suffer the disrespect and lose the confidence of the very society we seek to protect." Quoted in Thompson, "Locking Up the Vote."

15. *Personal Responsibility and Work Opportunity Reconciliation Act of 1996, HR 3734,* Public Law 104-193, 104th Cong., 2d sess., Sept. 22, 1996.

16. Marc Maurer, "Invisible Punishment, Block Housing, Education, Voting," *Focus* (published by the Joint Center for Political and Economic Studies) (May–June 2003), 4; Harry J. Holzer and Steven Raphael, "Can Employers Play a More Positive Role in Prisoner Reentry?" http://www.Urban.org/UploadedPDF/410803_PositiveRole.pdf (accessed June 16, 2005); John Riley, "Day 2: A New Set of Bars; Laws Block Ex-Cons from Jobs, Aid Due to Old Crimes," http://www.newsday.com/news/nationworld/nation/NY-uspris043401476aug04,D,745971l.story (accessed June 15, 2004).

17. Riley, "Day 2"; Joan Petersilia, "When Prisoners Return to the Community: Political, Economic, and Social Consequences," in *Sentencing and Corrections: Issues for the 21st Century,* papers from the executive sessions on sentencing and correction, no. 9 (Nov. 2000), U.S. Department of Justice, Office of Justice Programs, National Institute of Justice, available at http://www.ncjrs.org/pdffiles1/nij/184253.pdf (accessed June 16, 2005).

18. Harry J. Holzer, Steven Raphael, and Michael Stoll, "Employer Demand for Ex-Offenders: Recent Evidence from Los Angeles, March 2003, http://www.sscnet.ucla.edu/issr/csup/pubs/papers/pdf/csup7.pdf (accessed June 16, 2005).

19. "A Stigma That Never Fades," *The Economist*, Aug. 10, 2002, 9; "Barriers to Re-Entry."

20. Michael S. Anderson, "Strategies to Help Move Ex-Offenders from Welfare to Work" (July 22, 2002), http://www.prisonactivist.org/pipermail/prisonact-list/2002-July/005528.htm (accessed June 17, 2005).

21. Legal Action Center, "After Prison."

22. *De Veau v. Braisted*, 363 U.S. 144 (1960).

23. Anderson, "Strategies to Help Move Ex-Offenders." See also Bruce Western, Becky Pettit, and Josh Guetzkow, "Locking up Inequality," in Mauer and Chesney-Lind, *Invisible Punishment.*

24. "Reformer's Calendar," April 12, 2002, http://www.stopthedrugwar.org/chronicle/232/eventcalendar.html (accessed June 17, 2005).

25. Roy Lewis, "The Hope Scholarship Credit (The Hope Credit)," http://www.fool.com/school/taxes/1998/taxes981016.htm (accessed June 17, 2005).

26. Gabriel J. Chin, "Race, the War on Drugs, and the Collateral Consequences of Criminal Conviction," *Journal of Gender, Race, and Justice* 6 (2002), http://papers.ssrn.com/sol3/papers.cfm?abstract_id=390109 (accessed June 17, 2005).

27. John W. Perry Fund, "Scholarships for Students with Drug Convictions," Aug. 5, 2003, http://talkleft.com/new_archives/003366.html (accessed June 17, 2005).

28. *Personal Responsibility and Work Opportunity Reconciliation Act of 1996,* Public Law 104-193, 104th Cong. (Aug. 22, 1996), 110 Stat. 2105, http://wdr.doleta.gov/readroom/legislation/pdf/104-193pdf (accessed June 17, 2005). See Robin Levi and Judith Appel, "Collateral Consequences: Denial of Basic Social Services Based upon Drug Use" (Office of Legal Affairs, Drug Policy Alliance, June 16, 2003), http://www.drugpolicy.org/docUploads/Postincarceration_abuses_memo.pdf (accessed June 17, 2005).

29. Christopher Reinhart, "Consequences of a Felony Conviction," Office of Legislative Research, March 28, 2003, http://www.cga.ct.gov/2003/olrdata/jud/rpt/2003-R-0333.htm (accessed June 17, 2005).

30. Stephen Metraux and Dennis P. Culhane, "Homeless Shelter Use and Reincarceration Following Prison Release: Assessing the Risk," *Criminology and Public Policy* 3, no. 2 (2004).

31. Ibid. According to one study, at least 11 percent of people released from New York State prisons to New York City from 1995 to 1998 entered a homeless shelter within two years, more than half of them within the first month after their release. See Supportive Housing Network of New York, "Blueprint

to End Homelessness in New York City" (New York: Supportive Housing Network of New York, 2002), 13.

32. "Drug Laws Putting Too Many Women in Prison, Reform Group Says," Jan. 29, 2000, http://www.cnn.com/2000/us/01/29/women.prison/ (accessed June 17, 2005).

33. *Adoption and Safe Families Act of 1997,* Public Law 105-89, titles IV-B and IV-E, section 403(b), section 453, and section 1130(a) of the *Social Security Act,* Public Law 105-90, 105th Cong. For discussion, see Ann L. Jacobs, "Give 'Em a Fighting Chance: Women Offenders Reenter Society," *Criminal Justice* 16 (spring 2001), http://www.aba.net.org/crimjust/jacobs.html (accessed June 17, 2005).

34. Levi and Appel, "Collateral Consequences."

35. See Chandler Davidson, "The Recent Evolution of Voting Rights Laws Affecting Racial and Language Minorities," in *Quiet Revolution in the South,* ed. Chandler Davidson and Bernard Grofman (Princeton: Princeton University Press, 1994), 21. See also U.S. Department of Justice, Civil Rights Division, Voting Section, "Introduction to Federal Voting Rights Laws: The Effect of the Voting Rights Act," http://www.usdoj.gov/crt/voting/intro/intro_c.htm (accessed June 17, 2005).

36. Wyatt Olson, "Barred for Life: The Process for Restoring the Civil Rights of Felons in Florida Works Perfectly—If *Not* Restoring Their Rights Is the Goal," *Miami New Times,* Dec. 26, 2002, http.www.miaminewtimes.com/issues/2003-01-16/features.html. See also Jim Ash and George Bennett, "Felons Voting List Getting Scrutiny in Court, in Keys," *Palm Beach Post,* June 9, 2004, http://www.verifiedvotingfoundation.org/article.php?id=2350.

37. House Judiciary Committee, Subcommittee on the Constitution, *Hearing on the Civic Participation and Rehabilitation Act of 1999, HR 906,* 106th Cong., 1st sess., Oct. 21, 1999, 11.

38. Simson, "Felony Laws in the United States," 1.

39. Allard and Mauer, "Regaining the Vote," 7.

40. Alec Ewald, "The Racial History and Impact of Disenfranchisement Laws in the United States," Demos, April 2003, http://www.demos-usa.org/pubs/FD_-_Brief.pdf (accessed June 17, 2005).

41. Simson, "Justice Denied," 20.

42. Demos, *Democracy Dispatches* 30 (Jan. 30, 2002), http://www.demos-usa.org/pubs/Dispatches_15.pdf (accessed June 17, 2005).

43. For a discussion of disenfranchisement and clemency policies in Washington State, see Linda Greenhouse, "Supreme Court Declines to Hear Two Cases Weighing the Right of Felons to Vote," *New York Times,* Nov. 9, 2004, http://www.law.unc.edu/PDFs/lockenyt.pdf (accessed June 17, 2005).

44. Allard and Mauer, "Regaining the Vote," 5.

45. Sasha Abramsky, "Ex-Felons Fight for Right to Vote," *Jackson (Wyoming) Free Press,* July 22, 2004.

46. Nkechi Taifa, "Re-Enfranchisement: A Guide for Individual Restoration of Voting Rights in States That Permanently Disenfranchise Former Felons," Advancement Project, Washington, D.C., http://www.advancementproject. org/Re-Enforcement.pdf (accessed June 17, 2005).

47. U.S. Department of Justice, Civil Rights Division, "Fifty-State Report on Re-Enfranchisement—A Guide to Restoring Your Right to Vote," a report issued by the Lawyers' Committee for Civil Rights under Law, http:// www.lawyerscommittee.org/ep04/50stateguide.pdf (accessed June 17, 2005).

48. Taifa, "Re-Enfranchisement," 20, 15, 21.

49. Demos, *Democracy Dispatches* 45 (June 29, 2004), http://www.demos -usa.org/pub/Dispatches/Archives/pdf (accessed June 17, 2005).

50. Taifa, "Re-Enfranchisement," 20.

51. State laws governing the disenfranchisement and other civil disabilities confronting ex-felons are itemized in Department of Justice, Office of Pardon Attorney, "Civil Disabilities of Convicted Felons: A State-by-State Survey."

52. Dorf, "Do Symbolic Pardons Do More Harm than Good?"

53. "Black State Legislators, ACLU Voting Rights Project Challenge State's Failure to Help Ex-Offenders with Process of Restoring Voters Rights," March 14, 2001, www.Aclufla.org/news_events/archive/2001/exfelons_re lease.cfm (accessed June 17, 2005). For discussion, see Elizabeth Amon, "Felons Have Allies in Vote-Ban Case—Law Enforcement and Justice Department Officials File Amicus Brief," *National Law Journal* (Jan. 14, 2003). See also Lee Hubbard, "Denial of Vote to Felons Hurts African Americans," Progressive Media Project, Oct. 31, 2000, http://www.Progressive.org./ pmplh031.html (accessed June 17, 2005).

54. Carla Browder, "State's Ex-felons Start to Regain Voting Rights," *Birmingham News*, April 16, 2004.

55. Taifa, "Re-Enfranchisement," 21–22.

56. Ibid., 12, 21.

57. Simson, "Justice Denied," 20–21. Although convicted felons can vote in Idaho as soon as they have finished their sentences (unless their crime was treason), a survey undertaken by the *Idaho Statesman* revealed that almost one-third of the state's election offices were unaware of this fact. In Minnesota voting rights are restored to offenders once they complete their sentences and parole, but another study, conducted by the Minnesota Lawyers' Committee for Civil Rights, similarly discovered that there was no consistent procedure to notify ex-felons of this fact. Eric Alterman and Laleh Ispahani, "Voting Rights of the Convicted," Center for American Progress, http://www.progressivetrail.org/ articles/040116AltermanandLalehIspahani.shtml (accessed June 17, 2005).

58. "Felons and the Right to Vote," editorial, *New York Times*, July 11, 2004.

59. Chris Levister, "Silent Code: Don't Ask—Don't Know," *Black Voice News*, July 19, 2004, http://www.blackvoicenews.com/modules.php?file=ar ticle&name=News&op=modload&sid=2291 (accessed June 17, 2005).

60. Quoted in Jim Siegel, "Ex-Felons' Voting Rights Misstated," *Cincinnati Enquirer*, Aug. 4, 2004, http://www.enquirer.com/editions/2004/08/04/0c_exfelonsD4.htm (accessed June 17, 2005).

61. Levister, "Silent Code."

62. Sasha Abramsky "Ex-Felons Fight to Regain Political Voice," AlterNet, March 19, 2004, http://www.alternet.org/election04/18176/ (accessed June 17, 2005).

63. Demos, *Democracy Dispatches* 36 (July 29, 2003); 46 (July 15, 2004); 47 (Aug. 2, 2004); 48 (Aug. 19, 2004), http://www.demos-usa.org/pub/Dispatches/Archives/pdf (accessed June 17, 2005).

64. Quoted in Goodnough, "Disenfranchised Florida Felons Struggle to Regain Their Rights."

65. *Florida Conference of Black State Legislators, et al. v. Moore*, http://www.aclufl.org/legislature_courts/legaldepartment/briefs_complaints/ex-felons_voting_rights.cfm (accessed June 17, 2005). See also "ACLU Applauds Court Decision Ordering DOC to Assist Inmates with Voting Rights Restoration," July 14, 2004, http://www.aclu.org/votingrights/votingrights.cfm?id=161038c=167 (accessed June 17, 2005); "Black State Legislatures, ACLU Voting Rights Project Challenge State's Failure to Help Ex-Offenders with Process of Restoring Voting Rights," ACLU of Florida, March 14, 2001, http://www.aclufl.org/news_events/archives/2001/exfelons_release.cfm (accessed June 17, 2005). See also Dahleen Glanton, "Rehabbed Felons Seek Right to Vote," Voters Unite, July 19, 2004, http://www.votersunite.org/article.asp?id=2220 (accessed June 17, 2005).

66. Debbie Cenziper and Jason Grotto, "Clemency Proving Elusive for Florida's Ex-Cons," *Miami Herald*, Oct. 31, 2004. See also Maya Bell, "Push Grows to Let Ex-Cons Vote Again," *Orlando Sentinel*, Aug. 25, 2004.

67. Quoted in Cenziper and Grotto, "Clemency Proving Elusive."

68. *Florida Conference of Black State Legislators et al. v. James Crosby*, No. 1D03-3370, July 14, 2004, First District Court of Appeals.

69. David Royse, "Felons' Path to Rights Eased," *Tampa Tribune*, Dec. 10, 2004.

70. Quoted in the *Orlando Sentinel*, Nov. 20, 2004. See also Cenziper and Grotto, "Clemency Proving Elusive."

71. See Royse, "Felons' Path to Rights Eased."

72. Ibid.

73. Kai Erikson, "Notes on the Sociology of Deviance," in *The Other Side: Perspectives of Deviance*, ed. Howard S. Becker (New York: Free Press, 1964), 1–22. See also Petersilia, "When Prisoners Return to the Community."

74. Harrison M. Trice and Paul M. Roman, "Delabeling, Relabeling, and Alcoholics Anonymous," *Social Problems* 17 (1970): 538–46.

Chapter Five

1. See, e.g., Joshua Dressler, *Understanding Criminal Law,* 2d ed. (New York: Lexis Publishing, 1995), sec.2.03 [c][2] at 13; Demleitner, "Continuing Payment on One's Debt to Society," 789.

2. Demleitner, "Continuing Payment on One's Debt to Society," 755–56. Elsewhere Demleitner also discusses why disenfranchisement, not being considered a factor in criminal punishment, fails to serve a deterrent function: "U.S. exclusions from the ballot-box operate automatically, and do not require judicial explanation or even mention. Indicative is that '[n]either the judge nor the prosecutor usually feels called upon to go into specific, individual consequences of conviction and sentencing; they rely on counsel to relay these details to his client and to his client's family.' These consequences, including disenfranchisement, are not considered part of the sentence." "Disenfranchising Ex-Felons: A Comparative Study," http://www.law.strath.ac.uk/csr/resea rchchapters/1999/demleitner.htm (accessed June 17, 2005).

3. Harvey, "Ex-felon Disenfranchisement and Its Influence on the Black Vote," 1172.

4. *Trop v. Dulles,* 356 U.S. 86, 112 (1958) (concurring opinion).

5. In his dissenting opinion in *Suave v. Canada,* Judge Ganthier asserts that "denial of the right to vote is perceived as meaningful by the prisoners themselves … and can therefore contribute to the rehabilitation of prisoners." (Chief Electoral Officer), 2000 SCC 68 (Dec. 2002) par. 174. He reiterated this conviction later in his opinion: "[T]here is reason to believe that the disenfranchisement could have an ongoing positive rehabilitative effect. Since the vote is meaningful to these offenders, then perhaps its temporary loss will be a factor which these offenders will carry with them as they pursue reintegration into the community on their release" (183).

6. *Trop v. Dulles,* 356 U.S. 86, 111 (1958) (Brennan, J., concurring).

7. Christy A. Visher and Jeremy Travis, "Transitions from Prison to Community: Understanding Individual Pathways," *Annual Review of Sociology* 29 (Aug. 2003): 89–113.

8. National Advisory Commission on Criminal Justice Standards and Goals, Corrections, Standard 16.17 (1973), 592–93. See also Thomas Pangle: "[I]f we deprive prisoners of the vote, we are cutting them off from participation in the political process, and thereby diminishing the chances that they will take an active interest in the affairs of the community." "Should Felons Vote? A Pragmatic Debate over the Meaning of Civic Responsibility" (2002), unpublished article, http://sentencingproject.org/pdfs/jschall-harvard.pdf (accessed June 17, 2005).

9. For discussion, see Angel Manuel Rodriguez, "An Eye for an Eye," Biblical Research Institute, http://biblicalresearch.gc.adventist.org/Biblequestions/eyeforeye.htm (accessed June 17, 2005).

10. *Furman v. Georgia*, 408 U.S. 238, 309 (1972).

11. Dr. Laurence Boxer, a biblical scholar, explained why the phrase cannot be understood out of its context: One of the places "an eye for an eye" appears in the Bible is in Exodus 21:24. Note the clarifying follow-up verses 26–27: "And if a man smite the eye of his bondman, or of his bondwoman, and destroy it, he shall let him go free for his eye's sake. And if he smite out his bondman's tooth, or his bondwoman's tooth, he shall let him go free for his tooth's sake." Note that the master is punished not by being maimed to match his maiming of the victim, but by compensating the bondman with freedom and the generous material gifts that were to accompany a freed bondman (Deuteronomy 15:12–14). The larger point is that "an eye for an eye" calls for fair compensation, not for retaliatory mutilation. Letter to the editor, *Niagara Gazette,* July 19, 2003, http://faculty.niagara.edu/boxer/essays/rel/i4i/htm (accessed June 17, 2005). See also Justice Scalia's dissenting opinion in *Ewing v. California:* "Proportionality—the notion that punishment should fit the crime—is inherently a concept tied to the penological goal of retribution." 538 U.S. 11, 31 (2003). For a succinct summary of the proportionality requirement, see *Solem v. Helm*, 463 U.S. 277, 284–88 (1983).

12. See *R. v. M*, (C.A.), 1 SCR 500, 1996 CanII 230 (SCC), par. 82. Chief Justice Lamer, speaking for the British Columbia Court of Appeals, defended the measured use of retribution: "Retribution is an accepted, and indeed important, principle of sentencing in our criminal law. As an objective of sentencing, it represents nothing less than the hallowed principle that criminal punishment, in addition to advancing utilitarian considerations related to deterrence and rehabilitation, should also be imposed to sanction the moral culpability of the offender. Retribution represents an important unifying principle of our penal law by offering an essential conceptual link between the attribution of criminal liability and the imposition of criminal sanctions. The legitimacy of retribution as a principle of sentencing has often been questioned as a result of its unfortunate association with 'vengeance' in common parlance, but retribution bears little relation to vengeance. Retribution should also be conceptually distinguished from its legitimate sibling, denunciation. Retribution requires that a judicial sentence properly reflect the moral blameworthiness of the particular offender. The objective of denunciation mandates that a sentence should also communicate society's condemnation of that particular offender's conduct. Neither retribution nor denunciation, however, alone provides an exhaustive justification for the imposition of criminal sanctions. Retribution must be considered in conjunction with the other legitimate objectives of sentencing" (par. 81).

13. House Judiciary Committee, Subcommittee on the Constitution, *Hearing on the Civic Participation and Rehabilitation Act of 1999, HR 906,* 106th Cong., 1st sess., Oct. 21, 1999; "Voting Rights of Convicted Offenders: Defeat of Amendment to the Voting Rights Act of 2001," *Congressional*

Record, Feb. 14, 2002, S.Amdt 2879, amends S 565, http://www.tgorski. com/criminal_justice/voting_rights_of_convicted_offenders.htm   (accessed June 17, 2005).

14. Demleitner, "Continuing Payment on One's Debt to Society," 775.

15. See Ewald, "Punishing at the Polls."

16. *Suave v. Canada.*

17. *Canada Election Act, R.S.C.* 1985, C.E-2, S.51 (e).

18. Laurence Tribe, *American Constitutional Law,* 2d ed. (New York: Foundation Press, 1988), 1084, quoted in *Suave v. Canada,* par. 71.

19. *Suave v. Canada,* par. 75 (dissenting opinion).

20. Ibid., par. 76 (dissenting opinion).

21. Ibid., par. 145.

22. Ibid., par 140 (dissenting opinion).

23. Ibid., par. 90 (dissenting opinion).

24. Ibid., par. 98 (dissenting opinion).

25. Quoted in "Massachusetts Inmates Shouldn't Vote," *Boston Herald,* Oct. 24, 2000, 33.

26. Ibid.

27. See Clegg, "Who Should Vote?" 172; House Judiciary Committee, Subcommittee on the Constitution, *Hearing on the Civic Participation and Rehabilitation Act of 1999,* HR 906, 106th Cong., 1st sess., Oct. 21, 1999, 16–19 (testimony of Roger Clegg), 43–47 (testimony of Todd Gaziano).

28. Clegg, "Who Should Vote?" 172. See U.S. Department of Justice, Office of the Pardon Attorney, "Civil Disabilities of Convicted Felons: A State-by-State Survey."

29. Clegg, "Who Should Vote?" 172.

30. See, e.g., *Washington v. State:* "The manifest purpose [of denying ex-felons the franchise] is to preserve the purity of the ballot box, which is the only sure foundation of republican liberty, and which needs protection against the invasion of corruption, just as much as against that of ignorance, incapacity, or tyranny. The evil infection of the one is not more fatal than that of the other. The presumption is, that one rendered infamous by conviction of felony, or other base offense indicative of great moral turpitude, is unfit to exercise the privilege of suffrage, or to hold office, upon terms of equality with freemen who are clothed by the State with the toga of citizenship." 75 Ala. 582, 585 (1884). See also *Green v. Board of Elections,* 380 F.2d 445, 451 (1967).

31. Ewald, "'Civil Death.'" See also Ewald, "Punishing at the Polls."

32. See Clegg, "Who Should Vote."

33. Pinaire, Heumann, and Bilotta, "Barred from the Vote," 7.

34. Gordon Wood, *The Creation of the American Republic 1776–1787* (Chapel Hill: University of North Carolina Press, 1969), 68.

35. Quoted in Clegg, "Who Should Vote."

36. Quoted in John J. Miller, "Public Policy: Votes for Felons—National Campaign to Liberalize Voting Rights of Ex-Felons," *National Review*, April 3, 2000, 26–28.

37. *Washington v. State*, 75 Ala. 582 (1884).

38. See Thomas Hobbes, *Leviathan*, ed. C. B. McPherson (New York: Penguin, 1979); Jean-Jacques Rousseau, *The Social Contract*, trans. R. D. Masters and J. R. Masters (New York: St. Martin's Press, 1978); John Locke, *The Second Treatise of Government*, rev. ed., ed. J. W. Gough (New York: Macmillan, 1946); Locke, *Two Treatises of Government*, ed. Peter Laslett (New York: Cambridge University Press, 1988). See also Note, "The Disenfranchisement of Ex-Felons: Citizenship, Criminality, and the Purity of the Ballot Box," *Harvard Law Review* 102 (1989): 1300; Judith N. Shklar, *American Citizenship: The Quest for Inclusion* (Cambridge: Harvard University Press, 1991); Jesse Furman, Note, "Political Illiberalism: The Paradox of Disenfranchisement and the Ambivalence of Rawlsian Justice," *Yale Law Journal* 106 (1997): 1197.

39. John Locke, *An Essay Concerning the True, Original Extent and End of Civil Government* (Oxford: Blackwell, 1956), 889.

40. Thomas Hobbes, *Leviathan* (1651), Part II, chap. 28, "Of Punishments and Rewards," available at http://etext.library.adelaide.edu/au/h/hobbes/thomas/h68/chapter28.htm (accessed June 18, 2005).

41. Locke quoted in *Green v. Board of Elections*, 380 F.2d 445, 451.

42. Ibid.

43. Quoted in Margie Hyslop, "Some Maryland Felons to Get Vote," *Washington Times*, April 7, 2002.

44. Locke, *Two Treatises of Government*, 275, 451. Locke asserted that lawbreakers should be "punished to that degree, and with so much severity as will suffice to make it an ill bargain to the offender, give him cause to repent, and terrify others from doing the like" (275).

45. Hobbes, *Leviathan*, Part II, chapter 28.

46. *Williams v. Walker-Thomas Furniture Company*, 350 F.2d 445 (D.C. Cir. 1965).

47. Quoted in Thompson, "Locking Up the Vote," 21.

48. *Dillenburg v. Kramer*, 469 F.2d 1222, 1224 (CA9 1972).

49. *Suave v. Canada*, par. 67.

50. Ibid., par. 97.

Chapter Six

1. See Mauer, "Felon Disenfranchisement: A Policy Whose Time Has Passed?"

2. American Law Institute, Model Penal Code 306.3 (proposed official draft 1962), cited in *Richardson v. Ramirez*, 418 U.S. 24, 85n30 (1974). See also Mauer, "Felon Disenfranchisement: A Policy Whose Time Has Passed?" 1–2.

3. Fellner and Mauer, *Losing the Vote.*

4. Douglas R. Tims, "The Disenfranchisement of Ex-Felons: A Cruelly Excessive Punishment," *Southwestern University Law Review* 7 (spring 1975): 124.

5. Mike Burke, "Racist Reconstruction Era Law May Aid Bush in Florida," http://www.supersphere.com/FrontPage/Politics/Article.html (accessed June 18, 2005).

6. Gregory Palast, "The Great Florida Ex-Con Game," *Harper's* magazine, March 1, 2002. See Rebecca Perl, "The Last Disenfranchised Class," *The Nation,* Nov. 26, 2003.

7. United States Commission on Civil Rights, "Voting Irregularities in Florida during the 2000 Presidential Election," http://www.Theusccr.GOV/PUBS/VOTE2000/SUM0802.htm (accessed June 18, 2005).

8. See http://www.reformelections.org/data/reports/99_full_report.pdf (accessed June 18, 2005).

9. "Electoral Reform after Florida: The Need for State Innovation with a Strong Federal Foundation," *Voting and Democracy Review* no. 14 (Aug. 2001), http://www.fairvote.org/library/brochure/news/rtf (accessed June 18, 2005).

10. Quoted in Simson, "Justice Denied," 42.

11. NAACP, "Election Reform since November 2001," Oct. 2002, 5, http://www.pewtrusts.com/pdf/public_policy_electionline_2000pdf (accessed June 18, 2005).

12. Ibid.

13. "Former Felons Have a Right to Vote," editorial, *New York Times,* Oct. 17, 2002, A32.

14. See "Making Citizens of Ex-Felons," *Christian Science Monitor,* Oct. 23, 2001; "Let Ex-Felons Vote," *Washington Post,* June 17, 2004, A28; "Give Ex-Prisoners a Voice," *USA Today,* Aug. 26, 2003; "Ex-Felons in Florida Fight for Their Rights," *Baltimore Sun,* July 15, 2002; "Votes That Will Never Be Counted," *Chicago Tribune,* Nov. 12, 2000.

15. See Manza, Brooks, and Uggen, "Public Attitudes toward Felon Disenfranchisement in the United States"; Pinaire, Heumann, and Bilotta, "Barred from the Vote."

16. See Pinaire, Heumann, and Bilotta, "Barred from the Vote," 31.

17. Quoted ibid., 18.

18. Manza, Brooks, and Uggen, "Public Attitudes toward Felon Disenfranchisement in the United States," 283.

19. Marc Mauer, "State Laws Banning Ex-Convicts from Voting Face Scrutiny," in *Internet Bankruptcy Library: Class Action Reporter* 4 (Oct. 23, 2004).

20. Robert D. Putnam, *Bowling Alone: The Collapse and Revival of American Community* (New York: Simon & Schuster, 2000).

21. Readers can visit the organization's website at http://www.sentencingproject.org/.

22. See, e.g., the websites of ACORN (www.acorn.org); the Lawyers' Committee (www.lawyerscom.org); the NAACP (www.naacp.org); Human Rights Watch (www.hrw.org); the ACLU (www.aclu.org); and the Brennan Center (www.brennancenter.org).

23. 214 F.Supp.2d 1333 (S.D. Fla. 2002).

24. See http://www.brennancenter.org/programs/downloads/JvBush—11thCircuitDecision (accessed June 18, 2005).

25. See this group's website at http://www.svrep.org/. See also http://www.tulane.edu/~so-inst/catalyst/prisonjail.html (accessed June 18, 2005).

26. John Cole Vodicka, "Foundation Fellows," the Petra Foundation newsletter, http://www.petrafoundation.org/fellows/John_Cole_Vodicka/ (accessed June 18, 2005). See also "Inmate Advocate Relishes Role as 'Agitator,'" Atlanta Journal-Constitution, Nov. 30, 2003.

27. See, e.g., www.rockthevote.com; www.bigvote.org; www.youthvote.org; www.dogonvillage.com.

28. See Progressive Leadership Alliance of Nevada (PLAN), http://www.planevada.org/profile/htm; http://www.planevada.org/newsletter.htm (accessed June 18, 2005).

29. "Ex-Offenders Gain the Right to Vote," PLAN newsletter (fall 2001), http://www.planevada.org/nov2001/htm#one.

30. Alvin J. Bronstein, "Prison Reform Revisited: The Unfinished Agenda," Pace Law Review 24 (2004): 839–46, http://www.library.law.pace.edu/PLR24-2/PLR230.pdf (accessed June 18, 2005).

31. Steven Kalogenas, "Legislative Changes on Felony Disenfranchisement, 1996–2003," Sentencing Project, September 2003, 1–11, http://www.sentencingproject.org/media/legchanges/pdf (accessed June 18, 2005).

32. Common Dreams News Center, http://www.commondreams.org/community.htm (accessed June 18, 2005).

33. Posted by Benjamin T. Greenberg, May 5, 2005, http://minorjive.typepad.com/hungryblues/2005/05 (accessed June 18, 2005).

34. See www.blog.drugpolicy.org/2004/09/felondisenfranchisement-animation.html (accessed June 18, 2005).

35. In addition to http://VotingExCons.com/, see http://www.Prison talkOnline/.

36. See, e.g., www.Heritage.org; www.fed-soc.org; www.Focus_on_the_Family; www.nationalreview.com; www.washtimes.com.

37. See, e.g., House Judiciary Committee, Subcommittee on the Constitution, Hearing on the Civic Participation and Rehabilitation Act of 1999, HR 906, Oct. 21, 1999 (testimony of Todd F. Gaziano, senior fellow at the Heritage Foundation), http://www.house.gov/judiciary/gazi/1021.htm.

38. See, e.g., the Fraternal Order of Police newsletter at http://www.grandlodgefop.org/; the National Sheriffs' Association newsletter at http://www.Sheriffs.org/default_html.

39. See, e.g., Advocacy Partnerships Benefit Crime Victim, http://www.doc.wa.gov/stories/crimevictimadvocacypartnership.htm (accessed June 18, 2005); "The Role of the Victim in Offender Reentry," http://www.doc.wa.gov/stories/victimwrap.htm (accessed June 18, 2005).

40. See Demos, *Democracy Dispatches* 14 (Jan. 15, 2002), http://www.demos-usa-org/pubs//@demos—usa.org/pubs/Dispatches_14.pdf (accessed June 18, 2005).

41. Quoted in Mike Sherman, "Legislators Try to Bridge Gaps," *Montgomery Advertiser,* Sept. 21, 2003. See also Joyce Howard Price, "More States Allow Felons to Regain Vote, Study Finds," *Washington Times,* Dec. 28, 2003.

42. See Price, "More States Allow Felons to Regain Vote." See also Allard and Mauer, "Regaining the Vote," 1–2.

43. See Michael Coyle, "State-Based Advocacy on Felony Disenfranchisement," Sentencing Project, Feb. 2003, http://www.sentencingproject.org/pdfs/508.3pdf (accessed June 18, 2005).

44. Quoted in Kenneth Green, "Description of the Voting Rights Restoration Coalition," DemocracyWorks, March 22, 2003, http://www.democracyworksct.org/urrcdescription.shtml (accessed June 18, 2005).

45. Demleitner, "Continuing Payment on One's Debt to Society," 781–82, 799, 781, 804.

46. For an excellent discussion, see Simson, "Justice Denied," 34–45.

47. Jyl Josephson, director of Women's Studies, Rutgers University, phone interview by author, July 26, 2004. See also Adrienne Rich, "Compulsory Heterosexuality and Lesbian Existence," in Adrienne Rich, *Blood, Bread, and Poetry: Selected Prose, 1979–1985* (New York: W. W. Norton, 1987), 23–75.

48. Simson, "Justice Denied," 36.

49. Quoted in Jeffrey S. Solochek, "Former Felons Fight for Vote," *St. Petersburg Times,* Jan. 21, 2001.

50. Simpson, "Justice Denied," 43.

51. *Furman v. Georgia,* 408 U.S. 238, 393 (1972).

52. See John D. Skrentny, *The Minority Rights Revolution* (Cambridge: Harvard University Press, 2003).

53. See, e.g., Larry M. Bartels, "Partisanship and Voting Behavior, 1952–1996," *American Journal of Political Science* 44 (Jan. 2000): 35–50; Jerome M. Clubb, William H. Flanagan, and Nancy H. Zingale, *Partisan Realignment: Voters, Parties, and Government in American History* (Beverly Hills, Calif.: Sage Publications, 1980).

Chapter Seven

1. Testimony of Scott Harshbarger regarding election reform before the National Commission on Election Reform at the Lyndon Baines Johnson Library, Austin, Texas, May 24, 2001, 12, http://www.commoncause.org/HARSH

BARGER%20TESTIMONY%200N%20ELECTION%20SYSTEMS.PDF (accessed June 18, 2005).

2. "Fact Sheet: Funding the Help America Vote Act of 2002," http://www.nass.org/Funding%20HAVA%20FACT%Sheet.pdf (accessed June 19, 2005).

3. Mauer, "Race, Poverty and Felon Disenfranchisement."

4. Mauer, "Felon Voting Disenfranchisement: A Policy Whose Time Has Passed?"

5. Sentencing Project, "Legislative Changes on Felon Disenfranchisement, 1996–2003" (Washington, D.C.: Sentencing Project, Sept. 24, 2003), http://www.sentencingproject.org/pdfs/legchanges-report.pdf (accessed June 19, 2005).

6. Ibid.

7. Demos, Democracy Dispatches 38 (Nov. 11, 2003), http://www.demos-usa.org/pub78.cfm (accessed June 19, 2005).

8. "States Study Voting Rights for Felons," Washington Times, Sept. 24, 2003.

9. Allard and Mauer, "Regaining the Vote."

10. Demos, "A Wake Up Call: History and Impact of Disenfranchisement Laws in the United States," April 2003, http://www.demos-usa.org/pubs/FD_-_Brief.pdf (accessed June 19, 2005).

11. Allard and Mauer, "Regaining the Vote."

12. Uggen and Manza, "Democratic Contraction?" 792.

13. Ibid.; Gregory Palast, "Florida's Flawed 'Voter-Cleansing' Program," http://www.Dir.salon.com/politics/feature/2000/12/04/voterfile/index.html (accessed June 19, 2005); Earl Ofari Hutchinson, "Black Ex-felons and Gore," Christian Science Monitor, Dec. 24, 2000. See also Demos, "A Wake Up Call."

14. "Florida Rights Restoration Coalition," in ACLU newsletter, March 25, 2003, http://www.aclufl.org.news_events/archive/2003/votingrightscoalition032502.cfm (accessed June 19, 2005).

15. Quoted in "Comment," Sarasota Herald-Tribune Newscoast, Jan. 11, 2001, http://www.legitgov.com/wefile.pdf (accessed July 11, 2005).

16. Florida Governor's Select Task Force on Election Procedures, Standards, and Technology, "Revitalizing Democracy in Florida," March 1, 2001, http://www.collinscenter.org/usr%5Fdoc/Elect%20Report.pdf (accessed June 19, 2005).

17. Bev Conover, "Florida's 'Fixed it' Farce," May 11, 2001, http://www.onlinejournal.com/evoting/051101/Conover/051101conover.html (accessed June 19, 2005).

18. Quoted in Solochek, "Former Felons Fight for Vote."

19. Quoted in Michael A. Fletcher, "Voting Rights for Felons Win Support," Washington Post, Feb. 22, 1999.

20. *Florida Conference of Black State Legislators, et al. v. Moore,* http://www.aclufl.org/legislature   courts/legaldepartment/briefs_complaints/ex-felons_voting_rights.cfm (accessed June 19, 2005).

21. "National Movement to Restore Ex-Felon Voting Rights Grows with Legislative Changes in Eight States."

22. Excellent background material and analysis on Maryland and several other states that adopted election reform is provided by Coyle, "State-Based Advocacy on Felony Disenfranchisement."

23. Quoted in Bobby White, "Some Maryland Legislators Want to Give Vote Back to Felons," *Capital News Service,* Oct. 26, 2001, http://www.journalism.umd.edu/cns/wire/2001/editors/10-Oct.-editions-011-026-Friday/Felony/Fight_CNS-UMCP.html (accessed June 19, 2005).

24. Coyle, "State-Based Advocacy on Felony Disenfranchisement."

25. Quoted in Elaine Shen, "Maryland's Disenfranchisement of Felons May Be Easing," *Baltimore Chronicle and Sentinel,* http://www.baltimorechronicle.com/disenranchisement_felons/02.html (accessed June 19, 2005). See also Afefe Tyehimba, "Election Rejection: Activists Take Aim at Law Barring Repeal Ex-Felons from the Voting Booth," *Mobtown Beat,* Jan. 30, 2002, http://www.9-society.us/rejection_5htm-33K-supplementalresult (accessed June 19, 2005).

26. Ibid.

27. Coyle, "State-Based Advocacy on Felony Disenfranchisement."

28. Quoted in Shen, "Maryland's Disenfranchisement of Felons May be Easing."

29. Coyle, "State-Based Advocacy on Felony Disenfranchisement."

30. Ibid.

31. Marc Lightdale, "Felons Appeal to Lawmakers for Improved Voting Rights," *Capital News Service,* Feb. 19, 2004, http://www.newsline.umd.edu/politics/specialreports/elections04/felonsvote021904.htm (accessed June 19, 2005). See also Bobby White, "Some Maryland Legislators Want to Give Vote Back to Felons," *Capital News Service,* Oct. 26, 2001, http://www.journalism.umd.edu/cns/wire/2001-edition/10-October-edition s-011026-Friday/FelonyFight_CNS-UMCP.html (accessed June 19, 2005).

32. Coyle, "State-Based Advocacy on Felony Disenfranchisement."

33. Ibid.

34. Christopher Uggen and Jeffrey Manza, with Melissa Thompson and Sara Wakefield, "Impact of Recent Legal Changes in Felon Voting Rights in Five States," briefing paper prepared for the National Symposium on Felony Disenfranchisement, Sept. 30–Oct. 1, 2002, Washington, D.C. Michael Coyle's figures differ from those cited by Manza and Uggen. According to Coyle's calculations, during the 2000 presidential election, 1,200 former felons applied to register to vote, of whom 800 were granted the right. Coyle, "State-Based Advocacy on Felony Disenfranchisement." See also the Delaware Center

for Justice newsletter for spring 2004, http://www.dcjustice.org/ (accessed June 19, 2005).

35. Conn, "Excerpts from the Partisan Politics of Ex-Felon Disenfranchisement Laws."

36. Coyle, "State-Based Advocacy on Felony Disenfranchisement."

37. Ibid. See also Conn, "Excerpts from the Partisan Politics of Ex-Felon Disenfranchisement Laws."

38. Ibid. See also Coyle, "State-Based Advocacy on Felony Disenfranchisement."

39. Sentencing Project, "Legislative Changes on Felon Disenfranchisement," http://www.sentencingproject.org/legislativechanges.cfm.

40. "Celluci: No Vote from Jail," *SouthCoast Today*, Aug. 3, 1997, http://www.southcoasttoday.com/daily08-97/08-03-97/digest.html (accessed June 19, 2005).

41. Ibid.

42. *Massrail* 14 (Feb.–June 1999), http://www.etext.org/Politics/MIM/rail/hr14.htm (accessed June 19, 2005).

43. "Celluci: No Vote from Jail."

44. David Alvin, letter to the editor, *Boston Globe*, Oct. 22, 2000, E6.

45. Carolyn Ryan, "Governor Looks to Strip Cons' Voting Rights," *Boston Herald*, Aug. 12, 1997; Hyslop, "Special Report: Right to Vote?"

46. Allard and Mauer, "Regaining the Vote," 8.

47. Phillips, "Lawmakers Push to Ban Inmate Votes." See also Michael Crowley, "Lawmakers Favor Ban of Felons' Voting Rights," *Boston Globe*, June 29, 2000, B3.

48. Conn, "Excerpts from the Partisan Politics of Ex-Felon Disenfranchisement Laws," 45n72.

49. Sandeep Kaushik, "Blackball Vote: Washington's Secret Membership in Jim Crow Justice Club," Aug. 14, 2002, http://www.thestranger.com/seattle/content?oid=11555 (accessed June 19, 2005).

50. Maureen O'Hagan, "Felons Call Voting Ban Unfair to Minorities," *Seattle-Times*, March 2, 2004; Rottinghaus, "Incarceration and Enfranchisement."

51. O'Hagan, "Felons Call Voting Ban Unfair." See also Kaushik, "Blackball Vote."

52. "How Can I Get My Right to Vote Back?" ACLU, Washington, Oct. 4, 2004, http://www.aclu-wa.org/ISSUES/voting_rights/Restore.vote.html (accessed June 19, 2005).

53. Sam Skolnik, "Freed from Bars but Barred from Voting," *Seattle Post-Intelligencer*, Jan. 17, 2000.

54. "Disenfranchising Felons by State and Correctional Status," table 3, in Fellner and Mauer, *Losing the Vote*.

55. Ibid., table 2.

56. Ibid., table 3.

57. Quoted in Kaushik, "Blackball Vote."
58. Ibid. See also O'Hagan, "Felons Call Voting Ban Unfair."
59. Skolnik, "Freed from Bars."

Chapter Eight

1. See *Alexander v. Mineta*, no. 99-2062 (Oct. 16, 2000), http://www.usdoj.gov/osg/briefs/2000/0responses/1999-2062.resp.html (accessed June 19, 2005) (see *Alexander v. Daley*, 90 F.Supp.2d 35, 66 [DDC 2000]); Jamin B. Rankin, "A Right to Vote," *American Prospect* 12 (Aug. 27, 2001).
2. Thomas Paine, *Dissertation on First Principles of Government* (Paris, July 1795), quoted at http://www.quote.wikipedia.org/wiki/Thomas_Paine (accessed June 19, 2005).
3. For a comprehensive breakdown of the voting policies of other countries, see Rottinghaus, "Incarceration and Enfranchisement."
4. *Murphy v. Ramsey*, 114 U.S. 15, 43 (1885).
5. *Reynolds v. Sims*, 377 U.S. 533, 555 (1964).
6. See, e.g., *Help America Vote Act of 2002* [HAVA], Public Law 107-252, Oct. 2002. This act establishes requirements for voting systems used in federal elections that will allow voters to verify and amend their selections before officially casting their ballots, eliminate language barriers, and permit provisional voting whenever eligible voters are not listed on registration rosters. The law mandates that every precinct in the county must have at least one voting machine or system accessible to disabled individuals, including those with sight impairment, no later than January 1, 2006. See also the *1990 Americans with Disabilities Act* (ADA), 42 U.S.C., sections 12131–34. Section 203 of the Voting Rights Act, in addition, forbids election employees from discriminating in voting on the basis of anyone's membership in a minority-language group. The VRA also requires particular jurisdictions to print ballots and anything else related to the election process in the minority as well as in the English language, and to have available translators for those requiring assistance. See Code of Federal Regulations at the end of 28 C.F.R., part 55, http://www.usdoj.gov/crt/voting/misc/voterev.htm (accessed June 19, 2005).
7. Uggen and Manza, "Democratic Contraction?" 803.
8. *Reynolds v. Sims*, 377 U.S. 533, 541.
9. Ibid. Other fundamental rights include the right to travel between states, *Shapiro v. Thompson*, 394 U.S. 618 (1969); the right to free exercise of religion, *Sherbert v. Verner*, 351 U.S. 374, 398 (1963); the right to freedom of association, *Bates v. City of Little Rock*, 361 U.S. 516 (1960); and the right to a criminal appeal, *Griffin v. Illinois*, 351 U.S. 12 (1956).
10. The classes considered "suspect" by the Supreme Court are national origin, *Castaneda v. Partida*, 430 U.S. 482 (1977); race, *Loving v. Virginia*,

388 U.S. 1 (1967); and alienage, *In Re Griffiths*, 413 U.S. 717 (1973). See Chapter 9 on "suspect classes."

11. U.S. Constitution, Amendment 14, Section 2 reads: "Representatives shall be apportioned among the several States according to their respective numbers, counting the whole number of persons in each State, excluding Indians not taxed. But when the right to vote at any election for the choice of electors for President and Vice-President of the United States, Representatives in Congress, the Executive and Judicial officers of a State, or the members of the Legislature thereof, is denied to any of the male inhabitants of such State, being twenty-one years of age, and citizens of the United States, or in any way abridged, except for participation in rebellion, or other crime, the basis of representation therein shall be reduced in the proportion which the number of such male citizens shall bear to the whole number of male citizens twenty-one years of age in such State."

12. *Richardson v. Ramirez*, 418 U.S. 24 (1974).

13. *Nixon v. Herndon*, 273 U.S. 536, 541 (1927).

14. In *McGowan v. Maryland*, 366 U.S. 420 (1961), Chief Justice Earl Warren explained the reasoning behind the Court's application of the "rational relationship" standard: "State legislatures are presumed to have acted within their constitutional power despite the fact that, in practice, their laws result in some inequality. A statutory discrimination will not be set aside if any state of facts reasonably may be conceived to justify it" (425–26, citations omitted).

15. *Skinner v. Oklahoma*, 316 U.S. 535 (1942).

16. Ibid., 541.

17. See, e.g., *Washington v. State*, 75 Ala. 582 (1884), quoted above, Chapter 5, note 30.

18. Quoted in Simson, "Justice Denied," 49.

19. *Green v. Board of Elections*, 380 F.2d 445 (1967).

20. House Judiciary Committee, Subcommittee on the Constitution, *Hearing on the Civic Participation and Rehabilitation Act of 1999, HR 906,* 106th Cong., 1st sess., Oct. 21, 1999 (testimony of Marc Mauer), 11.

21. House Judiciary Committee, Subcommittee on the Constitution, *Hearing on the Civic Participation and Rehabilitation Act of 1999, HR 906.*

22. Matthew Cardinale, "Jeff Manza Speaks at UCI on Felon Disenfranchisement," *Irvine Progressive*, June 2004.

23. See Simson, "Justice Denied," 54.

24. See "National Movement to Restore Ex-Felon Voting Rights Grows with Legislative Changes in Eight States."

25. U.S. Congress, *Debate on Equal Protection of Voting Rights Act of 2001*, 107th Cong., 2d sess., *Congressional Record* 148 (2002): S797-809.

26. Ibid.

27. Quoted in Simson, "Justice Denied," 50.

28. *Help America Vote Act of 2002* [HAVA], Public Law No. 107-252, 116 Stat. 1666. The HAVA is codified at 42 U.S.C. 15301–545. For text of the law, see http://fecweb1.fec.gov/hava/law_ext.txt (accessed June 19, 2005).

29. Quoted in Miles Rapoport, "Election Reform Initiative Shifts to the States," Demos, *Democracy Dispatches* 19 (Oct. 9, 2001), http://www.demos-usa.org/pubs/Dispatches.pdf (accessed June 19, 2005).

30. See Shapiro, "Challenging Criminal Disenfranchisement under the Voting Rights Act," 540.

31. See John Mabry Mathews, *Legislative and Judicial History of the Fifteenth Amendment* (New York: DaCapo Press, 1997), 65.

32. Quoted in Election Reform Information Project, "Election Reform since November 2001—What's Changed, What Hasn't, and Why," http://www.reformelections.org/data/whats%5Fnew/archive/electionline%2D2002.pdf (accessed June 19, 2005).

33. Center for Voting and Democracy, "Background on the Voting Rights Act," http://www.fairvote.org/ura/#background (accessed June 19, 2005).

34. *Ex parte Siebold*, 100 U.S. 371, 383–84 (1880).

35. *Cook v. Gralike*, 531 U.S. 510 (2001), quoting *Smiley v. Holm*, 285 U.S. 355, 366 (1932).

36. *Foster v. Love*, 522 U.S. 67, 69 (1997).

37. *Tashjian v. Republican Party*, 479 U.S. 208 (1986).

38. House Judiciary Committee, Subcommittee on the Constitution, *Hearing on the Civic Participation and Rehabilitation Act of 1999, HR 906*, 106th Cong., lst sess., Oct. 21, 1999 (testimony of Gillian Metzger), 56, http://www.house.gov/judiciary/metz1021.htm (accessed June 19, 2005).

39. *Tashjian v. Republican Party*, 479 U.S. 208, 229.

40. *United States v. Classic*, 313 U.S. 299, 315 (1941).

41. *National Voter Registration Act of 1993*, 42 U.S.C. sec. 1973 qq *et seq.* (1994).

42. See Rebekah Evenson, "Approaching the Goal of Universal Enfranchisement, 1995 Motor Votes in the States," Feb. 22, 2003, http://www.fairvote.org/reports/1995/chp6/evenson.html (accessed June 19, 2005).

43. *Acorn v. Edgar*, 56 F.3d 791, 794 (7th Cir. 1995).

44. House Judiciary Committee, Subcommittee on the Constitution, *Hearing on the Civic Participation and Rehabilitation Act of 1999, HR 906*, Oct. 21, 1999 (statement of Assistant Attorney General Viet Dinh), http://www.house.gov/judiciary/dinh 1021.htm (accessed June 19, 2005).

45. Ibid., testimony of Roger Clegg.

Chapter Nine

1. *Davis v. Beason*, 138 U.S. 333, 347 (1890).

2. *Richardson v. Ramirez*, 418 U.S. 24 (1974), citing *Davis v. Beason*, 345–47.

3. *Green v. Board of Elections,* 380 F.2d 445 (1967).

4. *Otsuka v. Hite,* 64 Cal. 2d 596, 414 P.2d 412 (1966), 603, 611.

5. Ibid., 604, 608.

6. Mari D'Alessandro suggested this analogy to me on August 11, 2004.

7. *Stephens v. Yeomans,* 327 Supp. 1182, 1185, 1188 (D.N.J. 1970).

8. *Dillenburg v. Kramer,* 469 F.2d 1222, 1224 (1972).

9. *Ramirez v. Brown,* 9 Cal. 3d 199, 507 P.2d 1345, 1357 (1973).

10. Keyssar, *Right to Vote,* 305.

11. *Ramirez v. Brown,* 9 Cal. 3d 199, 507 P.2d 1345, 214.

12. *Richardson v. Ramirez,* 418 U.S. 24, 25, 43.

13. *Green v. Board of Elections,* 380 F.2d 445, 454–55.

14. *Richardson v. Ramirez,* 56.

15. Ibid., at 75–76.

16. Ibid.

17. Gary Reback, "Disenfranchisement of Ex-felons: A Reassessment," *Stanford Law Review* 25 (1973): 851.

18. See Note, "The Equal Protection Clause as a Limitation on the States' Power to Disenfranchise Those Convicted of a Crime," *Rutgers Law Review* 21 (1967): 318.

19. Demleitner, "Continuing Payment on One's Debt to Society," 774n109.

20. *Richardson v. Ramirez,* 418 U.S. 24, 45.

21. David E. Rosenbaum, "Seeking a Formula for Voting Laws," *New York Times,* Dec. 20, 2000, A31.

22. John W. Burgess, *Reconstruction and the Constitution* (New York: Charles Scribner's Sons, 1907), 120.

23. David L. Shapiro, "Mr. Justice Rehnquist: A Preliminary View," *Harvard Law Review* 90 (Dec. 1976): 303–4. Shapiro adds that "[e]ven within the Section 2 formula itself, the text distinguishes between those who are not male citizens over 21, for whom the right to vote may be 'denied,' and those who have participated in rebellion or other crime, whose right may be 'abridged.' " "It might be argued," he continues, "that under this distinction, *permanent denial* of the right to vote to an ex-convict, who has completed his sentence and thus paid his debt, was not contemplated by the Section 2 formula for representation, no such textual analysis was considered by the majority" (303n34).

24. William W. Van Alstyne, "The Fourteenth Amendment, the 'Right' to Vote, and the Understanding of the Thirty-Ninth Congress," *Supreme Court Law Review* (1965): 65.

25. Fletcher, "Disenfranchisement as Punishment," 1900.

26. *Nixon v. Herndon,* 273 U.S. 536, 541.

27. 575 F.2d 1110, 1114–15 (5th Cir. 1978).

28. *McLaughlin v. City of Canton,* 947 F.Supp. 954, 974–75 (S.D. Miss. 1995).

29. Thompson, "Locking Up the Vote," quoting Heywood Fennell.

30. See, e.g., Constitutional Rights Foundation, "Race and Voting in the Segregated South," http://www.crf-usa.org/brown50th/race_voting.html (accessed June 19, 2005).

31. Shapiro, "Challenging Criminal Disenfranchisement under the Voting Rights Act," 541, quoting Francis B. Simpkins, "Pitchfork Ben Tillman."

32. *Harper v. Virginia State Board of Elections,* 383 U.S. 663, 667–68 (1966).

33. See U.S. Department of Justice Civil Rights Division—Voting Section, "The Voting Rights Act of 1965," http://www.usdoj.gov/crt/voting/intro/into_b.htm (accessed June 19, 2005).

34. See Marquita Sykes, "The Origin of Affirmative Action," http://www.now.org/nnt/08-95/affirmhs.html (accessed June 19, 2005).

35. Section 2 of the Voting Rights Act, 42 U.S.C. § 1973, prohibits the use of any voting procedure or practice which "results in" a denial or abridgement of the right to vote on account of race or color or membership in a language minority.

36. *South Carolina v. Katzenbach,* 383 U.S. 301, 309 (1966).

37. President Lyndon B. Johnson's Remarks on the Capitol Rotunda at the signing of the Voting Rights Act, August 6, 1965, http://www.lbjlib.utexas.edu/johnson/archives/hom./speeches/hom/650806.asp (accessed June 19, 2005).

38. *Voting Rights Act of 1965,* Public Law 89-110, 79 Stat. 445 (current version at 42 U.S.C. §§ 1971, 1973 to 1973 gg-8 [2003]).

39. Ibid.

40. *Bolden v. City of Mobile,* 466 U.S. 55 (1980).

41. Public Law 97-205. For an excellent discussion, see Lawyers' Committee for Civil Rights under Law, "Preserving a Fundamental Right: Reauthorization of the Voting Rights Act," June 2003, http://www.Lawyersc omm.org/features/40thpapers/ura.pdf+Congress+amends+voting+rights+Act+to+prohibit+vote+dilution (accessed June 19, 2005).

42. *Thornburg v. Gingles,* 478 U.S. 30, 36 (1986).

43. Ibid., 32.

44. See http://www.brennancenter.org/programs/downloads/johnson_plt_app_brief.pdf (accessed June 19, 2005).

45. See Amon, "Felons Have Allies in Vote-Ban Case."

46. *Wesley v. Collins,* 605 F. Supp. 802, 804–14 (M.D. Tenn. 1985), aff'd, 791 F.2d 1255 (6th Cir. 1986). See Public Law 97-205, 96 Stat. 131 (1982), codified as amended at 42 U.S.C. Sec. 1973(a)-(b) (1988).

47. Harvey, "Ex-Felon Disenfranchisement and Its Influence on the Black Vote," 1147, 1184.

48. *Wesley v. Collins,* 813.

49. Ibid., 812.

50. *Wesley v. Collins*, 791 F.2d 1255, 1261 (6th Cir. 1986) (quoting *Bolden v. City of Mobile*).

51. Voting Rights Amendment of 1982, S. Rep. No. 417, 29n114, reprinted in 1982 U.S.C. Can. at 207. See Harvey, "Ex-Felon Disenfranchisement and Its Influence on the Black Vote," 1183.

52. Ibid.

53. *Baker v. Pataki*, 85 F.3d 919, 938 (2d Cir. 1996). As the Second Circuit stated in this case, "Because it is not unmistakably clear that, in amending Section 1973 in 1982 to incorporate the 'results' test, Congress intended that the test be applicable to felon disenfranchisement statutes, we conclude that Section 1973 does not apply." As a consequence, it concluded, the plaintiffs-appellants "have failed to state a claim under the Voting Rights Act."

54. New York State's disenfranchisement provisions were originally challenged in the mid-1990s. See *Baker v. Cuomo*, 58 F.3d 814, 819–22 (2d Cir. 1995), vacated in part on other grounds; *Baker v. Pataki*, 85 F.3d 919 (2d Cir. 1996) (en banc). In September 2000 a third suit was filed, *Hayden v. Pataki*, and on July 15, 2004, the Southern District Court of New York dismissed all the claims of *Hayden v. Pataki*. See NAACP Legal Defense Fund, press release, June 16, 2004, http://www.naacpldf.org/content.aspx?article=304 (accessed June 19, 2005). The *Hayden* decision was the second federal court opinion in New York State in 2004 to dismiss a challenge to the state's felon disfranchisement laws. In April, the U.S. Court of Appeals for the Second Circuit also threw out a second lawsuit in which plaintiffs argued that New York's law disproportionately targets African Americans, in violation of the Voting Rights Act. See *Muntaqim v. Coombe*, no. 94-CV-1237 (N.D.N.Y., Jan. 24, 2001); press release, Brennan Center, June 16, 2004, http://www.brennancenter.org/origrams/downloads/Muntaqim-AmicusBrief.pdf (accessed June 19, 2005).

55. Fellner and Mauer, *Losing the Vote*. This enormously influential study provides a comprehensive breakdown of each state's disenfranchisement policies and an analysis of their cumulative impact. The second study, Jeff Manza and Christopher Uggen's *Locked Out: Felon Disenfranchisement and American Democracy* (New York: Oxford University Press, 2005), is a well-documented study of the political consequences resulting from disenfranchisement laws.

56. *Johnson v. Bush*, 214 F.Supp.2d 1333 (S.D. Fla. 2002). See also http://www./brennancenter.org/programs/downloads/dem_VR_LIT_JOHNSON.html (accessed June 19, 2005). See also Amon, "Felons Have Allies in Vote-Ban Case."

57. See draft staff report, chapter 6, at http://www.brennancenter.org/programs/dem_fepp_Lit_BrandX.html (accessed June 19, 2005).

58. *Johnson v. Bush*, 353 F.3d 1287 (11th Cir. 2003). In remanding the case, a divided panel from the Eleventh Circuit instructed the lower court to gather additional findings on two of plaintiffs' claims—those alleging violations

of the equal protection clause and the Voting Rights Act. On July 20, 2004, the Eleventh Circuit granted the state's request to rehear the case before the entire court. Finally, on April 11, 2005, the tribunal upheld Florida's law prohibiting ex-felons from voting. *Johnson v. Bush*, no. 02-14469, April 12, 2005. The text of the opinion is available at http://www.brennancenter.org/programs/downloads/jvbushruling_11thCircuit_41205c.pdf (accessed June 19, 2005).

59. Brief of Defendants—Appellees, *Johnson v. Bush*, Nov. 19, 2002, no. 02-14469C, http://www.brennancenter.org/programs/downloads/Johnson_def_app_brief.pdf (accessed June 19, 2005).

60. Ibid.

61. *Johnson v. Bush*, Complaint—Class Action, Preliminary Statement, Plaintiff's Brief at Section 74, http://www.Brennancenter.org/programs/dowloads/JvBush-11thCircuitDecision(12-19-03).pdf (accessed June 19, 2005).

62. *Johnson v. Bush*, 214 F.Supp.2d 1333, 1340-42.

63. See Jay Weaver, "Ex-Felons Seeking Voting Rights Get Trial," Dec. 20, 2003, http://www.miami.com/mld/miamiherald/7538535.htm (accessed June 19, 2005).

64. Jeffrey Solochek, "Flareforms," *St. Petersburg Times,* April 8, 2003. See also Jeffrey Solochek, "Blacks: Allow Ex-felons to Vote," ibid., Feb. 19, 2001.

65. *Rogers v. Lodge*, 458 U.S. 613, 625 (1982).

66. See, e.g., Isabel V. Sawhill, "Poverty in the United States," Library of Economics and Liberty on-line, *Concise Encyclopedia of Economics,* ed. David R. Henderson, http://www.econlib.org/library/enc/povertyintheunitedstates. html (accessed June 19, 2005); Michael Yates, "Poverty and Inequality in the Global Economy," *Monthly Review* (Feb. 2004), http://www.monthlyreview. org/0204yates.htm.

67. *Hunter v. Underwood*, 471 US 222 (1985).

68. Alabama Constitution, Art. 3, sec. 182 (1901); see 471 U.S. at 224, 226.

69. Ibid., 229.

70. *Wesley v. Collins*, 791 F.2d, at 1262-63.

71. *Farrakhan v. Washington*, 338 F.3d. 1009, no. CV-96-000 76–RHW (July 25, 2003), 10131. On November 8, 2004, the Supreme Court declined to hear, on appeal, both *Washington v. Farrakhan*, (no. 03-1597), and a closely related case from New York, *Muntaqim v. Coombe* (no. 04-175). The Court will undoubtedly revisit the issue in the future, however, given both the controversy that disenfranchisement occasions and the inconsistency in appellate court rulings. Whereas the Ninth Circuit had permitted the challenge against Washington's voting restrictions to proceed, the Second Circuit had concluded just the opposite—i.e., that the Voting Rights Act did not apply to disenfranchisement policies in the absence of a "clear statement" from Congress. See Linda Greenhouse, "Supreme Court Declines to Hear Two Cases Weighing the Right of Felons to Vote," *New York Times,* Nov. 9, 2004, A19; Kristen Wyatt,

"Appeals Court Hears Cases in Felons' Voting Suit," *The Ledger*, Oct. 27, 2004, http://www.theledger.com/apps/pbcs.dll/article?AID=/20041027/NEWS/410270392/-1/elections20 (accessed June 19, 2005).

72. *Farrakhan v. Washington*, 338 F.3d. 1009 (9th Cir., 2003), at 1047–48.

73. Goodnough, "Felons Struggle to Regain Their Rights." Before the trial court could conduct this analysis, the state filed a petition asking the Supreme Court to determine whether the VRA applies to felon disfranchisement laws. On July 28, 2004, plaintiffs and amici filed a brief opposing Supreme Court review, maintaining that it is premature until the VRA's applicability is first determined at the appellate level and the trial court has an opportunity to develop a record. See *Farrakhan v. Washington*, no. 01-35032 D.C. No. CV-96-00076-RHW. The Supreme Court denied certiorari on November 8, 2004, and as a result the case is now scheduled for trial in district court in Washington State. Motion of Thomas Johnson, et al., for Leave to File *Amici Curiae* Brief Out of Time and *Amici Curiae* Brief in Support of Respondents, *Washington v. Farrakhan*, no. 03-1597, August 19, 2004.

Chapter Ten

1. See Anthony F. Granucci, " 'Nor Cruel and Unusual Punishment Inflicted': The Original Meaning," *California Law Review* 57 (October 1969): 860.

2. *Furman v. Georgia*, 408 U.S. 238, 332 (1972) (dissenting opinion).

3. Tims, "Disenfranchisement of Ex-Felons," 158.

4. See Granucci, " 'Nor Cruel and Unusual Punishment Inflicted.' "

5. *O'Neil v. Vermont*, 144 U.S. 323, 340 (1892).

6. *Weems v. United States*, 217 U.S. 349, 377, 372 (1910).

7. Ibid., 373.

8. *Robinson v. California*, 370 U.S. 660, 666 (1962).

9. *Stanford v. Kentucky*, 492 U.S. 361, 371 (1989) (plurality opinion).

10. See, e.g., *R. v. Smith* (1987), 1 S.C.R. 1045, 1068; *Gregg v. Georgia*, 428 U.S. 153, 183 ("The death penalty is said to serve two principal social purposes: retribution and deterrence of capital crimes by prospective offenders"); see also *People v. Anderson*, 6 Cal. 3d 628, 651, 493 P.2d 880, 896, *cert denied* (406 U.S. 958 [1992]); Tims, "Disenfranchisement of Ex-Felons," 145.

11. *Helling v. McKinney*, 509 U.S. 25 (1993).

12. See, e.g., *Rudolph v. Alabama*, 375 U.S. 889 (1963) (Goldberg, in dissent, said the majority should decide whether executing someone convicted of rape violated the "evolving standards of decency that mark the progress of [our] maturing society," or "standards of decency more or less universally accepted") (889–90). See also *Trop v. Dulles*, 356 U.S. 86, 101 (1958); *Robinson v. California*, 370 U.S. 660.

13. *Helling v. McKinney*, 509 U.S. 25, 32.

14. Ibid., citing *Estelle v. Gamble*, 429 U.S. 97, 103–4 (1976).

15. *Thompson v. Oklahoma,* 487 U.S. 815, 823–31 (1988).

16. *Atkins v. Virginia,* 536 U.S. 304 (2002), quoting *Penry v. Lynaugh,* 492 U.S. 302, 334 (1989).

17. Ibid. See O'Hagan, "Felons Call Voting Ban Unfair."

18. See Amnesty International, "U.S. Supreme Court Decision in Atkins vs. Virginia to Bring U.S. in Line with International Standards of Decency," June 20, 2002, http://www.amnesty.org/LIBRARY/index/ENGAMR5100 32004-28K (accessed June 20, 2005).

19. At least twenty-six states and the federal government have laws similar to California's, requiring that upon a person's third conviction he or she receive a sentence anywhere from twenty-five years to life. Another fourteen states have "enhanced penalty" laws that subject repeat offenders to longer prison terms than nonrepeaters receive for the same offense. See Phyllis Raybin Emert, "Three Strikes and You're Out," New Jersey State Bar Foundation, http://www.njsbf. com/njsbf/student/eagle/spring03-1/cfm (accessed June 20, 2005).

20. *Rummel v. Estelle,* 445 U.S. 263, 274n11, 284–85.

21. *Solem v. Helm,* 463 U.S. 277, 286–88 (1983).

22. *Harmelin v. Michigan,* 501 U.S. 957, 961 (1991).

23. *Ewing v. California,* 538 U.S. 11 (2003); *Lockyer v. Andrade,* 539 U.S. 63 (2003).

24. *Ewing v. California,* citing *Rummel v. Estelle,* 445 U.S. 263, 265.

25. Ibid., citing *Solem v. Helm,* 297n22.

26. Ibid., citing *Atkins v. Georgia,* 536 U.S. 304, 311 (2002); *U.S. v. Bajakajian,* 524 U.S. 321, 334–36 (1998) (excessive bail prohibited); *Stack v. Boyle,* 342 U.S. 1, 5 (1951) (other forms of excessive punishment prohibited).

27. *Ewing v. California,* citing *Solem v. Helm,* 294.

28. Ibid.

29. Ibid., citing *BMW of North America, Inc. v. Gore,* 517 U.S. 559, 562 (1996).

30. Ibid., citing *Doggett v. U.S.,* 605 U.S. 647 (1992).

31. The Court has never inquired whether long sentences further any penal objectives (never questioning, for instance, the "retributive" effectiveness of a prison term that is imposed regardless of the severity of the triggering offense). For discussion, see Michael Vitiello, "Three Strikes: Can We Return to Rationality?" *Journal of Criminal Law and Criminology* (1997): 427 (California's three strikes law, like other "[h]abitual offender statutes, [is] not retributive" because the prison term is "imposed without regard to the culpability of the offender or [the] degree of social harm caused by the offender's behavior" and "has little to do with the gravity of the offens[e]").

32. *Powell v. Texas,* 392 U.S. 514, 533 (1968) (dissenting opinion).

33. *Rudolph v. Alabama,* 375 U.S. 889, 889–90 (1963).

34. Eight states deny the vote to ex-offenders for life. Another twenty-nine disenfranchise anyone still on probation, and thirty-three withhold the vote

from individuals on parole. All but two states, moreover, deny voting privileges to anyone who is incarcerated. See Prison Policy Initiatives, "Disenfranchisement," http://www.prisonpolicy.org/prisonindex/disenfranchisement.shtml (accessed June 20, 2005).

35. International Covenant on Civil and Political Rights (ICCPR), 999 U.N.T.S. 171, entered into force March 23, 1976.

36. "General Comment Adopted by the Human Rights Committee under Art. 40, Par. 4 of the International Comment on Civil and Political Rights," General Comment No. 25 (57), Annex V (1), CC PR /C/21, Rev. 1, Add. 7, Aug. 27, 1996.

37. International Covenant on Civil and Political Rights, UN General Assembly resolution 2200A (XXI), 21 UN GAOR Supp. (No. 16) at 52, U.N. Doc. A/6316 (1966), 999 U.N.T.S. 171, entered into force March 23, 1976. Article 25 ratified by the United States June 8, 1992.

38. Ibid.

39. ICCPR, E/CN.4/SR. 364, p. 14. See also Fellner and Mauer, *Losing the Vote*, 20–22.

40. *Holland v. Ireland* (1988), 93-A.D.R. 15, 26–27.

41. *H. v. Netherlands* (1983), 33 D.R. 242, 245.

42. Ibid., 242.

43. See note 36 above.

44. Karl Josef Partsch, "Freedom of Conscience and Expression, and Political Freedoms," in *The International Bill of Rights: The International Covenant on Civil and Political Rights*, ed. Louis Henkin (New York: Columbia University Press, 1981).

45. See Lawyers' Committee for Civil Rights under Law, "Disenfranchisement Laws in the United States" (1998), http://www.hrw.org/reports 98/vote/usvot98.-06.htm (accessed June 20, 2005).

46. International Convention on the Elimination of all Forms of Racial Discrimination, adopted and opened for signature and ratification by General Assembly resolution 2106 (XX) of 21 December 1965, entry into force for January 1969, in accordance with Article 19.

47. UN Treaty Collection (as of Feb. 5, 2002), http://www.law.duke.edu/lib/ResearchGuides/treaties.htm (accessed June 20, 2005). See also http://www.lexisnexis.com/infopro/Zimmerman/disp.aspx?z=2027.

48. See UN Human Rights Committee, "General Comment 24 (52), on issues relating to reservations made upon ratification or accession to the Covenant or the Optional Protocols thereto, or in relation to declaration under article 41 of the Covenant, UN Doc. CCPR/C/21/rev.1/ADD 6" (1994), http://www.unhcr.ch/html/menu 3/b/treaty 2_asp.html (accessed June 20, 2005).

49. See Theodor Meron, "The Meaning and Reach of the International Convention on the Elimination of All Forms of Racial Discrimination," *American Journal of International Law* 79 (1985), 287–88.

50. UN General Assembly, "Measures for Securing the Implementation of Universal Suffrage for Prisoners," http://www.MeasuresForSecuringThe ImplementationOfUniversalSuffrageForPrisoners.html (accessed September 15, 2004). See also Jennifer Fitzgerald and George Zdenkowski, "Voting Rights of Convicted Persons," *Criminal Law Journal* 2 (1987).

51. Jerome Davidson, "Inside Outcasts: Prisoners and the Right to Vote in Australia," *Law and Bills Digests Section*, current issues brief no. 12 2003-04, May 24, 2004, 3–4.

52. Protocol No. 1 (P3-1), par. 42; DowningStreetSays.org, "Prisoners' Voting Rights," March 31, 2004, http://www.downingstreetsays.org/ archives/000427.html (accessed June 20, 2005). See also Clare Dyer, "Prisoners Must Get Right to Vote, Says Court," *The Guardian* (Manchester), March 31, 2004, http:www.politics.guardian.co.uk/homeaffairs/story/ 0,11026,1182356,00.html (accessed June 20, 2005).

53. Among the countries that have ratified the European Convention, eighteen grant prisoners full voting rights, while another thirteen deny them the franchise. The rest, including Britain, allow some categories of prisoners to vote. See Dyer, "Prisoners Must Get Right to Vote." For discussion, see http:// www.obv.org.uk/ (accessed June 20, 2005).

Chapter Eleven

1. Christopher Uggen and Jeff Manza, "Lost Voices: The Civic and Political Views of Disenfranchised Felons," in *Imprisoning America: The Social Effects of Mass Incarceration,* ed. Mary Pattillo, David Weiman, and Bruce Western, 165–204 (New York: Russell Sage Foundation, 2004). The following seven paragraphs rely on this article; page citations are given parenthetically in the text.

2. Malcolm X, assisted by Alex Haley, *The Autobiography of Malcolm X* (New York: Ballantine Books, 1981), 450–51, 207.

3. See Amy Goldstein and Richard Morin, "U.S. Electorate Is Aging as Young Desert the Polls, *Washington Post,* Oct. 21, 2002. This study, undertaken by the *Washington Post,* the Henry J. Kaiser Family Foundation, and Harvard University, concluded that "young adults hold beliefs quite distinct from those of their parents and grandparents—more conservative in many of their views of government, more tolerant in many of their social values."

4. See Sarah Lawrence and Jeremy Travis, "The New Landscape of Imprisonment: Mapping America's Prison Expansion," 2004, http://www. urban.org/urlprint.cfm?ID=8848.

5. See "The New York State Judicial Commission on Minorities," available at http://www.COURTS.STATE.NY.US/ip/minorities/2005-leadership-development-conference.pdf (accessed June 20, 2005).

6. I am drawing here from an article by Christopher Uggen and Jeffrey Manza: "Democratic Contraction? Political Consequences of Felon Disfranchisement in the United States," *American Sociological Review* 67 (Dec. 2002): 777–803.

7. Ibid. See "If Felons Could Have Voted, National Election Outcomes Would Have Been Different," American Sociological Association, Jan. 9, 2003, http://www.asa.net.org/media/felons.html (accessed June 20, 2005).

8. Uggen and Manza, "Lost Voices," 20.

9. Ibid., 17.

10. Ibid., 16.

11. In this paragraph and the next I am drawing on Manza and Uggen, "Democratic Contraction?" 786–94.

12. Manza and Uggen, "Political Consequences of Felon Disenfranchisement," 16; "Democratic Contraction?" 787.

13. Manza and Uggen, "Political Consequences of Felon Disenfranchisement," 3.

14. See Pinaire, Heumann, and Bilotta, "Barred from the Vote," 15–16; Jeffrey Manza, Clem Brooks, and Christopher Uggen, " 'Civil Death' or Civil Liberties? Public Attitudes toward Felon Disenfranchisement in the United States," Institute for Policy Research Working Paper 02-39 (fall 2002), 13–16.

15. Quoted in Simson, "Justice Denied," 41.

16. Katharine Seelye, "Congress Plans Study of Voting Processes and TV Coverage," *New York Times,* Feb. 9, 2001.

17. National Commission on Federal Election Reform, hearing 1, panel 2: "Outside Assessments," March 26, 2001, http://www.reformelections.org/data/transcripts/hi/hearing1_p.2php (accessed June 20, 2005).

18. Evan Gahr, "Criminal Voters: Democrats Pursue a Major Cell, er, Voting Bloc," *American Spectator,* June 1, 2000, 60.

19. Simson, "Justice Denied," 46.

20. Dan Greenberg, Backgrounder #1003, "A Report Card on the 103rd Congress: Failing Grades on Reform" (Washington, D.C.: Heritage Foundation, Sept. 28, 1994), http://www.heritage.org/Research/GovernmentReform/BG1003.cfm (accessed June 20, 2005).

21. Thomas Mann, "An Agenda for Election Reform," Brookings Institute policy brief 82-2001, http://www.brookings.edu/comm/policyubriefs/PB82.htm (accessed June 20, 2005).

22. Goodnough, "Disenfranchised Florida Felons Struggle to Regain Their Votes."

23. Gregory Palast, "Florida's 'Disappeared Voters': Disenfranchised by the GOP," *The Nation,* Feb. 5, 2001.

24. Gregory Palast, "Florida's Flawed "Voter-cleansing Program," *Washington Post,* Dec. 4, 2000.

25. John Lantigua, "How the GOP Gamed the System in Florida," *The Nation*, April 30, 2001.

26. "The Wrong Way to Fix the Vote," *Washington Post*, June 9, 2001, B1; Lantigua, "How the GOP Gamed the System in Florida."

27. Palast, "Florida's 'Disappeared Voters.' "

28. Ibid.

29. Quoted in Robert E. Pierre, "Botched Name Purge Denied Some the Right to Vote," *Washington Post*, May 31, 2001, A1.

30. Palast, "Florida's 'Disappeared Voters.' "

31. Quoted in Pinaire, Heumann, and Bilotta, "Barred from the Vote," 2.

32. Ibid. Manza and Uggen calculated that if felons had been allowed to cast ballots in the 2000 election, George Bush would have lost to Al Gore in Florida by roughly 60,000 votes. If this figure were halved by as much as fifty percent, Gore still would have won the contest by a 30,000-vote margin. In fact, the researchers pointed out, he would have won even if their calculations were off by 59,000 votes. "Democratic Contraction?" 792.

33. Lantigua, "How the GOP Gamed the System in Florida."

Chapter Twelve

1. Sarah Walton, president, Maine chapter of the League of Women Voters, statement before the Maine legislature's Joint Standing Committee on Legal and Veterans Affairs, concerning LD 1058, "Resolution, Proposing an Amendment to the Constitution of Maine to Revoke Voting Rights of Convicted Felons While in Prison," April 13, 2001.

2. Prison Reform Trust, "Prisoners Should Be Granted the Right to Vote," May 25, 2001, http://www.prisonreformtrust.org.uk/news-pr12.html (accessed June 20, 2005).

3. *August v. Election Commission*, 1999(3)SALR 1, par. 17.

4. *Suave v. Canada*, pars. 9, 41.

5. See "Voting Rights," on the official website of the U.S. House of Representatives, the Honorable John Conyers, January 9, 2003, http://www.house.gov/CONYERS/news_major_issues.htm (accessed June 20, 2005).

6. The phrase was used by Howard Itzkowitz and Lauren Oldak in Note, "Restoring the Ex-Offender's Right to Vote: Background and Developments," *American Criminal Law Review* 11 (spring 1973): 736.

7. Interview on BBC South West Television, Dec. 5, 2000, reprinted on the website of Prison Reform Trust, May 2001, http://www.prisonreformtrust.org.uk/news-pr12.html (accessed September 12, 2004).

8. Quoted in Pamela S. Karlan, "The Court Finds Room for Racial Candor," *New York Times*, Aug. 23, 2001, A15.

9. UN General Assembly, "Measures for Securing the Implementation of Universal Suffrage for Prisoners," Resolution for Adoption of the UN General Assembly.

10. Prison Reform Trust, "Barred from Voting," May 25, 2001, http://www.prisonreformtrust.org.uk/news-pr.12.html (accessed June 20, 2005).

11. Ibid.

12. UN General Assembly, "Measures for Securing the Implementation of Universal Suffrage."

13. NAACP Legal Defense Fund press conference, Jan. 15, 2003, http://www.naacpldf.org/printable,aspx?article=78 (accessed September 12, 2004).

14. Human Rights Watch Press Backgrounder, "Race and Incarceration in the United States," Feb. 27, 2002, http://www.hrw.org/backgrounder/usa/race/ (accessed June 20, 2005).

15. *Suave v. Canada*, par. 48.

16. Uggen and Manza, "Democratic Contraction?" As Uggen and Manza note, restrictions on the voting rights of felons and ex-felons constitute "a rare and potentially significant counter-example to the universalization of the franchise in democratic societies.... Felon disenfranchisement constitutes a growing impediment to universal political participation in the United States because of the unusually severe state voting restrictions imposed upon felons and the rapid rise in criminal punishment since the 1970s" (778).

17. *Ramirez v. Brown*, 9 Cal. 3d 199, 507 P.2d 1345, 41–46, rev'd sub nom. *Richardson v. Ramirez*, 418 U.S. 24 (1974).

18. House Judiciary Committee, Subcommittee on the Constitution, *Hearing on the Civic Participation and Rehabilitation Act of 1999, HR 906*, 106th Cong., 1st sess., Oct. 21, 1999 (testimony of Todd F. Gaziano), 93.

19. Uggen and Manza, "Lost Voices."

20. *Carrington v. Rash*, 380 U.S. 89, 94 (1965).

21. Keyssar, *Right to Vote*.

22. John Stuart Mill, "Thoughts on Parliamentary Reform," in *The Collected Works of John Stuart Mill*, ed. J. M. Robson (Toronto: University of Toronto Press, 1977).

23. According to the Bureau of Justice Statistics, 67 percent of the inmates released from state prisons in the United States in 1994 were reincarcerated within three years. U.S. Department of Justice Bureau of Justice Statistics, "Recidivism of Prisoners Released in 1994," http://www.ojp.usdoj.gov/bjs/abstract/rpr94.htm (accessed June 20, 2005). See also Shadd Maruna, Russ Immarigeon, and Thomas P. LeBel, "Ex-Offender Reintegration: Theory and Practice," in *After Crime and Punishment: Pathways to Offender Reintegration*, ed. Shadd Maruna and Russ Immarigeon (Devon, UK: Willan Publishing Co., 2004); John Laub, Daniel Nagin, and Robert Sampson, "Trajectories of Change in Criminal Offending: Good Marriages and the Desistance Process," *American Sociological Review* 63 (1998): 225–38; Shadd Maruna, *Making*

Good: How Ex-Convicts Reform and Rebuild Their Lives (Washington, D.C.: American Psychological Association, 2001).

24. See Hobbes, *Leviathan;* Rousseau, *Social Contract;* Ewald, " 'Civil Death,' " 1045–1137; Note, "The Disenfranchisement of Ex-Felons: Citizenship, Criminality, and the Purity of the Ballot Box," *Harvard Law Review* 102 (1989); Shklar, *American Citizenship;* Furman, "Political Illiberalism," 1197.

25. *Wesley v. Collins,* 813.

26. Michael Tonry, *Malign Neglect; Race, Crime, and Punishment in America* (New York: Oxford University Press, 1995), quoted in Simson, "Justice Denied," 4.

27. Travis, "Invisible Punishments."

28. Fletcher, "Disenfranchisement as Punishment," 1907.

29. Uggen and Manza, "Lost Voices."

30. Russell Watson, with Joseph Contreras, "Black Power," *Newsweek* on-line, May 9, 1994, http://curry.edschool.virginia.edu/go/capetown/ B-black.html (accessed June 20, 2005).

31. Warren Richey, "Black Men Hit Hard by Voting Bans for Convicts," *Christian Science Monitor,* Oct. 23, 1998.

32. Testimony of Diana Morris, president of the Baltimore branch of the Open Society Institute, before the Baltimore City Council, Nov. 29, 2000, http://www.soros.org./initiatives/issues/law (accessed September 12, 2004).

33. "Race and Prisons," *Drug War Facts,* July 1999, http://www.csdp. org/factbook/factbook.pdf (accessed June 20, 2005).

34. Rev. Jesse L. Jackson Sr., "Liberty and Justice for Some: More Incarceration Comes at a Moral Cost to Every American," *Mother Jones,* July 10, 2001.

35. See Thompson, "Navigating the Hidden Obstacles to Ex-Offender Reentry."

36. *August v. Electoral Commission,* 1999 (8) SALR 14 (CC).

Afterword

1. Michael Peltier, "International Election Monitors Take on Florida," Reuters, March 9, 2004, http://www.commondreams.org/headlines04/ 0309-13.htm (accessed June 20, 2005).

2. "U.S. Elections under a Microscope," Ballotpaper.org, Oct. 5, 2004, http://www.ballotpaper.org/archives/000731.html (accessed June 20, 2005).

3. Jo Becker, "Groups Say GOP Moves to Stifle Vote," *Washington Post,* Aug. 26, 2004, A5. See also Ann Doss Helms, "Activists to Help Watch Poll Sites," *Charlotte Observer,* Oct. 10, 2004.

4. Sarah Childress, "Felons: Registering Voters One Jail at a Time," *Newsweek,* Oct. 11, 2004.

5. Quoted in Brendan Farrington, "Florida's New Secretary of State Endures Skepticism," *Baltimore Sun*, July 23, 2004.

6. Danielle Worthy, "Florida Felon Purge List Made Public," *Westside (Florida) Gazette*, Sept. 1, 2004.

7. Abby Goodnough, "Election Troubles Already Descending on Florida," *New York Times*, July 15, 2004. See also "About Those Election Results," editorial, ibid., Nov. 14, 2004, 10.

8. Erika Bolstad, Jason Grotto, David Kidwell, "Thousands of Eligible Voters Are on Felon List" *Miami Herald*, July 2, 2004.

9. "2004 U.S. Presidential Election Controversy and Irregularities," *Wikipedia*, Nov. 25, 2004, http://en.wikipedia.org/w/index.php?title=2004_U.S._Election_controversies_and_irregularities&redirect=no (accessed June 20, 2005). See also http://www.voteprotect.org/.

10. "What Counts in Ohio Recount," editorial, *Christian Science Monitor*, Dec. 20, 2004; "Late Ruling Allows GOP to Challenge Ohio Voters," *Los Angeles Times*, Nov. 2, 2004.

11. Bob Fitrakis and Harvey Wasserman, "Hearings on Ohio Voting Put 2004 Election in Doubt," *Columbus (Ohio) Free Press*, Nov. 18, 2004, http://www.freepress.org/departments/display/19/2004/886 (accessed June 20, 2005).

12. James Dao, Ford Fessenden, and Tom Zeller Jr., "Voting Problems in Ohio Spur Call for Overhaul," *New York Times*, Dec. 24, 2004.

13. "Analysis of Election 2004 Finds Reason for Concern: Margin of Victory Covered Faults, But Did Not Diminish Problems," Election Reform Briefing #9, at ElectionLine.org (sponsored by the Pew Charitable Trust), December 2004, http://www.pewtrusts.com/pdf/ERIP_Brief_9_1204.pdf (accessed June 20, 2005). See also http://www.tallahassee.com/mld/tallahassee/news/local/10539608.htm (accessed January 10, 2005).

14. Kymberli Hagelberg, Carol Chancellor, and David Knox, "Voters' Stories Triggering Probe by Democrats Could Spur Fixes," *Akron Beacon Journal*, Dec. 11, 2004. See also Greg Palast, "Kerry Won," Nov. 4, 2004, http://www.tompaine.com/articles/kerry_won_.php (accessed June 20, 2005).

15. Alan Elsner, " 'Discouraged from Voting,' " Reuters, Sept. 22, 2004, http://www.commondreams.org/headlines04/0922-03.htm (accessed June 20, 2005).

16. Demos, *Democracy Dispatches* 48 (Aug. 19, 2004), http://www.demos-usa.org/pub271.cfm (accessed June 20, 2005). *New York Times* columnist Bob Herbert also disclosed that elderly blacks in Orlando, Florida, had been paid unexpected visits by Florida police officers who then warned them about the prison sentences facing anyone who engaged in "electoral fraud." Bob Herbert, "Suppress the Vote," *New York Times*, Aug. 18, 2004, 15. See also Becker, "Groups Say GOP Moves to Stifle Vote," www.washingtonpost.com/wp-dyn/articles/A33798-2004Aug25.html.

17. Danny Duncan Collum, "Race and Politics in 2004," *Sojourners*, August 2004.

18. See Demos, *Democracy Dispatches* 48 (Aug. 19, 2004). See also Elizabeth Daniel, "The New Voter Identification Requirement," *GothamGazette.com*, April 2002, http://www.gothamgazette.com/article/voting/20020401/17/728 (accessed June 20, 2005); Chet Brokaw, "Lawmakers Asked to Repeal Voter Identification Law," *AbdereenNews.Com*, July 15, 2004, http://www.aberdeennews.com/mld/aberdeennews/9163428.htm (accessed June 20, 2005).

19. Chris Levister, "Ex-Felons' Voting Rights Misstated," *Black Voice News*, Aug. 19, 2004, http://www.blackvoicenews.com/modules.php?file=article & name=News&op=modload&sid=2291 (accessed June 20, 2005).

20. Kristy Douglas, "Four Area Election Boards in Lawsuit, *Times Reporter.Com*, Aug. 18, 2004, http://www.timesreporter.com/left.php?external=repsearch_detail.php&ID=32716 (accessed June 20, 2005).

21. Bob Fitrakis and Harvey Wasserman, "Twelve Ways Bush Is Now Stealing the Ohio Vote," *Columbus (Ohio) Free Press*, Nov. 16, 2004, http://www.freepress.org/departments/display/19/2004/810 (accessed June 20, 2005). See also Demos, *Democracy Dispatches* 49 (Sept. 22, 2004), http://www.earthisland.org/project/newsPage2.cfm?newsID (accessed June 20, 2005).

22. "Felons and The Right to Vote," editorial, *New York Times*, July 11, 2004.

23. See Jason Grotto and Debbie Cenziper, "200,000 Rights Applications Rejected Since '99," *Miami Herald*, Oct. 31, 2004. See also http://www.votelaw.com/blog/archives/election_administration/voter_qualification/ (accessed January 15, 2005).

24. "ACLU Calls Changes in the Clemency Process a Lost Opportunity to Address Florida's Civil and Voting Rights Crisis," Dec. 9, 2004, http://www.aclufl.org/news_events/index.ctm?year=2004 (accessed June 20, 2005). See also Cenziper and Grotto, "Clemency Proving Elusive."

25. Jason Grotto and Debbie Cenziper, "The Long Road to Clemency," *Miami Herald*, Nov. 7, 2004.

26. William March, "Delays, Purge Hit Voter Rolls," June 7, 2004, http://news.tbo.com/news/MGB7TQUZ5VD.html (accessed July 11, 2005). See also Debbie Cenziper and Jason Grotto, "Clemency Revisions to Restore Rights to Felons," *Miami Herald*, Dec. 12, 2004.

27. Brendan Farrington, AP, July 23, 2004. Ohio secretary of state Kenneth Blackwell boasted that he had helped "deliver" his state for President Bush and that he was "truly pleased" to announce that the president had won Ohio; see http://www.bluelemur.com/index.php?p=528 (letter) (accessed June 20, 2005); http://rawstory.rawprint.com/105/blackwell_campaign_letter_105.php (accessed January 15, 2005).

28. Benjamin Dangl and Brendan Coyne, "Voter Suppression Becomes Biggest Election 'Issue,'" *New Standard,* Oct. 31, 2004, http://newstandardnews.net/content/?action=show_item&itemid=1174 (accessed June 20, 2005).

29. Oliver Burkeman, "Dirty Tricks Return to the Sunshine State," *The Guardian* (Manchester), Oct. 19, 2004.

30. Robin Templeton, "Allow Ex-convicts to Vote," Knight-Ridder News Service, Sept. 2, 2004, http://www.justicepolicy.org/article.php?id=446/// Justice Policy Institute (accessed June 20, 2005).

Selected Bibliography

Abramsky, Sasha. "Ex-Felons Fight for Right to Vote." *Jackson Free Press*, July 22, 2004.

Allard, Patricia, and Marc Mauer. "Regaining the Vote: An Assessment of Activity Relating to Felon Disenfranchisement Laws." Washington, D.C.: Sentencing Project, January 2000. http://www.sentencingproject.org/.

Alterman, Eric, and Laleh Ispahani. "Voting Rights of the Convicted." Center for American Progress, January 16, 2004. http://www.progressivetrail.org/.

American Civil Liberties Union. "Florida Rights Restoration Coalition." *ACLU Newsletter*, March 25, 2003. http://www.aclufl.org.news.

Amnesty International. "U.S. Supreme Court Decision in *Atkins vs. Virginia* to Bring U.S. in Line with International Standards of Decency." June 20, 2002. http://www.amnestyusa.org/.

Amon, Elizabeth. "Felons Have Allies in Vote-Ban Case—Law Enforcement and Justice Department Officials File Amicus Brief." *National Law Journal* (January 14, 2003).

Anderson, John. "Electoral Reform after Florida: The Need for State Innovation with a Strong Federal Foundation." *Voting and Democracy Review* 14 (August 2001).

Andrews, Richard Mowery, ed. *Perspectives on Punishment: An Interdisciplinary Exploration.* New York: Peter Lang, 1997.

Ash, Jim, and George Bennett. "Felons Voting List Getting Scrutiny in Court, in Keys." *Palm Beach Post*, June 9, 2004.

"A Stigma That Never Fades." *The Economist*, August 8, 2002, 25.

Avakian, Sarkaris. "Racial Disparity among the Incarcerated." *Law, Social Justice, and Global Development Journal* 1 (2002).

Bartels, Larry M. "Partisanship and Voting Behavior, 1952–1996." *American Journal of Political Science* 44 (January 2000): 35–50.

Beck, Allen J. "Prisoners in 1999" (NCJ 1834 76). Washington, D.C.: U.S. Department of Justice, Bureau of Justice Statistics (revised February 8, 2001).

Beck, Allen J., J. Karberg, and P. Harrison. "Prison and Jail Inmates at Midyear 2001." Washington, D.C.: U.S. Department of Justice, Bureau of Justice Statistics, 2001.

Becker, Jo. "Groups Say GOP Moves to Stifle Vote." *Washington Post*, August 26, 2004, A5.

Behrens, Angela, Christopher Uggen, and Jeffrey Manza. "Ballot Manipulation and the 'Menace of Negro Domination': Racial Threat and Felon Disenfranchisement in the United States, 1850–2000." *American Journal of Sociology* 109 (November 2003): 559–609.

Bell, Maya. "Push Grows to Let Ex-cons Vote Again." *Orlando Sentinel,* August 25, 2004.

Brookings Institute. "An Agenda for Election Reform." Policy Brief #82-2001. Washington, D.C.: Brookings Institute, June 2001.

Brooks, Clem, and Jeffrey Manza. "Social Cleavages and Political Alignments: U.S. Presidential Elections, 1960–1992." *American Sociological Review* 62 (1997): 937–46.

Browder, Carla. "State's Ex-felons Start to Regain Voting Rights." *Birmingham News,* April 16, 2004.

Brown, Deborah M. S. "Right to Vote Enhanced Women's Struggle for Other Rights." U.S. Department of State, International Information Programs. http://usinfo.state.gov/usa/womrts/75years.htm.

Burkeman, Oliver. "Dirty Tricks Return to the Sunshine State." *The Guardian* (Manchester), October 19, 2004.

Butterfield, Fox. "Many Black Men Barred from Voting." *New York Times,* January 30, 1997.

———. "U.S. 'Correctional Population' Hits New High." *New York Times,* July 26, 2004.

Campaign to End Felon Disenfranchisement. "Felons and the Right to Vote." February 17, 2003. http://www.righttovote.org/.

Campbell, Duncan. "Drug War Denied Vote to Two Million Blacks." *The Guardian* (Manchester), November 14, 2000.

Cenziper, Debbie, and Jason Grotto. "Clemency Revisions to Restore Rights to Felons." *Miami Herald,* December 12, 2004.

Clegg, Roger. "Who Should Vote?" *Texas Review of Law and Policy* 6 (2001): 160–71.

Clubb, Jerome M., William H. Flanagan, and Nancy H. Zingale. *Partisan Realignment: Voters, Parties, and Government in American History.* Beverly Hills, Calif.: Sage Publications, 1980.

Collum, Danny Duncan. "Race and Politics in 2004." *Sojourners* magazine, August 2004.

Conaway, Carrie. "Doing Well by Doing Time." Boston: Federal Reserve Bank of Boston, Fourth Quarter Report, 2002.

"Conference Focuses on Inmate Rights; Many Ex-Prisoners Unable to Vote." *Washington Post,* October 1, 2002, 29.

Conn, Jason Belmont. "Excerpts from the Partisan Politics of Ex-Felon Disenfranchisement Laws." Senior honors thesis, Cornell University, Department of Government, 2003.

Coyle, Michael. "State-by-State Advocacy on Felony Disenfranchisement." Washington, D.C.: Sentencing Project, February 2001. http://www.sentencingproject.org/.

Criminal Victimization 2001: Changes 2000–2001 with Trends 1993–2001. Washington, D.C.: U.S. Government Printing Office, 2001.

Crowley, Michael. "Lawmakers Favor Ban of Felons' Voting Rights." *Boston Globe*, June 29, 2000, B3.

Dangl, Benjamin, and Brendan Coyne. "Voter Suppression Becomes Biggest Election 'Issue.'" *New Standard*, October 31, 2004.

Dao, James Ford Fessenden, and Tom Zeller Jr. "Voting Problems in Ohio Spur Call for Overhaul." *New York Times*, December 24, 2004.

Davidson, Jerome. "Inside Outcasts: Prisoners and the Right to Vote in Australia." *Law and Bills Digests Section*, current issues brief no. 12 2003–04, May 24, 2004, 3–4.

Demeo, Marisa J., and Steven A. Ochoa. "The Lost Latino Vote: A Preliminary Analysis of Latino Felony Disenfranchisement in Ten States." Mexican American Legal Defense and Education Fund, June 27, 2003. http://www.maldef.org/publications.

Demleitner, Nora V. "Continuing Payment on One's Debt to Society: The German Model of Felon Disenfranchisement as an Alternative." *Minnesota Law Review* 84 (April 2000): 753–804.

Democracy Now. "Felon Disenfranchisement: Purging the Minority Vote." July 9, 2004. http://www.democracynow.org/.

Demos: A Network for Ideas and Action. "A Wake Up Call: History and Impact of Disenfranchisement Laws in the United States." April 2003. http://www.demos-usa.org/.

"Disenfranchised for Life." *The Economist*, October 24, 1998, 31.

Dressler, Joshua. *Understanding Criminal Law.* 2d ed. New York: Lexis Publishing, 1995.

Drinan, Robert. "Let Prisoners Keep the Right to Vote." *Boston Globe*, July 14, 2000.

Drug Policy Alliance. "Barriers to Re-Entry for Convicted Drug Offenders." April 2003. http://www.drugpolicy.org/.

Dyer, Clare. "Prisoners Must Get Right to Vote, Says Court." *The Guardian* (Manchester), March 31, 2004.

Election Reform Information Project. "Election Reform since November 2001—What's Changed, What Hasn't, and Why." October 2002. http://www.electionline.org/.

Equal Employment Opportunity Commission. "Employment Discrimination Based on Religion, Ethnicity, or Country of Origin." http://www.eeoc.gov/.

Erikson, Kai. "Notes on the Sociology of Deviance." In *The Other Side: Perspectives of Deviance*, ed. Howard S. Becker, 1–22. New York: Free Press, 1964.

Ewald, Alec C. "'Civil Death': The Ideological Paradox of Criminal Law in the United States." *University of Wisconsin Law Review* 5 (2002): 1045–1138.

————. "Punishing at the Polls: The Case against Disenfranchising Citizens with Felony Convictions." Demos: A Network for Ideas and Action, November 24, 2003. http://www.demos-usa.org/.

Federal Bureau of Investigation. *Crime in the United States—2000.* Washington, D.C.: U.S. Government Printing Office, 2001.

Fellner, Jamie, and Marc Mauer. *Losing the Vote: The Impact of Felony Disenfranchisement Laws in the United States.* Washington, D.C.: Sentencing Project, and New York: Human Rights Watch, 1998.

"Felons and the Right to Vote." Editorial, *New York Times,* July 11, 2004.

"Felony Disenfranchisement Removes 1.4 Million Black Men from the Voting Rolls." *Journal of Blacks in Higher Education* 22 (January 31, 1999): 61–62.

Fitrakis, Bob, and Harvey Wasserman. "Hearings on Ohio Voting Put 2004 Election in Doubt." November 18, 2004. http://www.FreePress.org/.

Fletcher, George P. "Disenfranchisement as Punishment: Reflections on the Racial Issues of Infamia." *UCLA Law Review* 46 (August 1999): 1895–1907.

Fletcher, Michael A. "Voting Rights for Felons Win Support." *Washington Post,* February 22, 1999.

Florida Governor's Select Task Force on Election Procedures, Standards, and Technology. "Revitalizing Democracy in Florida." *Election Law Journal* 1 (March 2002): 125–36.

"Florida's 'Disappeared Voters': Disenfranchised by the GOP." *The Nation,* February 5, 2001.

Foner, Eric. *Freedom's Lawmakers: A Directory of Black Officeholders during Reconstruction.* New York: Oxford University Press, 1993.

————. *Reconstruction: America's Unfinished Revolution, 1863–1877.* New York: Harper & Row, 1988.

Friscolanti, Michael. "Convicts 'Morally' Fit to Vote: Supreme Court Ruling; 5–4 Decision Extends Franchise to Prisoners Inside Federal Institutions." *National Post,* October 31, 2002.

Furman, Jesse. Note, "Political Illiberalism: The Paradox of Disenfranchisement and the Ambivalence of Rawlsian Justice." *Yale Law Journal* 106 (1997): 1197–1232.

Gahr, Evan. "Criminal Voters: Democrats Pursue a Major Cell, er, Voting Bloc." *American Spectator,* June 1, 2000, 60.

"Give Ex-Prisoners a Voice." *USA Today,* August 26, 2003.

Glanton, Dahleen. "Rehabbed Felons Seek Right to Vote." July 19, 2004. http://www.votersunite.org/.

Goldstein, Amy, and Richard Morin. "U.S. Electorate Is Aging as Young Desert the Polls." *Washington Post,* October 21, 2002.

Goodnough, Abby. "Disenfranchised Florida Felons Struggle to Regain Their Rights." *New York Times,* March 28, 2004, A1.

Granucci, Anthony F. "'Nor Cruel and Unusual Punishment Inflicted': The Original Meaning." *California Law Review* 57 (October 1969): 839–65.

Green, Kenneth. "Description of the Voting Rights Restoration Coalition." March 22, 2003. http://www.democracyworksct.org/.

Greenberg, Dan. "A Report Card on the 103rd Congress: Failing Grades on Reform." Washington, D.C.: Heritage Foundation, September 28, 1994.

Greenhouse, Linda. "Felons Struggle to Regain Their Rights." *New York Times*, March 28, 2004, A1.

———. "Supreme Court Declines to Hear Two Cases Weighing the Right of Felons to Vote." *New York Times*, November 9, 2004, A19.

Grotto, Jason, and Debbie Cenziper. "200,000 Rights Applications Rejected Since '99." *Miami Herald*, October 31, 2004.

———. "The Long Road to Clemency." *Miami Herald*, November 7, 2004.

Hagelberg, Kymberli, Carol Chancellor, and David Knox. "Voters' Stories Triggering Probe by Democrats Could Spur Fixes." *Akron Beacon Journal*, December 11, 2004.

Hals, Kristina. *From Locked Up to Locked out: Creating and Implementing Postrelease Housing for Ex-Prisoners.* Boston: AIDS Housing Corp., 2003.

Harvey, Alice E. "Comment: Ex-felon Disenfranchisement and Its Influence on the Black Vote: The Need for a Second Look." *University of Pennsylvania Law Review* 142 (January 1994): 1145–90.

Help America Vote Act of 2002, Public Law 107-252, 116 Stat. 1666 (2002). The HAVA is codified at 42 U.S.C., 15301 to 15545 (2000).

Herbert, Bob, "Whiff of Voter Suppression Fouls the Air." *New York Times*, August 18, 2004, 15.

Hobbes, Thomas. *Leviathan.* Edited by C. B. McPherson. New York: Penguin, 1979.

Holzer, Harry J., and Steven Raphael. "Can Employers Play a More Positive Role in Prisoner Reentry?" http://www.urban.org/.

Hubbard, Lee. "Denial of Vote to Felons Hurts African Americans." Progressive Media Project, October 31, 2000. http://www.Progressive.org/.

Human Rights Watch. "Race and Incarceration in the United States." February 27, 2002. http://www.hrw.org/.

———. "U.S.: Incarceration Rates Reveal Striking Racial Disparities." Human Rights Watch World Report, February 27, 2002. http://www.hrw.org/.

Hutchinson, Earl Ofari. "Black Ex-felons and Gore." *Christian Science Monitor*, December 24, 2000.

Hyde, Philip. "Former Felons Have a Right To Vote." *Prison Stories*, October 17, 2002, A32.

Hyslop, Margie. "Right to Vote? More States Debate Giving Felons Ballot Access." *Washington Times*, July 14, 2002, A1.

———. "Some Maryland Felons to Get Vote." *Washington Times*, April 7, 2002.

———. "Special Report: Right to Vote?" *Washington Times*, July 14, 2002, A1.
"If Felons Could Have Voted, National Election Outcomes Would Have Been Different." American Sociological Association, Media Releases, January 9, 2003. http://www.asa.net.org/.

Immerwahr, John, and Jean Johnson. "Exploring Public Attitudes toward Prisoner Reentry." Washington, D.C.: Urban Institute, March 20, 2002. http://www.urban.org/.

"Inmate Advocate Relishes Role as 'Agitator.'" *Atlanta Journal-Constitution*, November 30, 2003.

Inter-Parliamentary Union. "Declaration on Criteria for Free and Fair Elections." Unanimously adopted by the Inter-Parliamentary Council at its 154th session, Paris, March 26, 1994.

Itzkowitz, Howard, and Lauren Oldak. Note, "Restoring the Ex-Offender's Right to Vote: Background and Developments." *American Criminal Law Review* 11 (spring 1973): 721–70.

Jackson, Jesse L., Sr. "Liberty and Justice for Some: More Incarceration Comes at a Moral Cost to Every American." *Mother Jones*, July 10, 2001.

Jacobs, Ann L. "Give 'Em a Fighting Chance: Women Offenders Reenter Society." *Criminal Justice* 16 (spring 2001).

Karlan, Pamela Susan. "The Court Finds Room for Racial Candor." *New York Times*, August 23, 2001, A15.

Keyssar, Alexander. *The Right to Vote: The Contested History of Democracy in the United States.* New York: Basic Books, 2000.

Knowlton, Brian. "Some States Seek to Give the Vote Back to Felons." *International Herald Tribune*, February 23, 1999.

Kousser, J. Morgan. *Colorblind Injustice: Minority Voting Rights and the Undoing of the Second Reconstruction.* Chapel Hill: University of North Carolina Press, 1999.

———. *The Shaping of Southern Politics.* New Haven: Yale University Press, 1974.

Lampo, David. "Felon Voters a Growing Menace." *National Review*, May 2, 2003.

Lantigua, John. "How the GOP Gamed the System in Florida." *The Nation*, April 30, 2001.

Laub, John, Daniel Nagin, and Robert Sampson. "Trajectories of Change in Criminal Offending: Good Marriages and the Desistance Process." *American Sociological Review* 63 (1998): 225–38.

Lawrence, Sarah, and Jeremy Travis, "The New Landscape of Imprisonment: Mapping America's Prison Expansion." Urban Institute, 2004. http://www.urban.org/.

Lawyers' Committee for Civil Rights under Law. "Preserving a Fundamental Right: Reauthorization of the Voting Rights Act." June 2003. http://www.Lawyerscomm.org/.

Leadership Conference on Civil Rights. "Justice on Trial: Racial Disparities in the American Criminal Justice System." Washington, D.C.: Leadership Conference on Civil Rights, May 2000. http://www.civilrights.org/publications.

Legal Action Center. "After Prison: Roadblocks: A Report on State Legal Barriers Facing People with Criminal Records." New York: Legal Action Center, 2004. http://www.lac.org/.

———. *Housing Laws Affecting Individuals with Criminal Convictions.* New York: Legal Action Center, 2000. http://www.lac.org/.

"Let Ex-Felons Vote." Editorial, *Washington Post*, June 17, 2004, A28.

Levenson, Joe. "On the Edges of Democracy: Prisoners and the Democratic Process." *Prison Service Journal* 130 (2000): 8.

Levi, Robin, and Judith Appel. "Collateral Consequences: Denial of Basic Social Services Based upon Drug Use." Drug Policy Alliance, Office of Legal Affairs, June 16, 2003. http://www.drugpolicy.org/.

Levister, Chris. "Ex-Felons' Voting Rights Misstated." *Black Voice News*, August 19, 2004. http://www.blackvoicenews.com/.

Lewin, Tamar. "Crime Costs Many Black Men the Vote, Study Says." *New York Times*, October 23, 1998.

———. "Silent Code: Don't Ask—Don't Know." *Black Voice News*, July 19, 2004. http://www.blackvoicenews.com/.

Lightdale, Marc. "Felons Appeal to Lawmakers for Improved Voting Rights." *Capital News Service*, February 19, 2004. http://www.newsline.umd.edu/.

Locke, John. *The Second Treatise of Government.* Rev. ed. Edited by J. W. Gough. New York: Macmillan, 1946.

———. *Two Treatises of Government.* Edited by Peter Laslett. New York: Cambridge University Press, 1988.

Lowenstein, Daniel Hays. *Election Law: Cases and Materials.* Durham: Carolina Academic Press, 1995.

"Making Citizens of Ex-Felons." Editorial, *Christian Science Monitor*, October 23, 2001.

Malcolm X, with Alex Haley. *The Autobiography of Malcolm X.* New York: Grove Press, 1965.

Manfredi, Christopher P. "Judicial Review and Criminal Disenfranchisement in the United States and Canada." *Review of Politics* 60 (spring 1998): 277–305.

Manza, Jeffrey, and Clem Brooks. *Social Cleavages and Political Change: Voter Alignments and U.S. Party Coalitions.* New York: Oxford University Press, 1999.

Manza, Jeffrey, and Christopher Uggen. *Locked Out: Felon Disenfranchisement and American Democracy.* New York: Oxford University Press, 2005.

———. "Lost Voices: The Civic and Political Views of Disfranchised Felons." In *Imprisoning America: The Social Effects of Mass Incarceration,* ed. Mary

Pattillo, David Weiman, and Bruce Western, 165–204. New York: Russell Sage Foundation, 2004.

———. "Punishment and Democracy: Disenfranchisement of Nonincarcerated Felons in the United States." *Perspectives on Politics* 2 (September 2004): 491–505.

Manza, Jeffrey, Clem Brooks, and Christopher Uggen. " 'Civil Death' or Civil Liberties? Public Attitudes toward Felon Disenfranchisement in the United States." Institute for Policy Research Working Paper 02-39 (fall 2002).

———. "Public Attitudes toward Felon Disenfranchisement in the United States." *Public Opinion Quarterly* 68 (2004): 275–86.

Manza, Jeffrey, Fay Lomax Cook, and Benjamin I. Page, eds. *Navigating Public Opinion: Polls, Policy, and the Future of American Democracy.* New York: Oxford University Press, 2002.

Maruna, Shadd. *Making Good: How Ex-Convicts Reform and Rebuild Their Lives.* Washington, D.C.: American Psychological Association, 2001.

Maruna, Shadd, Russ Immarigeon, and Thomas P. LeBel. "Ex-Offender Reintegration: Theory and Practice." In *After Crime and Punishment: Pathways to Offender Reintegration,* ed. Shadd Maruna and Russ Immarigeon. Devon, UK: Willan Publishing Co., 2004.

"Massachusetts Inmates Shouldn't Vote." Editorial, *Boston Herald,* October 24, 2000, 33.

Mathews, John Mabry. *Legislative and Judicial History of the Fifteenth Amendment.* New York: DaCapo Press, 1997.

Mauer, Marc. "A Policy Whose Time Has Passed?" *American Bar Association Journal* 31 (winter 2004): 17–19.

———. "Race, Poverty, and Felon Disenfranchisement." *Poverty and Race* 11 (July–August, 2002): 2.

Mauer, Marc, and Meda Chesney-Lind, eds. *Invisible Punishment: The Collateral Consequences of Mass Imprisonment.* Washington, D.C.: New Press, 2003.

Meron, Theodor. "The Meaning and Reach of the International Convention on the Elimination of All Forms of Racial Discrimination." *American Journal of International Law* 79 (April 1985): 283–318.

Metraux, Stephen, and Dennis P. Culhane. "Homeless Shelter Use and Reincarceration Following Prison Release: Assessing the Risk." *Criminology and Public Policy* 3 (March 2004): 139–60. Reprinted in *Preventing Homelessness among People Leaving Prison,* ed. Nino Rodriguez and Bremer Brown. New York: Vera Institute of Justice, 2003.

Mill, John Stuart. "Thoughts on Parliamentary Reform." In *The Collected Works of John Stuart Mill,* ed. J. M. Robson. Toronto: University of Toronto Press, 1977.

Miller, John J. "Public Policy: Votes for Felons—National Campaign to Liberalize Voting Rights of Ex-Felons." *National Review,* April 3, 2000, 26–28.

NAACP Legal Defense and Educational Fund. "Felon Disenfranchisement." January 15, 2003. http://www.naacpldf.org/.

Nakagawa, Scot. "Voting Rights Battle in Washington State." Western Prison Project, spring 2004. http://www.westernprisonproject.org/.

National Advisory Commission on Criminal Justice Standards and Goals. *Report of the Task Force on Courts, Corrections Standard 16.17.* Washington, D.C.: National Legal Aid and Defender Association, 1973.

National Commission on Federal Election Reform. *To Assure Pride and Confidence in the Electoral Process: Final Report.* New York: Century Foundation, 2001.

Nelson, James F. "Disparities in Processing Felony Arrests in New York State, 1990–1992." Albany: New York State Division of Criminal Justice Services, September 1995.

Northrup, Nancy. "Votes That Will Never Be Counted." *Chicago Tribune,* November 12, 2000.

Note, "The Disenfranchisement of Ex-Felons: Citizenship, Criminality, and the Purity of the Ballot Box." *Harvard Law Review* 102 (April 1989): 1300–1317.

Note, "The Equal Protection Clause as a Limitation on the States' Power to Disenfranchise Those Convicted of a Crime." *Rutgers Law Review* 21 (1967): 297–321.

Note, "Restoring the Ex-Offender's Right to Vote: Background and Developments." *American Criminal Law Review* 11 (spring 1973): 725.

O'Hagan, Maureen. "Felons Call Voting Ban Unfair to Minorities." *Seattle Times,* March 2, 2004.

Olson, Wyatt. "Barred for Life: The Process for Restoring the Civil Rights of Felons in Florida Works Perfectly—If Not Restoring Their Rights is the Goal." *Miami New Times,* December 26, 2002.

———. "Florida's Flawed 'Voter-Cleansing' Program." *Washington Post,* December 4, 2000.

Organization of American States. *American Convention on Human Rights,* OAS Treaty Series No. 36, 1144 U.N.T.S. 123, entered into force July 18, 1978.

Palast, Gregory. *The Best Democracy Money Can Buy.* London: Pluto Press, 2002.

———. "The Great Florida Ex-Con Game." *Harper's* magazine, March 1, 2002.

———. "The Wrong Way to Fix the Vote." *Washington Post,* June 9, 2001, B1.

Pangle, Thomas. "Should Felons Vote? A Pragmatic Debate over the Meaning of Civic Responsibility." Washington, D.C.: Sentencing Project, 2002. http://www.sentencingproject.org/.

Partsch, Karl Josef. "Freedom of Conscience and Expression, and Political Freedoms." In *The International Bill of Rights: The International Covenant on Civil and Political Rights,* ed. Louis Henkin. New York: Columbia University Press, 1981.

Penal Reform International. "PRI information Collection Sheet no. 13: Prisoners' Voting Rights." Memorandum by the Prison Reform Trust, UK Parliament, session 1997–98. http://www.publications.parliament.uk/.

Perl, Rebecca. "The Last Disenfranchised Class." *The Nation,* November 24, 2003.

Perman, Michael. *Struggle for Mastery: Disenfranchisement in the South, 1888–1908.* Chapel Hill: University of North Carolina Press, 2001.

Petersilia, Joan. "Parole and Prisoner Reentry in the United States." *Prisons: Crime and Justice* 26 (1999): 479–529.

———. "When Prisoners Return to the Community: Political, Economic, and Social Consequences." Washington, D.C.: Department of Justice, Office of Justice Programs, National Institute of Justice. November 2000.

Phillips, Frank. "Lawmakers Push to Ban Inmate Votes; Amendment Would Target Those Convicted of Felonies." *Boston Globe,* June 28, 2000, B1.

Pierre, Robert E. "Botched Name Purge Denied Some the Right to Vote." *Washington Post,* May 31, 2001, A1.

Pinaire, Brian, Milton Heumann, and Laura Bilotta. "Barred from the Vote: Public Attitudes toward the Disenfranchisement of Felons." Paper presented at the annual meeting of the Northeastern Political Science Association, Philadelphia, November 8–10, 2001.

Planinc, Zdravko. "Should Imprisoned Criminals Have a Constitutional Right to Vote?" *Canadian Journal of Law and Society* 2 (1987): 153–64.

Preuh, R. R. "State Felon Disenfranchisement Policy." *Social Science Quarterly* 82 (December 2001): 733–48.

Price, Howard Price. "More States Allow Felons to Regain Vote, Study Finds." *Washington Times,* December 28, 2003.

Prison Reform Trust. "Barred from Voting." May 25, 2001. http://www.prisonreformtrust.org.uk/.

———. "Prisoners Should Be Granted the Right to Vote." May 25, 2001. http://www.prisonreformtrust.org.uk/.

"Public Policy: Votes for Felons (Nationwide Campaign to Liberalize Voting Rights of Ex-Felons)." *National Review,* April 3, 2000.

Putnam, Robert D. *Bowling Alone: The Collapse and Revival of American Community.* New York: Simon & Schuster, 2000.

Rankin, Jamin B. "A Right to Vote." *American Prospect* 12, August 27, 2001.

Rapoport, Miles S. "Restoring the Vote." *American Prospect* 12, August 27, 2001, 14.

Reback, Gary. "Disenfranchisement of Ex-felons: A Reassessment." *Stanford Law Review* 25 (1973): 845–76.

Reinhart, Christopher. "Consequences of a Felony Conviction." *OLR Research Report*, March 28, 2003. Washington, D.C.: Office of Legislative Research, 2003.

Richey, Warren. "Black Men Hit Hard by Voting Bans for Convicts." *Christian Science Monitor*, October 23, 1998.

———."The Right to Vote as Applied to Ex-Felons." *Federal Probation* 12 (March 1981).

Rosenbaum, David. "Seeking a Formula for Voting Laws." *New York Times*, December 20, 2000, A31.

Rottinghaus, Brandon, III. "Incarceration and Enfranchisement: International Practices, Impact, and Recommendations for Reform." Washington, D.C.: International Foundation for Election Systems, June–July 2003.

Rousseau, Jean-Jacques. *The Social Contract*. Translated by R. D. Masters and J. R. Masters. New York: St. Martin's Press, 1978.

Royse, David. "Felons' Path to Rights Eased." *Tampa Tribune*, December 10, 2004.

Ryan, Carolyn. "Governor Looks to Strip Cons' Voting Rights." *Boston Herald*, August 12, 1997.

Sawhill, Isabel V. "Poverty in the United States." In *The Concise Encyclopedia of Economics*, ed. David R. Henderson, Library of Economics and Liberty online (1993). http://www.econlib.org/library/enc/povertyintheunitedstates.html.

Seelye, Katharine Q. "Congress Plans Study of Voting Processes and TV Coverage." *New York Times*, February 9, 2001.

Sentencing Project. "Legislative Changes on Felon Disenfranchisement, 1996–2003." Washington, D.C.: Sentencing Project, September 24, 2003.

———. "National Movement to Restore Ex-Felon Voting Rights Grows with Legislative Changes in Eight States between 1996–2003; More Proposed." Washington, D.C. Sentencing Project, September 24, 2003.

Shapiro, Andrew L. "Challenging Criminal Disenfranchisement under the Voting Rights Act: A New Strategy." *Yale Law Journal* 103 (November 1993): 537–66.

Shapiro, David L. "Mr. Justice Rehnquist: A Preliminary View." *Harvard Law Review* 90 (December 1976): 293–357.

Sheldon, Randall. *Controlling the Dangerous Classes: A Critical Introduction to the History of Criminal Justice*. Boston: Allyn and Bacon, 2001.

Sherman, Mike. "Legislators Try to Bridge Gaps." *Montgomery (Alabama) Advertiser*, September 21, 2003.

Shklar, Judith N. *American Citizenship: The Quest for Inclusion*. Cambridge: Harvard University Press, 1991.

Siegel, Jim. "Ex-Felons Voting Rights Misstated." *Cincinnati Enquirer*, August 4, 2004.

Simson, Elizabeth. "Felony Laws in the United States." Washington, D.C.: Sentencing Project, 2001.

———. *How Felony Disenfranchisement Laws Undermine American Democracy.* Washington, D.C.: Americans for Democratic Action, 2002.

———. "Justice Denied: How Felon Disenfranchisement Laws Undermine American Democracy." Washington, D.C.: Americans for Democratic Action Education Fund, March 2002.

Skolnik, Sam. "Freed from Bars but Barred from Voting." *Seattle Post-Intelligencer,* January 17, 2000.

Skrentny, John D. *The Minority Rights Revolution.* Cambridge: Harvard University Press, 2003.

Solochek, Jeffrey S. "Blacks: Allow Ex-felons to Vote." *St. Petersburg Times,* February 19, 2001.

———. "Flareforms." *St. Petersburg Times,* April 8, 2003.

———. "Former Felons Fight for Vote." *St. Petersburg Times,* January 21, 2001.

Sontag, Deborah. " 'Second Israel' Hails First Big Election Triumph." *New York Times,* May 21, 1999, A3.

Sourcebook of Criminal Justice Statistics. Washington, D.C.: U.S. Government Printing Office, 2002.

"State Laws Banning Ex-Convicts from Voting Face Scrutiny." In *Internet Bankruptcy Library: Class Action Reporter* 4 (October 23, 2002).

"States Study Voting Rights for Felons." *Washington Times,* September 24, 2003.

Street, Paul. "Starve the Racist Prison Beast." *Black Commentator,* November 20, 2003. http://www.blackcommentator.com/.

Supportive Housing Network of New York. "Blueprint to End Homelessness in New York City." New York: Supportive Housing Network of New York, 2002.

Taifa, Nkechi. "Re-Enfranchisement: A Guide for Individual Restoration of Voting Rights in States that Permanently Disenfranchise Former Felons." Washington, D.C.: Advancement Project, September 2002. http://www.advancementproject.org/.

"They Don't Count." Editorial, *Boston Bay-State Banner,* April 8, 2004.

Thompson, Melissa, and Sara Wakefield. "Impact of Recent Legal Changes in Felon Voting Rights in Five States." Briefing paper prepared for the National Symposium on Felony Disenfranchisement, sponsored by the Sentencing Project, Washington, D.C., September 30–October 1, 2002.

Thompson, Nicholas. "Locking Up the Vote: Disenfranchisement of Former Felons Was the Real Crime in Florida." *Washington Monthly* (January–February 2001), 21.

Tims, Douglas R. "The Disenfranchisement of Ex-Felons: A Cruelly Excessive Punishment." *Southwestern University Law School Review* 7 (spring 1975): 124–60.

Tonry, Michael. *Malign Neglect: Race, Crime, and Punishment in America.* New York: Oxford University Press, 1995.

Trapp, Doug. "Vermont Takes First Steps to Legalize Same-Sex Unions." *City Beat,* March 30–April 5, 2000.

Travis, Jeremy. "Invisible Punishments: An Instrument of Social Exclusion." Washington, D.C.: Urban Institute, 2002.

Travis, Jeremy, Amy L. Solomon, and Michelle M. Waul. *From Prison to Home: The Dimensions and Consequences of Prisoner Reentry.* Washington, D.C.: Urban Institute Press, 2001.

Trice, Harrison, and Paul Roman. "Delabeling, Relabeling, and Alcoholics Anonymous." *Social Problems* 17 (1970): 538–46.

Tyehimba, Afefe. "Election Rejection: Activists Take Aim at Law Barring Repeat Ex-Felons from the Voting Booth." *Motown Beat,* January 30, 2002.

Uggen, Christopher, and Jeffrey Manza. "Democratic Contraction? The Political Consequences of Felon Disenfranchisement in the United States." *American Sociological Review* 67 (December 2002): 777–803.

United Nations General Assembly. *International Covenant on Civil and Political Rights,* UN General Assembly resolution 2200A (XXI), 21 UN GAOR Supp. (No. 16) at 52, U.N. Doc. A/6316 (1966), 999 U.N.T.S. 171, entered into force March 23, 1976, Article 25.

———. *International Convention on the Elimination of all Forms of Racial Discrimination.* Adopted and opened for signature and ratification by General Assembly resolution 2106 (XX) of 21 December 1965, entered into force January 1969, in accordance with Article 19.

U.S. Code of Federal Regulations. 28 C.F.R. Part 55.

U.S. Commission on Civil Rights. Staff Report, "Voting Irregularities in Florida during the 2000 Presidential Election" (approved by the Commissioners on June 8, 2001). http://news.findlaw.com/.

U.S. Congress. Senate. *Debate on Equal Protection of Voting Rights Act of 2001, S. 565/HR 1170,* 107th Cong., 2d sess. *Congressional Record* 148: S797–809. This became Public law 107-252 on October 29, 2002.

U.S. Congress. House Judiciary Committee, Subcommittee on the Constitution. *Hearing on the Civic Participation and Rehabilitation Act of 1999, HR 906.* 106th Cong., 1st sess., October 21, 1999.

U.S. Department of Justice. Civil Rights Division, Voting Section. "Introduction to Federal Voting Rights Laws: The Effect of the Voting Rights Act," March 28, 2005. http://www.usdoj.gov/.

———. Office of Pardon Attorney. "Civil Disabilities of Convicted Felons: A State-by-State Survey." Washington D.C.: U.S. Department of Justice, October 1996.

———. Bureau of Justice Statistics. Press Release: "State Prison Population Drops in Second Half of 2001; Federal Inmate Growth Continues." Washington, D.C.: U.S. Government Printing Office, 2002.

———. Press Release: "U.S. Correctional Population Reaches 6.6 Million." Washington, D.C.: U.S. Government Printing Office, 2002.

———. "Restoring Your Right to Vote." Washington, D.C.: U.S. Department of Justice, Civil Rights Division, December, 2000.

———. *Sourcebook of Criminal Justice Statistics.* Washington, D.C.: U.S. Government Printing Office, 1995.

Van Alstyne, William W. "The Fourteenth Amendment, the 'Right' to Vote, and the Understanding of the Thirty-Ninth Congress." *Supreme Court Law Review* (1965): 33–86.

Vitiello, Michael. "Three Strikes: Can We Return to Rationality?" *Journal of Criminal Law and Criminology* 87 (1997): 395–479.

Von Bar, Carl Ludwig. *A History of Continental Criminal Law.* Boston: Little, Brown, 1916.

Voting Rights Act, Public Law 89-110, Title 1, Sec. 2, 89th Cong., 1st sess., August 6, 1965, 79 Stat. 437.

Weinstein, Henry. "Late Ruling Allows GOP to Challenge Ohio Voters." *Los Angeles Times,* November 2, 2004.

Western, Bruce, Becky Pettit, and Josh Guetzkow. "Black Economic Progress in the Era of Mass Imprisonment." In *Invisible Punishment: The Collateral Consequences of Mass Imprisonment,* ed. Marc Mauer and Meda Chesney-Lind. Washington, D.C.: New Press, 2003.

Wisconsin Department of Workforce Development. Timeline History: 1883–2003. http://www.dwd.state.wi.us/.

Wood, Gordon. *The Creation of the American Republic, 1776–1787.* Chapel Hill: University of North Carolina Press, 1969.

Index

Page numbers in italics refer to tables.

211